D0721690

NO LONGER PROPERTY OF
ANYTHINK LIBRARIES/
RANGEVIEW LIBRARY DISTRICT

NO LONGER PROPERTY OF
ANYTHINK LIBRARIES/
RANGEVIEW LIBRARY DISTRICT

Machine Learning with Microsoft Technologies

Selecting the Right Architecture
and Tools for Your Project

Leila Etaati

Apress®

Machine Learning with Microsoft Technologies: Selecting the Right Architecture and Tools for Your Project

Leila Etaati
Aukland, Auckland, New Zealand

ISBN-13 (pbk): 978-1-4842-3657-4
https://doi.org/10.1007/978-1-4842-3658-1

ISBN-13 (electronic): 978-1-4842-3658-1

Copyright © 2019 by Leila Etaati

This work is subject to copyright. All rights are reserved by the Publisher, whether the whole or part of the material is concerned, specifically the rights of translation, reprinting, reuse of illustrations, recitation, broadcasting, reproduction on microfilms or in any other physical way, and transmission or information storage and retrieval, electronic adaptation, computer software, or by similar or dissimilar methodology now known or hereafter developed.

Trademarked names, logos, and images may appear in this book. Rather than use a trademark symbol with every occurrence of a trademarked name, logo, or image, we use the names, logos, and images only in an editorial fashion and to the benefit of the trademark owner, with no intention of infringement of the trademark.

The use in this publication of trade names, trademarks, service marks, and similar terms, even if they are not identified as such, is not to be taken as an expression of opinion as to whether or not they are subject to proprietary rights.

While the advice and information in this book are believed to be true and accurate at the date of publication, neither the author nor the editors nor the publisher can accept any legal responsibility for any errors or omissions that may be made. The publisher makes no warranty, express or implied, with respect to the material contained herein.

Managing Director, Apress Media LLC: Welmoed Spahr
Acquisitions Editor: Joan Murray
Development Editor: Laura Berendson
Coordinating Editor: Jill Balzano

Cover image designed by Freepik (www.freepik.com)

Distributed to the book trade worldwide by Springer Science+Business Media New York, 233 Spring Street, 6th Floor, New York, NY 10013. Phone 1-800-SPRINGER, fax (201) 348-4505, e-mail orders-ny@springer-sbm.com, or visit www.springeronline.com. Apress Media, LLC is a California LLC and the sole member (owner) is Springer Science+Business Media Finance Inc (SSBM Finance Inc). SSBM Finance Inc is a Delaware corporation.

For information on translations, please e-mail rights@apress.com or visit www.apress.com/rights-permissions.

Apress titles may be purchased in bulk for academic, corporate, or promotional use. eBook versions and licenses are also available for most titles. For more information, reference our Print and eBook Bulk Sales web page at www.apress.com/bulk-sales.

Any source code or other supplementary material referenced by the author in this book is available to readers on GitHub via the book's product page, located at www.apress.com/9781484236574. For more detailed information, please visit www.apress.com/source-code.

Printed on acid-free paper

To my lovely husband, Reza, without whose support
I could not have achieved this

To my mother, for her patience and courage, and to my brothers,
Kamran and Kouros, and my sister, Kiana, for all their encouragement

To all people who inspired me

Table of Contents

About the Author

Leila Etaati is a data scientist, BI consultant, trainer, and well-known speaker at many international conferences, such as MS Ignite, SQL PASS, Data Platform Summit, SQL Saturday, Power BI World Tour, in Europe, the United States, Asia, Australia, and New Zealand. She has more than 10 years of experience with databases and software systems. She is an active technical Microsoft AI blogger at RADACAD.

Leila is a codirector and data scientist at RADACAD, with many clients around the world. She is a co-organizer of the Microsoft Business Intelligence and Power BI User group in Auckland, New Zealand, which has more than 1,300 members. She is also a co-organizer of three principal conferences in Auckland: SQL Saturday Auckland (since 2015), Difinity (since 2017), and Global AI Bootcamp.

Leila is the first Microsoft AI MVP in New Zealand and Australia as well as a data platform MVP. She holds a Ph.D. from the University of Auckland.

About the Technical Reviewer

Christian Berg is a group product manager at Microsoft, where he is responsible for customer success with Power BI, with a focus on developing new solutions with R, Azure Machine Learning, and general AI integration.

PART I

Getting Started

CHAPTER 1

Introduction to Machine Learning

Machine learning allows decision makers to gain more insight from their data. Today, the application of machine learning is no longer limited to research and specific industries. In most fields, there is a valuable opportunity to use machine learning to obtain more concise and in-depth information from available data. As a result, most big software companies provide opportunities to their users to access machine learning via easy-to-use software. For example, Microsoft, a pioneer in developing business software, leverages machine learning in developing products such as the Bing search engine, Xbox, Kinect, and others. The use of machine learning in Microsoft is not limited to the production of new software. In many of Microsoft's software development tools, such as Microsoft SQL Server, Power BI, and .NET, there is an opportunity to use machine learning to create smarter applications and reposts.

In this chapter, you will learn the central concepts and approaches to machine learning, review machine learning types, and discover step-by-step the life cycle of machine learning. Also, you will learn about the highly useful machine learning tools that are available in Microsoft products.

Machine Learning Concepts

Machine learning is a subset of artificial intelligence (AI). Ian Goodfellow and his colleagues [1] introduced a diagram that shows the different approaches to AI. As you can see in Figure 1-1, machine learning is one of several methods of AI.

© Leila Etaati 2019
L. Etaati, *Machine Learning with Microsoft Technologies*, https://doi.org/10.1007/978-1-4842-3658-1_1

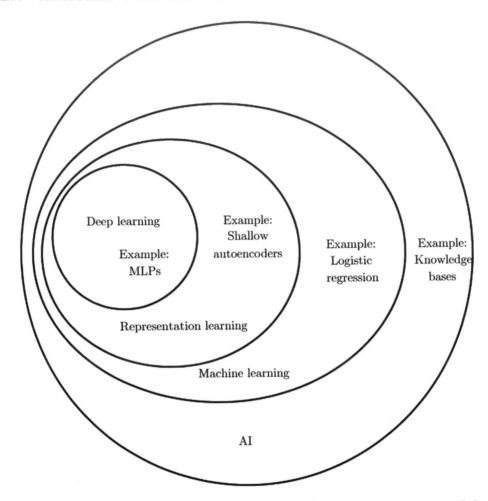

Figure 1-1. *A Venn diagram showing the AI category and subcategories [1]*

Academics and authors have proposed different definitions of machine learning. For example, Sebastian Raschka defined machine learning as tools for making sense of data, using algorithms [2]. He mentioned that we encounter a significant amount of structured (numbers) and unstructured (image, voice text, and so forth) data. Gaining insight from these data affects the decision-making process and helps managers to achieve a better understanding of what happened, why it happened, what will happen in future, and how to make it happen.

The concepts of machine learning are based on discovering common patterns from current data sets. Historically, we created reports and software to understand what happened in the past. Analyzing recent events and data always helps us to perform further analysis, such as finding key performance indicators (KPIs), and so forth.

Investigating what happened in the past is straightforward and provides us some value (Figure 1-2). For the next step, we want to become more agile regarding change, so analyzing live data is essential. Analyzing recent data obviously provides more insight than legacy data does. The process is a bit more difficult than following prior approaches but offers more value to an organization.

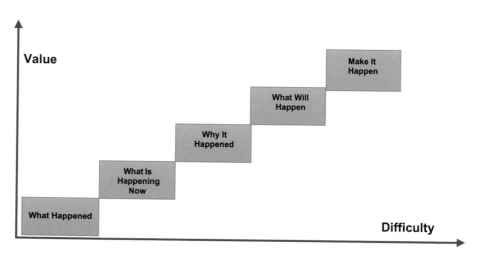

Figure 1-2. *Value and difficulty of various analyses, from past to future*

The third step is the root cause analysis, a type of data investigation focused on cause and effect. For example, analyzing the primary cause of a sales decrease in a specific branch can provide lots of value for a business owner.

A further step for getting better value out of data is analyzing what will happen in the future, or *predictive analysis*. Understanding what will happen in the future, or having insight about the data pattern, will help decision makers implement better informed company policies. "What will happen" analysis requires more effort and is more time-consuming than previous steps. However, it is an opportunity for a business to obtain even more valuable and actionable information.

Finally, the last stage is "how to make it happen." This *prescriptive analysis* recommends steps to take after predicting the future. This process brings more insight into any organization, but it is far more challenging to implement, compared to the other stages.

Machine Learning Approaches

There are two main approaches to machine learning:

>Supervised Learning

>Unsupervised Learning

In the following paragraphs, a brief explanation of each is provided. In Chapter 5, I will go into more detail about these and offer examples of both.

Supervised Learning

The primary goal of supervised learning is to learn how to predict a group or value from past data. By another definition, supervised learning is the machine learning task of inferring a function from labeled training data [2].

There are different approaches to supervised learning. One is to predict a value, for example, predicting the number of subscribers to a video channel, which could range from one to millions of individuals. Supervised learning makes it possibile to predict how many people will subscribe to this channel. Another example is predicting sales for a forthcoming year that could range from $1,000 to $200,000. By this approach, an algorithm predicts the number of sales for the company. We call this method a *regression approach*, in which the outcome is a continuous value.

The other approach to supervised learning involves predicting a group, for example, predicting whether a customer will stay with a company or leave it. In this example, the goal is to predict whether a current customer will remain with a group. Another case could consider a company that provides different tiers of customers, such as gold, silver, and bronze. In this case, the supervised learning approach might predict whether a new customer will belong to the gold, silver, or bronze group. In this type of supervised learning, the prediction column should be a *discrete class label*.

Unsupervised Learning

In supervised learning, we already have an idea of the answer before creating and training the model. In unsupervised learning, we do not predict a column, and we do not attach any label to the data. The main goal of unsupervised learning is to find the natural data pattern, to explore the data and extract its meaningful information.

Machine Learning Life Cycle

The machine learning life cycle consists of four main steps:

1. Business understanding

2. Data acquisition and understanding

    a. Data collection

    b. Feature selection

    c. Data wrangling

3. Modeling

    a. Model selection

    b. Split data set

    c. Train model

4. Deployment

    a. Evaluating the model

    b. Monitoring model

Microsoft has proposed a Team Data Science Process (TDSP) that illustrates these phases (Figure 1-3).

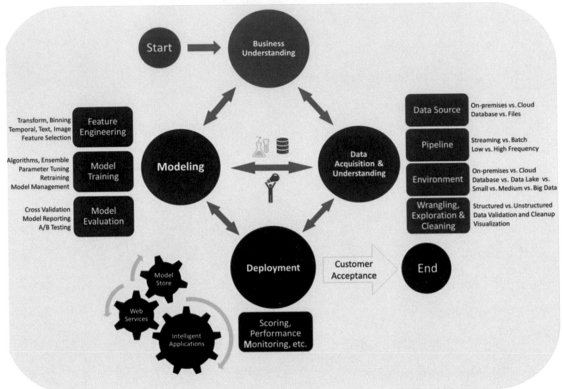

Figure 1-3. *The Team Data Science Process life cycle proposed by Microsoft [3]*

Step 1 is to understand the business problem. People who know their business are the best resources for identifying the company needs and issues that machine learning is able to solve. However, not all issues can be addressed by machine learning! In addition, use cases for machine learning should be prioritized in collaboration with business stakeholders and data scientists and engineers, so that you start with solutions that are valuable, affordable, and have a high probability of being successful.

Step 2 is to ingest data, which involves collecting required data from different resources and exploring and cleaning it. Finding relevant data columns to a problem, mainly for supervised learning, helps to create more accurate algorithms. Furthermore, for each algorithm, specific data transformation must be complete before the modeling stage.

Step 3 is modeling, which consists of model selection. This is done by analyzing the nature of a problem and data. Most data should be allocated for model creation (training), with a small percentage left for testing and evaluating the model. As you can see in Figure 1-3, the machine learning process is iterative. For example, after creating a model, there is a possibility that it might not be accurate. In this case, we would have to recheck the previous steps, such as business understanding or data acquisition.

Machine Learning Languages and Platforms

In order to create a machine learning model, you must be familiar with at least one language that facilitates machine learning. However, there are some tools, such as Microsoft Azure Machine Learning, that provide a drag-and-drop environment.

There are many different languages for doing machine learning, including Python, Java, R, C++, C, JavaScript, and so forth. However, among all these languages, Python and R are the most widely used, with a focus on creating models and the machine learning process.

There are also many different tools for doing machine learning. In this book, we will look specifically at the Microsoft tools that can help us perform machine learning, as well as how to use different Microsoft technologies to implement certain machine learning processes.

Microsoft has integrated machine learning in some of its tools, such as Bing search or Xbox, for many years now. In 2004, it embedded the data-mining tools in SQL Server. These tools helped SQL and business intelligence (BI) developers to leverage machine learning, to create more insightful reports.

SQL Server allows users to quickly produce mining models, using the current data in cubes. The main advantage of using data mining tools in SQL Server is that they are easy to deploy, have a great interface, and are user-friendly. However, there are some disadvantages. For example, there is no way to create custom code using R or Python, and only a limited number of algorithms are available.

Subsequently, Microsoft announced a cloud-based machine learning platform, Azure Machine Learning (AML), in 2014. This platform provides a smooth drag-and-drop environment and does not require any software to make it work. Azure Machine Learning supports R and Python and offers more than 25 algorithms specific to machine learning (Figure 1-4). You'll learn more about those in Chapter 12.

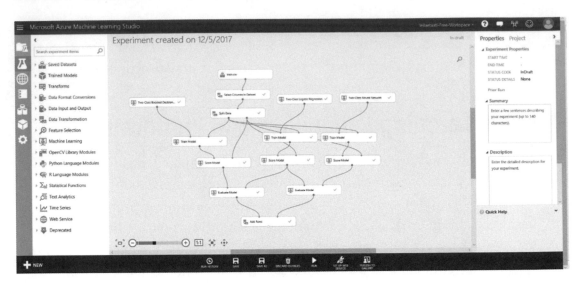

Figure 1-4. *The Azure Machine Learning environment is easy to use and flexible*

In addition to Azure Machine Learning, Microsoft provides the ability to embed the R or Python code in some of its other tools, such as Power BI, a self-service BI tool that is widely used for BI practices. In 2015, Microsoft began to offer new possibilities for machine learning in Power BI, for example, a custom visual in the reporting section that helps developers to write R code with the goals of visualization and machine learning. You will learn more about it in Chapter 4.

Another critical component of Microsoft Power BI is Power Query. Power Query helps developers to source data from different resources and offers many features for cleaning data. In 2016, Microsoft introduced the option of writing R code inside Power Query for machine learning. There is a difference between writing code in Power BI reporting and Power Query. In the former, you can create visuals (Figure 1-5), but not in the latter. Moreover, the code in the R visual runs every time the filter context changes or page opens, whereas the R scripts in Power Query Editor run only on refresh, unless there is a direct query connection. You will learn how to perform machine learning inside Power Query with R in Chapters 6, 7, and 8.

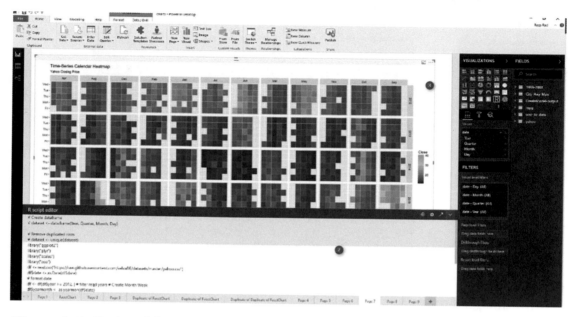

Figure 1-5. *R visual for machine learning in Power BI report*

Another Microsoft platform with embedded machine learning is Microsoft Azure, a cloud platform that includes various components for getting, storing, visualization, and output of data. Various parts of Microsoft Azure have the cabability for machine learning. As you can see in Figure 1-6, it is possible to write R or Python code in Microsoft Power BI, Microsoft SQL Server 2016 and 2017 (Chapters 9 and 10), Azure Data Lake (Chapter 11), Azure Stream Analytics (Chapter 13), Azure Machine Learning Studio (Chapter 12), and Azure Machine Learning Workbench (Chapter 14). Also some introduction on Azure HDInsight (Chapter 15) will be provided. Next in Chapter 16 an overview on Data Science Virtual Machine will be presented. In chapter 17 reader get familiar with CNTK concepts. Moreover, some services, such as cognitive services, provide different APIs for doing machine learning in natural language processing, text analysis, image and voice processing, and more. I will go into detail about these in Chapters 18 and 19. Figure 1-6 shows how all the Azure components interact with other Azure tools, to expedite the process of machine learning development.

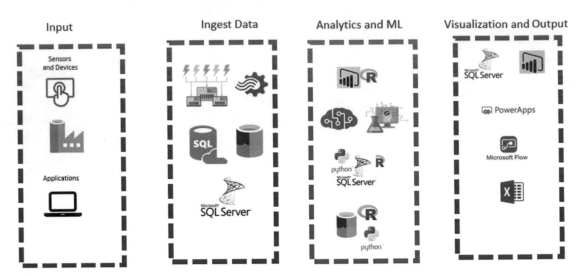

Figure 1-6. *Microsoft Azure components offering different possibilities for performing machine learning*

There is also an option to create a Data Science Virtual Machine (DSVM) in the Azure portal (Figure 1-7). DSVM supports a variety of languages (e.g., R, Python, C#), machine learning models (Azure Machine Learning Workbench, H2O), data ingestion tools, data exploration, and development. I will cover how to work with these components in depth in Part V.

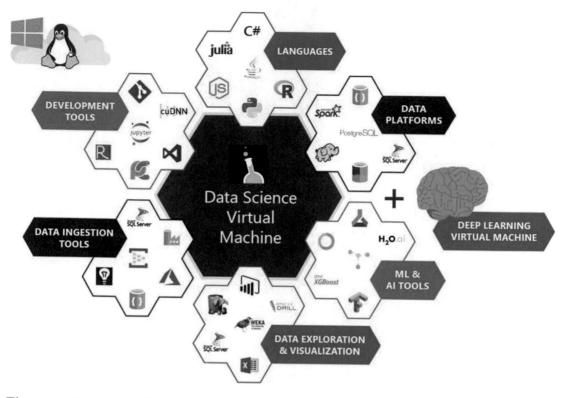

Figure 1-7. *Microsoft Data Science Virtual Machine (DSVM) components [4]*

Summary

This chapter offered an introduction to Microsoft machine learning products, providing a brief explanation of what machine learning is, the machine learning process, and the machine learning life cycle. In addition, some of the main machine learning approaches, such as descriptive, predictive, and prescriptive analysis were described. An overview of how we are able to leverage these tools for creating predictive, descriptive, and prescriptive analysis was provided. In the rest of the book, greater insight into most of the AI tools in the Microsoft stack will be introduced, and how to leverage them with the aim of machine learning will be explained.

References

[1]   Goodfellow, Ian; Bengio, Yoshua; and Courville, Aaron. *Deep Learning: Adaptive Computation and Machine Learning*. Cambridge, MA: MIT Press, 2016.

[2]   Raschka, Sebastian. *Python Machine Learning*. Birmingham, UK: Packt Publishing, 2015.

[3]   Microsoft Azure, "The Team Data Science Process lifecycle," `https://docs.microsoft.com/en-us/azure/machine-learning/team-data-science-process/lifecycle`, 2019.

[4]   Microsoft Azure, "Pre-Configured environments in the cloud for Data Science and AI Development," `https://azure.microsoft.com/en-us/services/virtual-machines/data-science-virtual-machines/`, 2019.

CHAPTER 2

Introduction to R

R is undoubtedly one of the most popular languages for machine learning. It is a programming language and free software environment used mainly for statistical computing and data visualization. R has been used by academics, data scientists, and statisticians for a long time. It is a statistical language, which is excellent for machine learning, statistics, and use as a visualization tool. There is an integration between Microsoft technologies and R language that enhances the capability of machine learning in Microsoft applications and reports. R is an open source and proprietory language that is available for the Windows and Mac operating systems. It can be extended via packages [1]. This chapter provides an overview on installing RStudio, and how to extend the R capability via installing packages, R data structures, machine learning, and statistical analysis and visualization with R will be explained.

Installing RStudio

To write and use R for machine learning and statistical analysis, you must install one version of R on your machine. There are different versions of R and different tools to write the R codes, but for this book, we are going to write R scripts in RStudio, which is an integrated development environment (IDE) for R with the possibility of using a syntax-highlighting editor. To install RStudio, you must go to the web site located at `www.rstudio.com/products/RStudio/`. It is also possible to run R scripts on your desktop and via a server. In this book, RStudio for desktop has been used. Moreover, the free version of RStudio for desktop has been installed and used. To start, install the RStudio desktop on your machine and open it. The RStudio environment has four main parts, as shown in Figure 2-1.

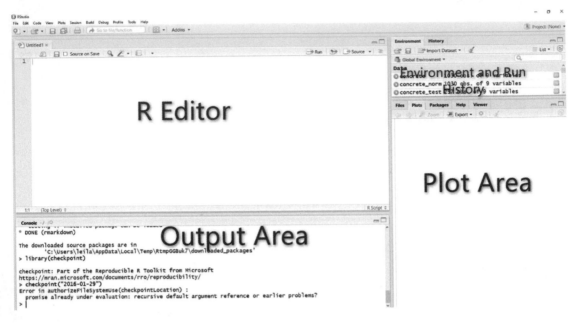

Figure 2-1. *RStudio environment*

You can write your R code in the R editor. The editor is more user-friendly compared to other R IDEs. The output or console area shows the result of running the codes. The plot area is where the visualization charts, help sections, etc., are shown. The last section, environment and run history, shows the variables and logs.

Let's start with a simple expression in R. We want to assign value 10 to variable name X. The simple statement is

```
X<-10
```

In R, the <- symbol is used to assign a value to a variable. To run the code, you just have to press Ctrl+Enter or click the run button in the editor window.

As you can see in Figure 2-2, I have run the statement x<-1, and the result is shown in the console editor. Now I am going to determine the type of the X variable. To do this, there is a function named typeof that gets a variable and identifies its type. RStudio also provides "intellisense" for each function.

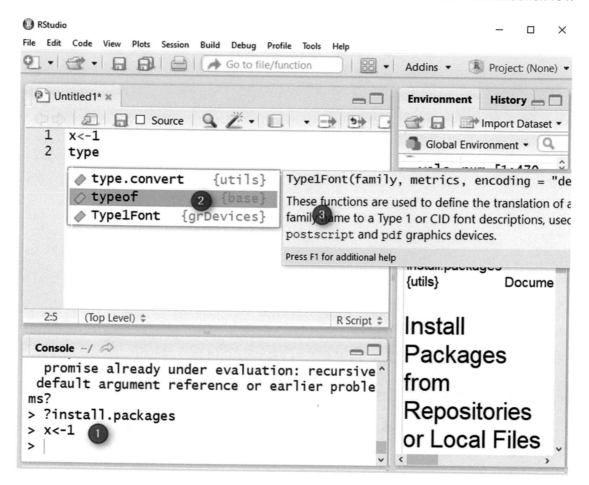

Figure 2-2. *Running a simple statement in R code*

After running the typeof function (Figure 2-3), you will see the output in the console window. The type of variable X is double. There are different data types and structures in R, discussed later in this chapter.

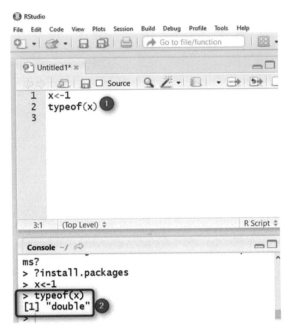

Figure 2-3. *Running the typeof function in RStudio to identify the type of variable*

Installing Packages

To extend the capability of R, additional packages can be installed. Each package has different functions that provide more functionality in working with R.

The main command for installing packages is `install.packages()`. When you install R, a library folder will be created on your machine that contains some of the basic packages for working with R, such as "Base" packages. However, in Chapter 4, you will see how to use this command to add some packages for assisting with machine learning.

R Data Structure

Every programming language has a specific data structure. R has some predefined data structures that each serves a specific purpose. For performing machine learning in R, we normally use a data structure, such as a vector, list, data frame, factor, array, and matrix. Following, I will explain some of these briefly.

Vector—C()

A vector stores the order set of values. Each value belongs to the same data type. A vector can hold data types such as integers (numbers without decimals), doubles (numbers with decimals), characters (text data), and logical (TRUE or FALSE values). See Figure 2-4.

Integer	Integer	Integer	Integer	Integer	Integer	Integer	Integer	Integer	Integer

Figure 2-4. *Simple visualization of a vector*

To create a vector data structure in R, we must use the function c(). To create a vector to store the name of a company employee, you would write the following code:

```
employee_name<-c("Jan","Jack","Mike")
```

The same would be done to store the employee's age and academic degree.

```
employee_age<-c(23,34,23)
employee_degree<-c("BS","MS","BS")
```

The resulting records for employee_name, employee_age, and employee_degree are as follows (Figure 2-5):

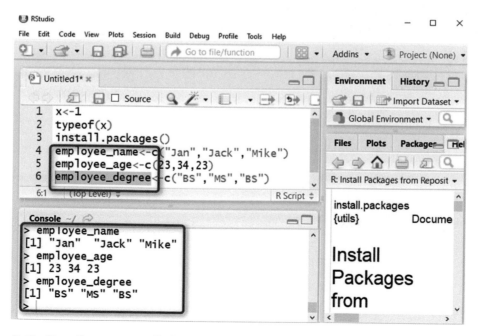

Figure 2-5. *Employee records for name, age, and degree*

Factor

Factors are a second data structure for a specific type of vector: categorical or ordinal values. For example, instead of storing the female and male types in a vector, a factor stores 1, 2, which takes less storage space. To define a factor, first we define a vector; the employee degree is a categorical variable. We use the common `Factor()` to convert a vector to a factor type, as follows:

```
employee_degreeFactor<-factor(c("BS","MS","BS"))
 the result of running the employee_degreefactor would be
employee_degreeFactor
[1] BS MS BS
Levels: BS MS
```

As you see in the preceding output, we have beside each employee's degree another parameter, named `Level`

Lists—list ()

List is another data structure that is similar to vector but can have a combination of data types (Figure 2-6). A vector has only one data type.

Integer	String	Double	character	Logical

Figure 2-6. *A simple visualization of list*

Lists help us to combine data types. For creating a list in R, we use the `list()` command, as follows:

```
employee_list<-list(employee_name,employee_age,employee_degree)
```

As you can see in the preceding code, the `list()` function gets a vector data structure, to create a list.

The output of running the variable `employee_list` would be as follows:

```
[[1]]
[1] "Jan"  "Jack" "Mike"
[[2]]
[1] 23 34 23
[[3]]
[1] "BS" "MS" "BS"
```

Data Frames—data.frame()

The primary data structure that we use for machine learning is the data frame. A data frame is very similar to a table structure in SQL Server and Power BI. It has columns and rows. The graphical representation of a data frame is shown in Figure 2-7.

Integer	String	Double	character	Logical
Integer	String	Double	character	Logical
Integer	String	Double	character	Logical
Integer	String	Double	character	Logical
Integer	String	Double	character	Logical

Figure 2-7. *Simple visualization of a data frame structure*

To define a frame, we use the data.frame syntax, as follows:

```
employee_DataFrame<-data.frame(employee_name,employee_age,employee_degree)
```

The result of running the variable employee_Dataframe is

```
employee_name employee_age employee_degree
1             Jan          23              BS
2             Jack         34              MS
3             Mike         23              BS
```

A data frame is like a table. We can access the cells, rows, and columns separately. For example, to retry a specific column in employee_Dataframe, such as an employee's age, we would use the following code:

```
employee_DataFrame$employee_age
```

Another way to access a row or column is via index number. The space before the comma stands for all rows, while the number after the comma is for column numbers. For example, we can extract all the rows of the first column using the following code:

```
employee_DataFrame[,1]
[1] Jan  Jack Mike
Levels: Jack Jan Mike
```

Similarly, to extract from all columns the data of a specific employee, we can leverage the following code:

```
employee_DataFrame[1,]
  employee_name employee_age employee_degree
1           Jan           23              BS
```

R for Statistical Analysis

R has been used widely for statistical analysis. It can be used for simple statistical analysis to complex statistical testing.

A simple statistical analysis would be to find the center of data. In R, there is a simple command for this, summary(), that provides a brief description of the data set.

Following is a data set of used cars (Figure 2-8):

year	model	price	mileage	color	transmission
2011	SEL	21992	7413	Yellow	AUTO
2011	SEL	20995	10926	Gray	AUTO
2011	SEL	19995	7351	Silver	AUTO
2011	SEL	17809	11613	Gray	AUTO
2012	SE	17500	8367	White	AUTO
2010	SEL	17495	25125	Silver	AUTO
2011	SEL	17000	27393	Blue	AUTO
2010	SEL	16995	21026	Silver	AUTO
2011	SES	16995	32655	Silver	AUTO
2010	SES	16995	36116	Silver	AUTO
2010	SES	16995	40539	Black	AUTO
2011	SES	16992	9199	Silver	AUTO
2011	SEL	16950	9388	Green	AUTO
2010	SES	16950	32058	Red	AUTO
2011	SE	16000	15367	White	AUTO
2011	SES	15999	16368	Blue	AUTO
2010	SEL	15999	19926	Silver	AUTO
2010	SES	15995	36049	Silver	AUTO
2011	SEL	15992	11662	Blue	AUTO
2011	SEL	15992	32069	Silver	AUTO
2010	SES	15988	16035	Silver	MANUAL
2010	SEL	15980	39943	White	AUTO
2011	SE	15899	36685	Silver	AUTO

Figure 2-8. *Used car data set*

As you can see in Figure 2-8, we have the price and mileage for each car. If we want to see the simple center measure of them, we can use the summary function.

```
summary(used cars)
```

After running the code in RStudio, we receive the following output (Figure 2-9):

```
> summary(usedcars)
      year          model              price           mileage            color          transmission
 Min.   :2000   Length:150        Min.   : 3800    Min.   :  4867    Length:150        Length:150
 1st Qu.:2008   Class :character  1st Qu.:10995    1st Qu.: 27200    Class :character  Class :character
 Median :2009   Mode  :character  Median :13592    Median : 36385    Mode  :character  Mode  :character
 Mean   :2009                     Mean   :12962    Mean   : 44261
 3rd Qu.:2010                     3rd Qu.:14904    3rd Qu.: 55125
 Max.   :2012                     Max.   :21992    Max.   :151479
```

Figure 2-9. *Output of running the* summary *function code in RStudio*

For a numeric variable, such as price or mileage, we have five measures: minimum (Min.) and maximum (Max.), mean (average), median, and first and third quarter (1st Qu., 3rd Qu.).

R for Machine Learning

R contains many packages and functions that help data scientists to perform machine learning. With the R language, you are able to undertake predictive, descriptive, and prescriptive analysis. The following R packages from the KDnuggets web site (Table 2-1) are especially popular for machine learning [2].

Table 2-1. *R Packages for Machine Learning*

Ranks	Package Name	Machine Learning
1	caret	Predictive analysis (classification and regression)
2	randomForest	Predictive analysis (classification and regression)
3	E1071	Descriptive analysis
4	rpart	Predictive analysis (classification and regression)
5	nnet	Predictive analysis (classification and regression)
6	arules	Descriptive analysis (data mining)
7	kernlab	Predictive analysis (classification and regression) and descriptive analysis

There are many packages and functions for machine learning. In this book, I will show how we can use them inside Power BI.

R for Visualization

R can be used for visualization. Ggplot2 packages are a popular package that helps us to draw different charts. With R visual, you can draw static, dynamic, and 3D charts. In Chapter 6, I will discuss some of the ways to draw charts using R codes inside Power BI.

We want to implement visualization for the following principal purposes:

> Comparison
>
> Composition
>
> Distribution
>
> Relationship [3]

The chart in Figure 2-10 shows the main goals of visualization.

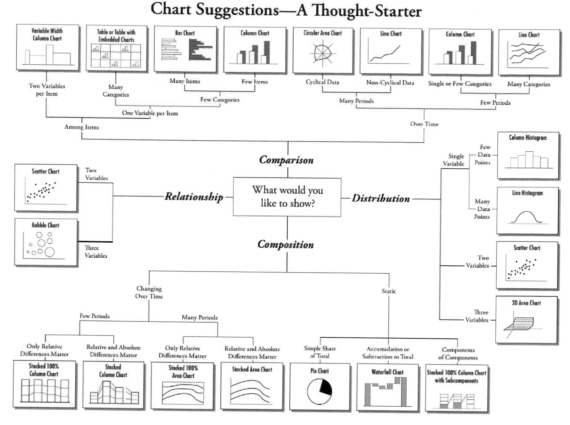

Figure 2-10. *Selecting the right chart for the purpose*

Figure 2-10 illustrates that the main purposes of visualization can be categorized by four main aspects: the relationship, distribution, comparison, and composition. This chart is a map to find the best matches for visualization. Most of the available visualization tools are able to follow this chart. However, using R scripts extends these capabilities, to draw all different chart types we want.

Summary

This chapter provided an overview of what R is and how to install it. It also offered a brief introduction to available packages and different data structures in the R language. Finally, a brief discussion on how we can use R for visualization and machine learning was presented. The rest of this book presents a more in-depth explanation on how to draw charts with the help R scripts.

References

[1]   R Foundation, "What is R," `www.r-project.org/about.html`.

[2]   KDnuggets, "Top R packages for Machine Learning," `www.kdnuggets.com/2017/02/top-r-packages-machine-learning.html`, February 2017.

[3]   Abela, A. Chart Suggestions—A Thought-Starter, `http://extremepresentation.typepad.com/.shared/image.html?/photos/uncategorized/choosing_a_good_chart.jpg`, 2006.

CHAPTER 3

Introduction to Python

Python is one of the main languages used for performing machine learning. It is a multi-purpose language that has been leveraged for device programming, object-oriented programming, machine learning, and so forth. In this chapter, you will learn

> Python IDE
>
> Install packages
>
> Python data structure
>
> Statistical analysis with Python
>
> Python for visualization
>
> Python for machine learning

However, the main aim of this chapter is to introduce R briefly.

Python IDE

According to the DataCamp web site (`www.datacamp.com/community/tutorials/data-science-python-ide`), there are five top integrated development environments (IDEs) in which to write code. A brief description of each follows.

- **Spyder** is an environment (Figure 3-1) very similar to RStudio, so if you are switching from R to Python, it is a really good choice. It is supported in Windows and MacOS. Spyder can be downloaded from the Anaconda web site (`www.anaconda.com/distribution/`) as well.

© Leila Etaati 2019

L. Etaati, *Machine Learning with Microsoft Technologies*, https://doi.org/10.1007/978-1-4842-3658-1_3

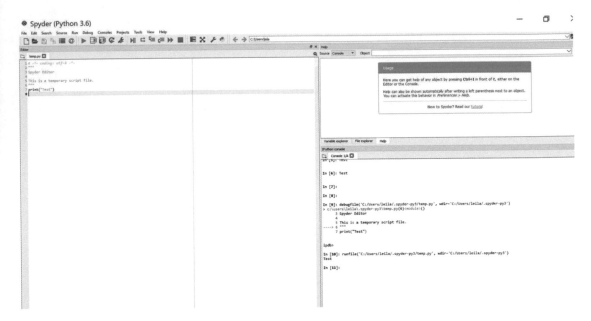

Figure 3-1. *Spyder environment*

- **Rodeo** is another Python IDE that is similar to RStudio. You can download it from (`https://rodeo.yhat.com/`). Rodeo has four main environments (Figure 3-2). There is one for writing code, a console for showing results, an area for installing packages, and another for showing plots.

Figure 3-2. *Rodeo environment*

- **PyCharm** is another IDE for writing Python codes. Current versions of Azure Machine Learning Workbench support this IDE (www.jetbrains.com/pycharm/).

- **Jupyter** is another IDE for writing Python code and can be accessed via a browser or desktop version.

- **Microsoft Visual Studio** is another IDE for writing Python. It is possible to edit Python code in Azure Machine Learning Workbench inside Microsoft Visual Studio. A detailed explanation of how to work with Azure Machine Learning and Visual Studio is provided in the following section.

Install Packages

To write Python codes inside Visual Studio, we must first install Visual Studio 2017 (https://docs.microsoft.com/en-us/visualstudio/install/install-visual-studio). From File, choose the New project option. Then select Python ➤ Python Application ➤ Put Location and click the OK button (Figure 3-3).

Figure 3-3. *Creating a Python application in Visual Studio 2017*

To extend the capability of Python programming, you must install some additional packages. Each package has different functions that offer us more functionality in working with Python. To install packages in Visual Studio, we must click View ➤ Other Windows ➤ Python Environment (Figure 3-4).

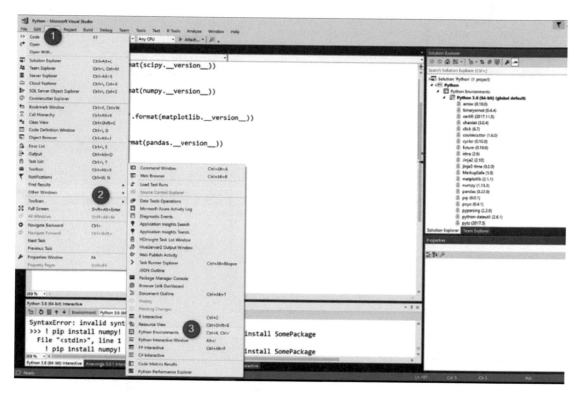

Figure 3-4. *Python environment in Visual Studio 2017*

In Python Environments, select Python version 3.6. In another tab, select Packages. In the search area, type the package name (Figure 3-5). For example, to install Pandas, click pip install pandas from PyPi.

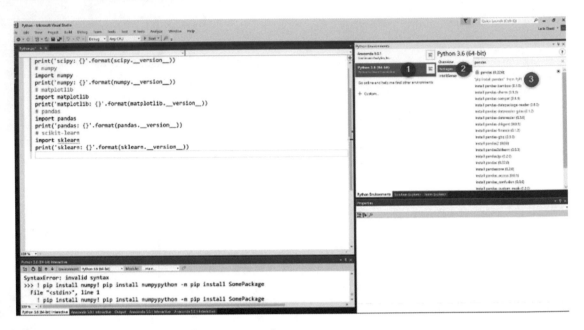

Figure 3-5. *Installing packages in Python*

After installing the package, you will see a message in the output. Figure 3-6 shows that the Panda package has been installed successfully.

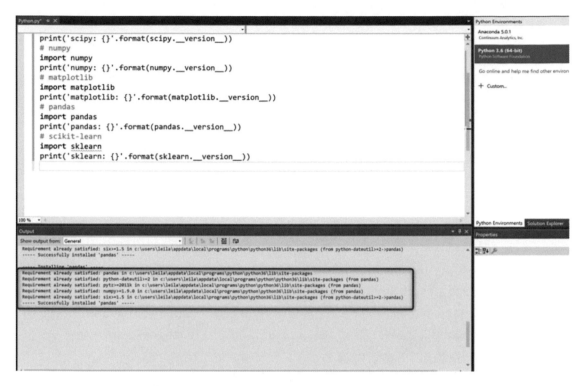

Figure 3-6. *Installing packages output result*

After installing the package, you will be able to check that it has been installed. In the interactive Python version 3.6, write the following codes, to check whether Pandas packages have been installed.

```
import pandas
print('pandas: {}'.format(pandas.__version__))
```

Now we must test the environment, to make sure that the packages have been installed successfully. You can run the code in a different environment. As you can see from Figure 3-7, it is possible to run the code in Anaconda 5.0.1, Python 3.6, and ProjectApplication 1.

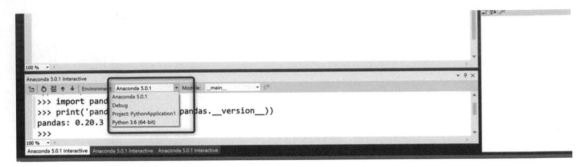

Figure 3-7. *Running Python code inside Visual Studio in different environments*

Python for Statistical Summary

The first step in doing any machine learning or statistical analysis is to summarize the data set. We are going to look at the data set with regard to dimensions, statistical summary of columns, and peek at the data. We can access a data resource about cars from the following link: https://archive.ics.uci.edu/ml/machine-learning-databases/auto-mpg/auto-mpg.data.

We are going to load data directly from the web site, then assign a name to each column. Assigning a name to each column will help us to explore the data better. Then we will use the Panda package to load and read the data.

```
URL = "https://archive.ics.uci.edu/ml/machine-learning-databases/auto-mpg/
auto-mpg.data"
names = ['MPG', 'Cyl', 'Disp', 'HorsePower', 'Weight','Acceleration','Model
Year','Origin','Car Name']
dataset = pandas.read_csv(URL, names=names)
```

Dimensions

To get the dimensions of the data, such as some rows and columns, we use the shape property, as follows:

```
print(dataset.shape)
```

result

```
(398, 9)
```

The preceding indicates that we have 398 rows and 9 columns. In addition, we can use the head property, to see the first 20 rows of data, as follows:

```
print(dataset.head(20)).
```

Statistical Distribution

To check the statistical summary of attributes, we can use the describe command, as follows:

```
print(dataset.describe())
```

Python for Visualization

Python allows users to create charts. It offers a variety of options for visualizing data. Matplotlib is the main package for visualization in Python. It is very powerful and can be used for complex charts. Matplot was the first visualization library, and other tools, such as Seaborn, ggplot, Bokeh, and so forth, have been built on top of it (see `https://blog.modeanalytics.com/python-data-visualization-libraries/`).

The ggplot2 package is also available in Python. ggplot2 is based on R's plotting system. It works based on layers.

Bokeh is another library similar to ggplot2, but it is native to Python. It helps developers to draw interactive and web-based charts.

Plotly is an online data visualization tool that is useful for creating interactive charts. Plotly can be used both in R and Python.

Python for Machine Learning

Python is a simple, elegant, and consistent language. It is more readable compared to R, for example.

Python is especially popular in applied data science. It has different packages for machine learning, such as NumPy, Pandas, Keras, TensorFlow, and so forth. However, it is a general-purpose language that can be used for data engineering, web site scraping, web application building, and so forth.

Summary

This chapter provided an overview of Python and related software and discussed how we can use it to perform machine learning.

CHAPTER 4

R Visualization in Power BI

Power BI is a self-service business intelligence (BI) software. This tool can be used for data visualization, data cleaning, modeling, analysis, and collaboration at enterprise scale. Many books and blogs have been published about how to use Power BI. In this chapter, I am going to show how we can leverage R to create better visualizations and get additional value from Power BI. In this chapter, I will explain how to set up R within Power BI, how to draw charts in Power BI using R scripts, how to set up the Power BI report environment, how to set up Power BI to write R code, and how to draw R charts in Power BI.

Power BI

The Power BI report environment helps us to visualize data. According to Dr. Abela [1], there are four main purposes of data visualization, as follows and represented graphically in Figure 4-1:

1. Data comparison

2. Data relationship

3. Data composition

4. Data distribution

© Leila Etaati 2019

L. Etaati, *Machine Learning with Microsoft Technologies*, https://doi.org/10.1007/978-1-4842-3658-1_4

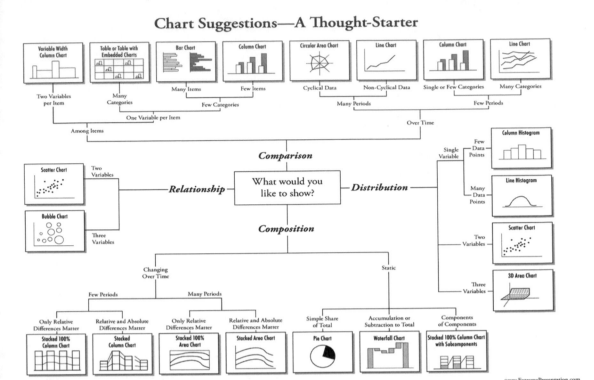

Figure 4-1. Data visualization diagram [1]

Power BI Desktop is a free application that you can download from https://powerbi.microsoft.com/en-us/desktop/. The Power BI Visualizations panel supports most of the charts suggested in Figure 4-1. It is possible to extend the visualization capabilities, by importing custom visuals from the marketplace or other sources.

Power BI Desktop helps users to get data from different sources with the Get Data options (Figure 4-2). To learn more about Power BI, go to http://radacad.com/online-book-power-bi-from-rookie-to-rockstar.

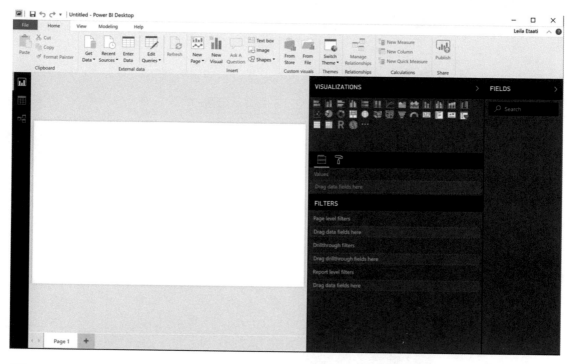

Figure 4-2. *Power BI Visualizations environment*

Setting Up R in Power BI

To draw an R chart in Power BI, the first step is to install at least one R version or Microsoft R Open. Now we must specify what R version we are going to use. To do this, we click the File menu, then click Options and Settings, then Options. Under the Global option, click R Scripting, to specify the R version (Figure 4-3).

Figure 4-3. *Setting up the R environment in Power BI*

As mentioned in Chapter 3, R is based on packages. Whenever you use a specific package, you must install it on your machine first. (If you are using Power BI Desktop, most of the packages are already installed in the service.) You can install packages using an R IDE, e.g., R Studio. Then, in the Power BI R editor, you must refer to that package. Moreover, you ensure that you are using the right version of the R package that you already installed (Figure 4-4).

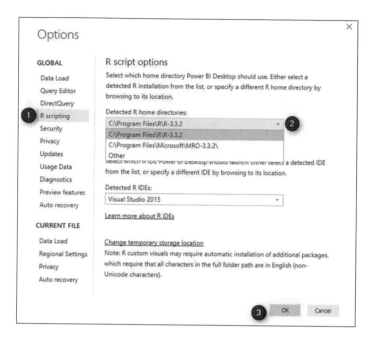

Figure 4-4. *Specifying an R version and environment in Power BI*

Writing R Code in Power BI

It is possible to write R code in Power BI's report area. To do that, we must import data into Power BI report.

A data set that includes car specifications, such as speed in town and along a highway, cylinders, and so forth, is available to download at `https://forge.scilab.org/index.php/p/rdataset/source/tree/master/csv/ggplot2/mpg.csv`. This data set is free and titled "mpg.csv." I am going to use this data set to show the speed of the car on the highway and the city, the number of cylinders the car has, its year of production, and type of drive (front wheel, rear wheel, and so on) in one picture. According to Figure 4-1, to show the comparison of the data among the different items, we must use a table chart. We are going to import data into Power BI Desktop via the Get Data option and import a CSV file (Figure 4-5).

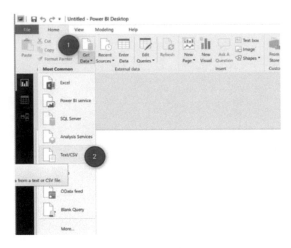

Figure 4-5. *Importing a CSV file into Power BI Desktop*

After importing the data, you should be able to see it under Fields. Click the R and drag it into the whitespace area (Figure 4-6).

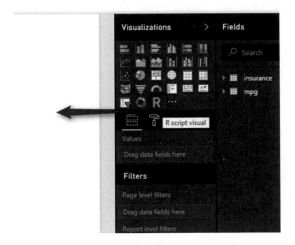

Figure 4-6. *Putting R into a whitespace area*

Expand the mpg data set (Figure 4-7) and choose cty (speed in the city), hwy (speed on the highway), and cyl (cylinder) options.

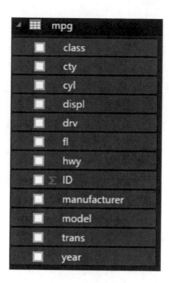

Figure 4-7. *Selecting related data from the mpg file*

The R scripts editor will be enabled. Under R script editor, you will see some R codes. The crosshatch (#) is a symbol for making comments in R and is not executed as script. Power BI automatically puts the selected fields in a variable named `dataset`, so all fields (cty, hwy, and cyl) will be stored in a data set variable equivalent to using the `<-` syntax. Also, Power BI automatically removes any duplicated rows. This is explained in the R script editor area (Figure 4-8).

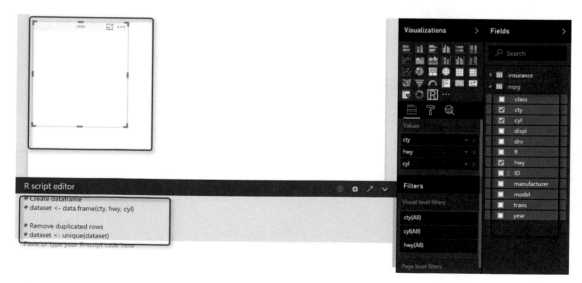

Figure 4-8. *Active Python environment in Visual Studio 2017*

Next, we are going to put R codes for drawing a two-dimensional graph in Power BI. In Power BI, to use any R scripts, install the package in R, using the `install.package()` function. In our case, we must install ggplot2. We use the function `library(ggplot2)` to refer to this package. The first line of code in the R editor is `library(ggplot2)`. This package contains some important functions for drawing charts.

To draw a chart, I first use the `ggplot` function, to configure a two-dimensional chart. The first argument is `dataset`, which holds our three fields. Then we have another function inside ggplot2, named `aes`, which identifies which file should be on the x or y axes. Finally, in the chart, I also want to indicate the number of the car's cylinders. This can be done by adding another layer in the `aes` function: Size. So, cars with more cylinders will have bigger dots (see Figure 4-9).

```
t←ggplot(dataset, aes(x=cty, y=hwy,size=cyl))
```

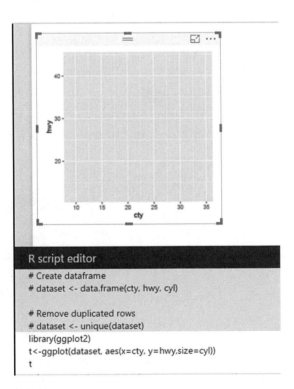

Figure 4-9. *R script editor*

However, the preceding figure shows the graph area without any specific charts. We need a scatter chart to indicate the city and highway speeds on x and y axes. ggplot2's `geom_point` function draws a scatter chart. This function has value of pch=21, which relates to the shape of the dot in the chart. For example, if I set this value as 20, it becomes a filled cycle; a value of 23 becomes a diamond shape. To run the code, click the run option (Figure 4-10).

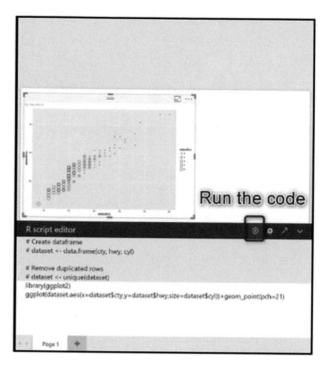

Figure 4-10. *How to run the R code*

After clicking the run code option, the charts will be shown in R visual (Figure 4-11).

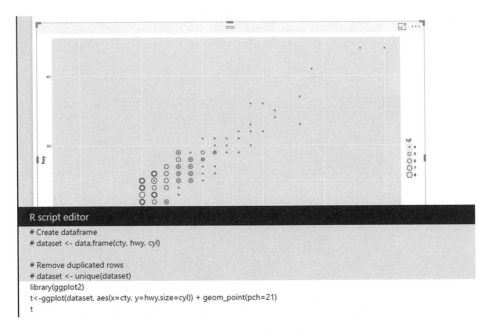

Figure 4-11. *Drawing a chart using the* ggplot *function*

In Figure 4-11, you can see that we have three different fields: highway and city speed, along the y and x axes, respectively. A car's cylinder variable is shown as a different cycle size. However, you might need a bigger cycle, to differentiate cars with 8 and 4 cylinders. We accommodate this need by adding another layer, by adding a function name, as follows:

```
scale_size_continuous(range=c(1,5))
```

Following, is the entire code:

```
t<-ggplot(dataset, aes(x=cty, y=hwy,size=cyl)) + geom_point(pch=23)+
scale_size_continuous(range=c(1,5))
in the scale_size_continues(range=c(1,5))
```

The difference between the lowest and highest value specified is 5. I can increase this difference by changing it from 5 to 10. The resulting scatter chart is shown in Figure 4-12.

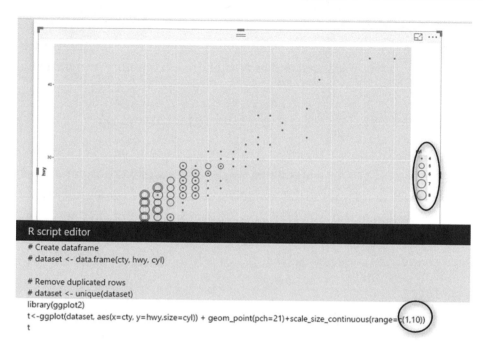

Figure 4-12. *Scatter chart showing speed in the city and on the highway, plus the number of cylinders*

In the next example, I have changed the pch value to 24 and added another code inside the aes function name: fill=Red. This means that the chart will show solid red rectangles (Figure 4-13).

```
t<-ggplot(dataset, aes(x=cty, y=hwy,size=cyl,fill="Red")) +
geom_point(pch=24)+scale_size_continuous(range=c(1,5))
```

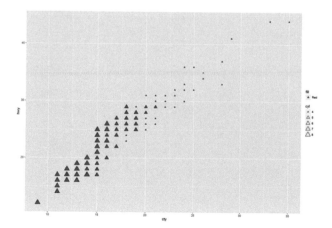

Figure 4-13. *The final chart*

By using the `facet` command in R, it is possible to show five different variables in just one chart. This helps us to have more dimension in our chart. For this we are going to show the year a car was produced and its type of drive. Therefore, we must change the code, as follows:

```
t← ggplot(dataset, aes(x=cty, y=hwy,color = factor(cyl))) +
geom_point(size=4)
```

By changing the aes function argument, we have replaced `size` argument with `color`. This indicates that I want to differentiate a car's cylinder values not just by cycle size, but that I am going to show them by allocating different colors to them. Hence, I change the aes function as in the preceding code snippet.

We must change the code, as follows:

```
library(ggplot2)
t<-ggplot(dataset, aes(x=cty, y=hwy,color = factor(cyl))) +
geom_point(size=4)
t<-t + facet_grid(year ~ drv)
```

Now, you can see the car's speed on the highway and in the city in y and x axes. Also, we have cylinders as a color and drive and year of production as a facet (Figure 4-14).

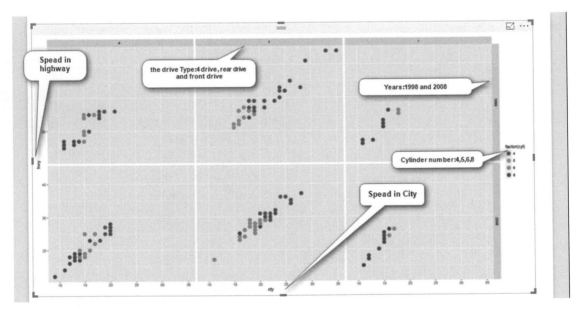

Figure 4-14. *Drawing a table chart showing five variables in the same chart*

R Features in Power BI

R script editor has some features that help us to better use Power BI Desktop, such as slice and dice and edit R code.

Slice and Dice

R visuals are interactive. It is possible to slice and dice them. We are going to use a slicer to slice the facet chart. We also are going to insert a year slicer in the report area, to filter the R visual (Figure 4-15).

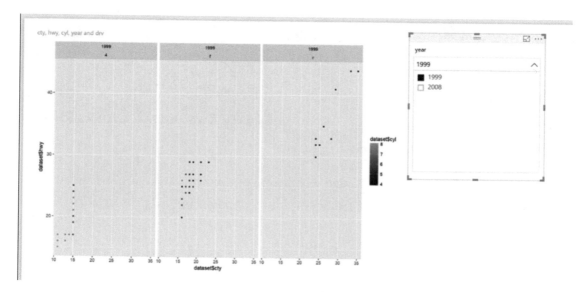

Figure 4-15. *Slicing and dicing the R visual*

Edit R Code in RStudio

It is possible to open the code in RStudio with the data. There is also an option to run the R code in RStudio using the data we have (Figure 4-16).

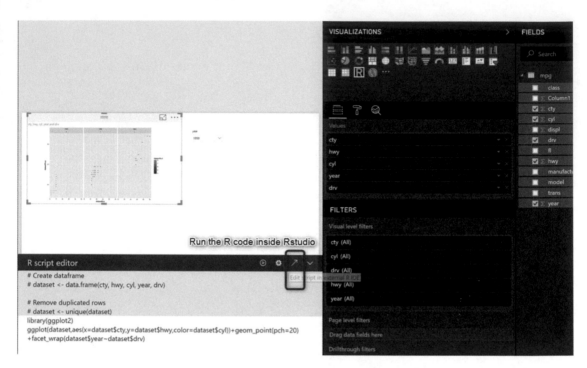

Figure 4-16. *Running the R code*

After clicking the Run option, a page will be open in RStudio that contains the data related to the car. The imported data set contains all changes in data (Figure 4-17).

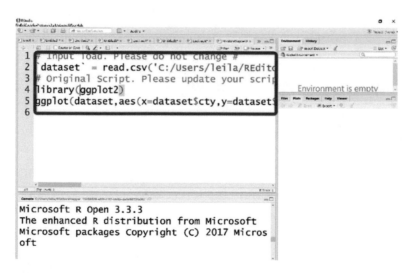

Figure 4-17. *Opening R code in RStudio*

Custom Visuals

Using custom visuals is another way to extend the capability of visualization in Power BI. There are two ways to access custom visuals:

1.   Use existing custom visuals available from the Office store

2.   Create custom visuals

Custom Visuals in the Power BI Office Store

The Office store provides a variety of custom visuals to the Power BI user. To access them, you must first sign in to your work account (Figure 4-18).

Figure 4-18. *Signing in to a Power BI account*

Then, in the Power BI Visualizations panel, click the three dots and select the Import from store option (Figure 4-19).

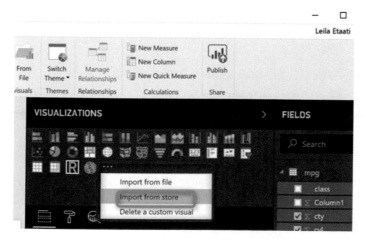

Figure 4-19. *Importing visuals from the Power BI store*

51

Next, you will see a page with the title "Power BI Custom Visuals." There are many categories listed here, such as filters, KPIs, Maps, Advanced Analytics, Time, Gauges, Infographics, and Data Visualizations (Figure 4-20).

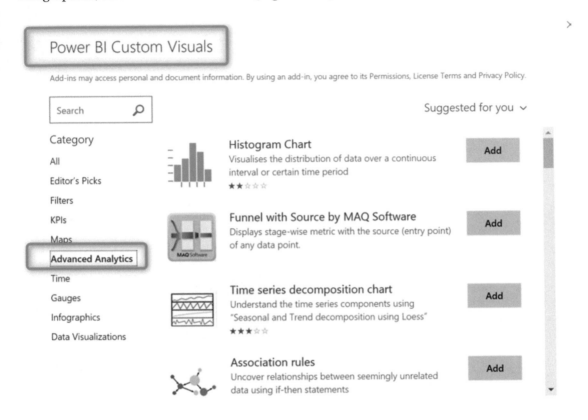

Figure 4-20. *Power BI Custom Visuals pane*

As mentioned, Power BI Custom Visuals includes an Advanced Analytics category. By clicking it, you will see such advanced analytics as time series, associative rules, clustering, and more. I am going to use one of these custom visuals to forecast milk production.

The first step is to import a milk data set into Power BI Desktop. The data has two columns: date of milk production and value of the milk (Figure 4-21).

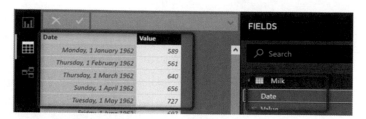

Figure 4-21. *Milk production data*

We must now import custom visuals from Power BI Custom Visuals, to forecast milk production (Figure 4-22).

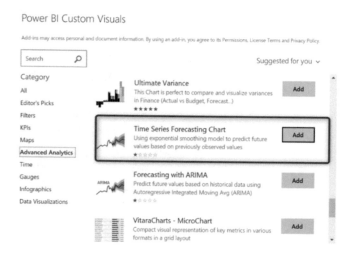

Figure 4-22. *Advanced Analytics time series custom visual*

After importing Custom Visuals, you will see that it has been added to the standard visual panel (Figure 4-23).

Figure 4-23. *Forecasting a custom visual*

Having imported the forecasting custom visual, we must now choose the date and value for the data field.

This custom visual uses an Exponential Smoothing algorithm for forecasting milk production over the next ten months (Figure 4-24).

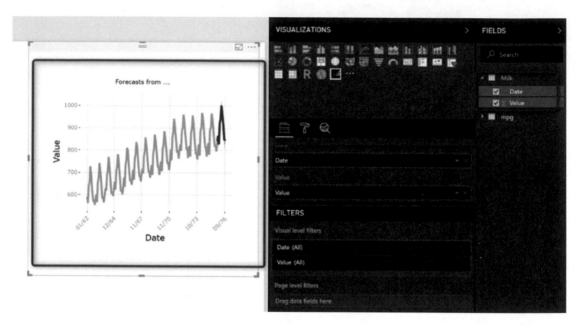

Figure 4-24. *Forecasting milk production*

The forecasting chart shows in yellow the actual data related to the production of milk in the previous months, and the forecasting for the later ten months is in red.

The algorithm behind the scenes is not accessible, and we are only able to change the parameters (Figure 4-25).

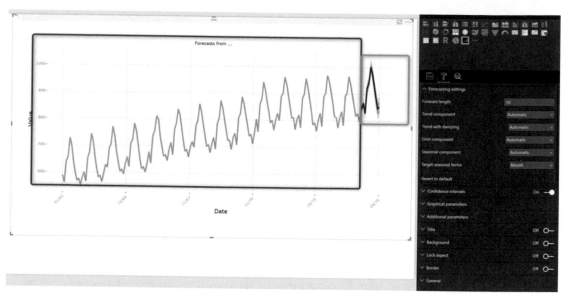

Figure 4-25. *Forecast milk production for the next ten months*

Custom visuals in Power BI extend the possibility of having different charts. However, the number of custom visuals created by the Microsoft team is limited. To extend visualization capabilities, there is a way to create custom visuals by using R scripts. In the next section, I will explain the process of creating custom visuals.

Creating Custom Visuals

Some of the main Power BI standard visuals in Power BI Desktop are widely used. However, as mentioned in the previous section, it is possible to extend these with custom visuals. To access the custom visuals, you must click Market Place in Power BI Desktop. There are two ways to create custom visuals using Java scripts or R codes.

I will explain briefly the process of creating custom visuals by using R codes.

1. The first step is to install NodeJS from `https://nodejs.org/`.

2. Next, install Power BI visuals tools using the command prompt (Figure 4-26):

```
npm install -g powerbi-visuals-tools
```

```
npm install -g powerbi-visuals-tools
```

```
C:\Users\leila\Documents>npm install -g powerbi-visuals-tools
npm WARN engine powerbi-visuals-package-validator@1.0.0: wanted: {"node":">=4.2.4"} (current: {"node":"0.12.2","npm":"2.
7.4"})
npm WARN engine typescript@2.1.5: wanted: {"node":">=4.2.0"} (current: {"node":"0.12.2","npm":"2.7.4"})
npm WARN engine gulp-debug@3.1.0: wanted: {"node":">=4"} (current: {"node":"0.12.2","npm":"2.7.4"})
npm WARN engine eslint@3.19.0: wanted: {"node":">=4"} (current: {"node":"0.12.2","npm":"2.7.4"})
npm WARN engine stringify-object@3.2.0: wanted: {"node":">=4"} (current: {"node":"0.12.2","npm":"2.7.4"})
npm WARN deprecated node-uuid@1.4.8: Use uuid module instead
npm WARN deprecated tough-cookie@2.2.2: ReDoS vulnerability parsing Set-Cookie https://nodesecurity.io/advisories/130
npm WARN deprecated minimatch@2.0.10: Please update to minimatch 3.0.2 or higher to avoid a RegExp DoS issue
npm WARN deprecated minimatch@0.2.14: Please update to minimatch 3.0.2 or higher to avoid a RegExp DoS issue
npm WARN deprecated graceful-fs@1.2.3: graceful-fs v3.0.0 and before will fail on node releases >= v7.0. Please update t
o graceful-fs@^4.0.0 as soon as possible. Use 'npm ls graceful-fs' to find it in the tree.
npm WARN engine babel-eslint@7.2.3: wanted: {"node":">=4"} (current: {"node":"0.12.2","npm":"2.7.4"})
npm WARN engine strip-bom@3.0.0: wanted: {"node":">=4"} (current: {"node":"0.12.2","npm":"2.7.4"})
npm WARN engine esprima@3.1.3: wanted: {"node":">=4"} (current: {"node":"0.12.2","npm":"2.7.4"})
npm WARN engine esprima@3.1.3: wanted: {"node":">=4"} (current: {"node":"0.12.2","npm":"2.7.4"})
npm WARN engine string-width@2.1.0: wanted: {"node":">=4"} (current: {"node":"0.12.2","npm":"2.7.4"})
npm WARN engine strip-ansi@4.0.0: wanted: {"node":">=4"} (current: {"node":"0.12.2","npm":"2.7.4"})
npm WARN engine is-fullwidth-code-point@2.0.0: wanted: {"node":">=4"} (current: {"node":"0.12.2","npm":"2.7.4"})
npm WARN engine request@2.81.0: wanted: {"node":">= 4"} (current: {"node":"0.12.2","npm":"2.7.4"})
npm WARN engine ansi-regex@3.0.0: wanted: {"node":">=4"} (current: {"node":"0.12.2","npm":"2.7.4"})
npm WARN engine har-validator@4.2.1: wanted: {"node":">=4"} (current: {"node":"0.12.2","npm":"2.7.4"})
```

Figure 4-26. *Installing Power BI custom visuals via the command prompt*

3. After installing the Power BI custom visuals, to ensure that they
    are properly installed, we must run the pbiviz command. After
    running this command, the information about Power BI Custom
    Visual Tool will be shown in the command prompt console
    (Figure 4-27).

```
:\Users\leila\Documents>pbiviz
      +3yysu+/
  oms/+osyhdhyso/
  ym/        /+oshddhys+/
  ym/             /+oyhddhyo+/
  ym/                     /osyhdho
  ym/                             sm+
  ym/                  yddy       om+
  ym/           shho /mmmm/       om+
   /     oys/ +mmmm /mmmm/        om+
  oso  ommmh +mmmm /mmmm/         om+
 ymmmy smmmh +mmmm /mmmm/         om+
 ymmmy smmmh +mmmm /mmmm/         om+
 ymmmy smmmh +mmmm /mmmm/         om+
 +dmd+ smmmh +mmmm /mmmm/         om+
       /hmdo +mmmm /mmmm/ /so+//ym/
              /dmmh /mmmm/ /osyhhy/
                //     dmmd
                       ++

    PowerBI Custom Visual Tool


Usage: pbiviz [options] [command]


Commands:

  new [name]       Create a new visual
  info             Display info about the current visual
  start            Start the current visual
  package          Package the current visual into a pbiviz file
  validate [path]  Validate pbiviz file for submission
  update [version] Updates the api definitions and schemas in the current visual. Changes the version if specified
  help [cmd]       display help for [cmd]

Options:

  -h, --help      output usage information
  -V, --version   output the version number
  --install-cert  Install localhost certificate


C:\Users\leila\Documents>
```

Figure 4-27. *Confirming Power BI custom visuals*

4. Next, we must create an rhtml template. To create a template folder, we first must create an empty folder in the C drive. After creating a new folder with the name CustomVisual in the C folder, then, using the command prompt, we must change the directory to C:\ CustomVisual. From the command prompt, we run the following code:

```
pbiviz new sampleRHTMLVisual -t rhtml
```

By running the code, a folder with the name sampleRHTMLVisual will be created in CustomVisual folder. In this folder, there is an R file with the name script.r (Figure 4-28).

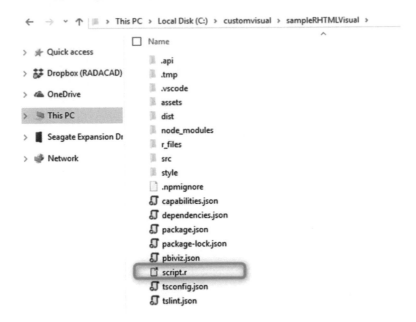

Figure 4-28. *A sample folder for custom visuals*

This is a folder that provides a template with which to create other R custom visuals. Check the file `script. R` inside the folder (Figure 4-29).

```
1  source('./r_files/flatten_HTML.r')
2
3  ############### Library Declarations ###############
4  libraryRequireInstall("ggplot2");
5  libraryRequireInstall("plotly")
6  ###################################################
7
8  ################## Actual code ##################
9  g = qplot(`Petal.Length`, data = iris, fill = `Species`, main :
10 ###################################################
11
12 ############# Create and save widget #############
13 p = ggplotly(g);
14 internalSaveWidget(p, 'out.html');
15 ###################################################
```

Figure 4-29. *R codes inside the script file*

Now, as you can see in the code in Figure 4-29, we require two libraries, Plotly and ggplot2, to draw a simple ggplot2 chart with Plotly.

Here, the data set has been hard-coded for `iris`, which is an open source data set in R. The plot gets the data from the `iris` data set and shows the petal and the length and species of the flower. Then we use the `ggplotly` function to show the data.

As a result, we have an R script. Now I first will create a package from this, then I will write my codes to create different charts. Hence, I return to the command prompt and type `pbiviz package` in the folder (Figure 4-30).

Figure 4-30. *Creating a custom visual in the command prompt*

5. Open the custom visual in the Power BI file. To do this, we must select the Import from file option in the Visualizations standard panel (Figure 4-31).

Figure 4-31. *Importing a custom visual into Power BI*

6. After choosing the Import from file option, we must browse the `sampleRHTMLVisual` folder and look for the `dist` folder. In this folder, there is a `pbiviz` file with the folder name. We must import this file into the Power BI Visualizations panel (Figure 4-32).

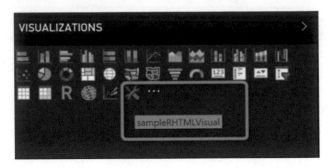

Figure 4-32. *Imported custom visual*

7. The last step is to drag and drop the custom visual into the Power BI report area (Figure 4-33). The visual is not related to the specific data.

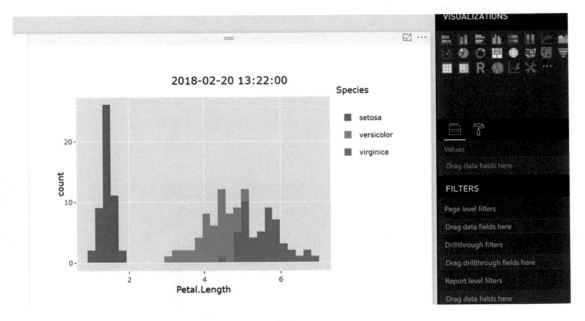

Figure 4-33. *Custom visual with R code*

We can change the R code and create a custom visual with a different name and icon. In another example, I am going to create a table chart. (I already explained the R codes for this earlier in the chapter.)

First, we must return to the sampleRHTMLVisual folder we have from the sample Power BI package, then copy the folder, to create a new custom visual. We change the name of the folder to TableChart. There is a pbiviz file here that contains information

about the name of the custom visual, the icon, and so forth. We must change the
pbiviz.json files content.

1. Change the name of the custom visual to "TableChart."

2. Create an icon for a custom visual with the dimension 20×20 and
   put it into the assets folder.

3. Change the address of the icon in the JSON file (Figure 4-34).

```
{
    "visual": {            TableChart
        "name": "sampleRHTMLVisual",
        "displayName": "sampleRHTMLVisual", TableChart
TableChart    "guid":
    "sampleRHTMLVisualFC0A875061A74051BC7B70D7B91B82F4",
        "visualClassName": "Visual",
        "version": "1.0.0",
        "description": "",
        "supportUrl": "",
        "gitHubUrl": ""
    },
    "apiVersion": "1.9.0",
    "author": {
        "name": "",
        "email": ""
    },                              we need to createn incon and put it in the assets fodler
    "assets": {
        "icon": "assets/icon.png"
    },
    "externalJS": [
        "node_modules/powerbi-visuals-utils-
    dataviewutils/lib/index.js"
    ],
    "style": "style/visual.less",
    "capabilities": "capabilities.json",
    "dependencies": "dependencies.json",
    "stringResources": []
}
```

Figure 4-34. *JSON file name must be changed*

4. After changing the name and creating a new icon for the custom
   visual, we must save the JSON file and put the created icon in the
   assets folder.

5. Next, we must change the R scripts in the `scripts.R` file. In the `actual code,` section, replace the existing code with the following one.

```
if(ncol(Values)==5)
{
  names(Values)[1]<-paste("X")
  names(Values)[2]<-paste("Y")
  names(Values)[3]<-paste("Z")
  names(Values)[4]<-paste("W")
  names(Values)[5]<-paste("M")
    g=ggplot(Values,aes(x=X,y=Y,color=Z))+geom_jitter()+facet_
    grid( M ~  W,scales = "free")
}
```

6. Save the file.

7. We must now return to the command prompt environment and change the directory to the `sampleRHTMLVisual` folder, by typing `pbiviz package` (Figure 4-35).

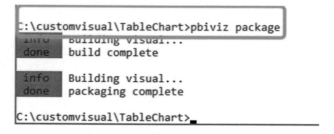

Figure 4-35. `pbiviz` *command in the command prompt*

8. After running the code, we should be able to see a new `pbiviz` file with name `TableChart` in the `dist` folder (Figure 4-36).

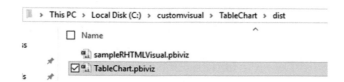

Figure 4-36. *Custom visual for a table chart*

9. Finally, we must import the created custom visual into Power BI
    Desktop and pass the data fields to the visual.

As mentioned, we must change the code, as follows:

```
if(ncol(Values)==5)
{
  names(Values)[1]<-paste("X")
  names(Values)[2]<-paste("Y")
  names(Values)[3]<-paste("Z")
  names(Values)[4]<-paste("W")
  names(Values)[5]<-paste("M")
    g=ggplot(Values,aes(x=X,y=Y,color=Z))+geom_jitter()+facet_grid
    ( M ~  W,scales = "free")
  }
```

The main data set is Values. The first item in the Values data set relates to the x axis,
the second to the y axis, and so forth.

So, in Power BI Desktop, be careful about the axis you specify in the R code.

As you can see in Figure 4-37, the imported visual has a name and icon. In addition,
in the data fields, we have Values as the main data set, and the sequence of the variable
we put there is as in the code we specify for each of them. For example, the cty field will
be located on the x axis, hwy on the y axis (the second value), and so on.

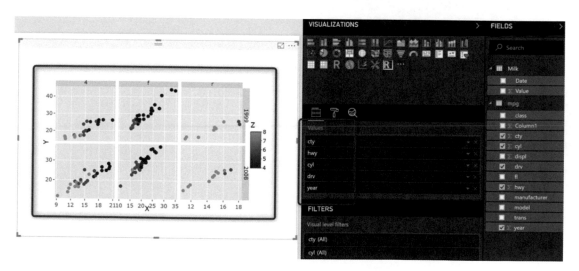

Figure 4-37. *Custom visual with a specific R code, name, and icon*

It is possible to change the Value fields to have separate x, y, legend, row, and column data fields. This can be done from capabilities.JSON. Additional information on how to change the data fields and how to add more settings is accessible via other Microsoft sources and the RADACAD web site.

Summary

This chapter explained how to set up Power BI Desktop to write R code. It also described how to draw a simple chart using R packages, such as ggplot2 and Plotly, inside Power BI. A very brief explanation of the available custom visuals for advanced analytics in Power BI was provided. Finally, the process of how we can create R custom visuals by writing R and JSON scripts was addressed briefly. In the next chapter, the main concepts for businesses to understand before initiating machine learning will be explained.

Reference

[1]   Dr. Abela, The Extreme Presentation ™ Method: Extremely effective communication of complex information, "Choosing a Good Chart," http://extremepresentation.typepad.com/ blog/2006/09/choosing_a_good.html, September 6, 2006.

PART II

Machine Learning with R and Power BI

Today, there is huge interest in using machine learning in various industries. Consider Power BI as a collaborative, self-service tool that supports the entire value chain for descriptive analytics (data ingestion, transformation, modeling, and visualization). In addition to these functionalities, Power BI provides really good tools for performing advanced analytics and machine learning. Chapters 5–8 focus mainly on the principal machine learning cycle inside Power BI. In Chapter 5, concepts related to what business problem we are going to solve by leveraging machine learning will be discussed. Chapter 6 focuses on the possibility of data wrangling (data cleaning) inside Power BI. Chapters 7 and 8 focus on the machine learning algorithm for predictive and descriptive analysis.

CHAPTER 5

Business Understanding

Business understanding is the main and first step in undertaking machine learning in any platform or language. Not all business problems can be addressed by machine learning approaches. There are some basic categories into which machine learning falls, including supervised learning and unsupervised learning.

Supervised learning is when both the input and output variables are identified. Unsupervised learning is when there is only input data, without corresponding variables.

Another machine learning classification is made up of three major groups:

- Descriptive analysis
- Predictive analysis
- Prescriptive analysis

Descriptive analysis uses mainly unsupervised learning approaches for summarizing, classifying, and extracting rules to answer something that has happened. Predictive analysis is about machine learning approaches for forecasting based on past data. Finally, prescriptive analysis uses optimization and recommendation algorithms to maximize expected outcomes.

However, there are other analytics, such as diagnosis analytics, that also help to provide a better understanding of a business. According to Gartner [1], these four analytics approaches help decision makers in an organization to make better decisions.

Each of these approaches (Figure 5-1) provides some values for a company, and implementing them requires some level of skills. Descriptive analysis is the simplest approach. It does not demand a high level of skill and can be done with different tools. Diagnosis and discovery analysis provides more insight into data and requires more skill.

© Leila Etaati 2019
L. Etaati, *Machine Learning with Microsoft Technologies*, https://doi.org/10.1007/978-1-4842-3658-1_5

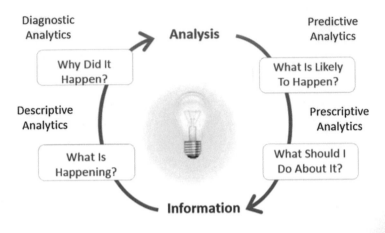

Figure 5-1. *Analysis and information [1]*

As you can see in Figure 5-2, the next two analyses, predictive and prescriptive, provide more insight into data and a better understanding of what may happen in the future, in addition to offering some prescriptive advice. These analyses bring more value for a company than the other three, and they require a greater degree of skill.

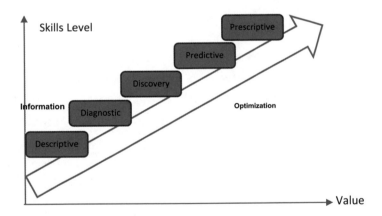

Figure 5-2. *Advanced analytics [1]*

In this chapter, I will explain the main concepts of each type of analysis and what different approaches we can take with each.

Descriptive Analysis

Descriptive analysis is the main approach with which to understand data and existing patterns. Descriptive analysis can be used to understand the structure of data, existing rules, or patterns in data, and so forth. Descriptive analysis can be grouped into three main categories.

- Operational reports

- Statistical analysis

- Data mining approaches

Operation reports are mainly traditional reports focused on analysis of past data. These reports are used principally to judge the performance of companies. Figure 5-3 shows such a report, illustrating the average total hourly rate of labor in different industries and income groups.

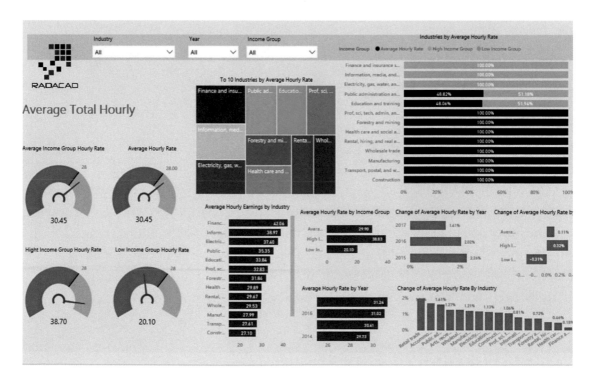

Figure 5-3. *Average total hourly report using Power BI*

This report provides a brief description of the hourly rate of workers in different industries. Other types of reports relate statistical facts about data.

Statistical analysis is another way of doing descriptive analysis, which gives us a better understanding of the statistical behavior of data. There are various kinds of statistical analysis, such as univariate analysis, in which each column of data is considered separately, such as a summary of data and data distribution (Figure 5-4). As you can see from the preceding figure, the average hourly rate of an employee is presented as a histogram, to show the distribution. In addition, we can see the minimum, maximum, and average distribution. The median of this data is plotted in a box or a table format. The box-plot chart shows that the data has been distributed smoothly at the median (the middle point), which is the same as the data average.

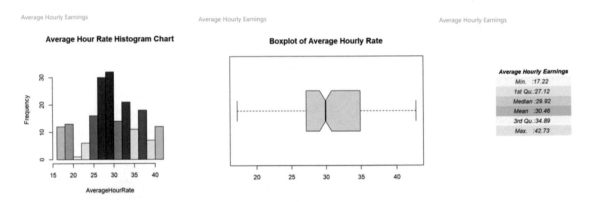

Figure 5-4. *Statistical analysis—univariate analysis*

Other forms of statistical analysis are concerned with the bivariate correlation and regression between two different data columns.

The other one is about finding the rules, natural cluster of data, and existing pattern, which can be done by data mining approaches (explained briefly in Chapter 8). In Chapter 8, I explain the code and concept of some algorithms aimed at descriptive analysis, such as clustering, market basket analysis, and decision trees.

Predictive Analysis

Another type of analysis related to machine learning is predictive analysis. Predictive analysis is about supervised learning, meaning that we want to learn from past data in order to predict future trends. Predictive analysis forecasts the future based on some probability. There is no way to predict the future with 100% probability. Predictive analysis is based mainly on the probability of the statistics. We can classify predictive analysis into two main approaches:

- Regression

- Classification

Regression approaches predict a value, for example, sales for the next three months, or the number of web site followers over the next three years.

Classification analysis is concerned with making predictions about a group. Classification predicts which person or thing belongs to which category or categories. For example, in analyzing a customer churn problem, classification analysis can predict whether a new customer belongs to a group that he or she may leave or remain in.

For both regression and classification approaches, there are many associated algorithms to help us. In Chapter 7, some of these algorithms will been explored.

For regression analysis, there are several related algorithms, such as linear regression, logistic regression, polynomial regression, stepwise regression, ridge regression, lasso regression, and elastic net regression. In addition, there are some other techniques, such as neural network, decision tree, and more (Figure 5-5).

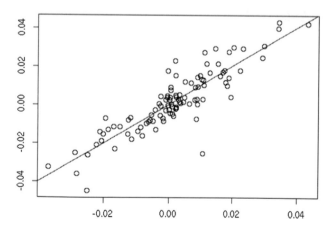

Figure 5-5. *Regression analysis [2]*

For classification analysis, there are also many related algorithms, including support-vector machine (SVM), decision tree, and k-nearest neighbors (KNN) (see Chapter 7). An example of classification analysis using Power BI is presented in Chapter 7.

Time series forecasting is a subdomain of predictive analysis and has some similarity to regression algorithms. Time series analysis forecast values are based on time. Time series data may relate to trends and/or seasonality (Figure 5-6).

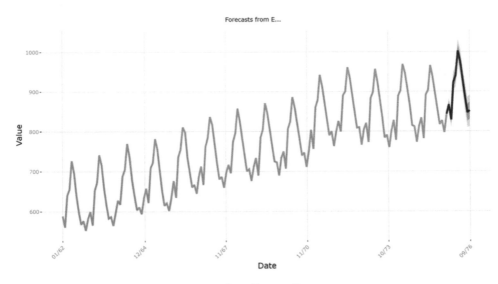

Figure 5-6. *Time series forecasting of milk production*

Prescriptive Analysis

Prescriptive analysis is about the recommendation system. A recommendation system predicts the rating or preference users express for an item. Recommendation systems can be categorized into two main classes:

- *Content-based systems*: These find similarities between items. Content-based recommendation systems analyze item descriptions and recommend those having greater similarity to a user's interests [3]. For example, if we want to recommend new movies to a customer, content-based filtering checks the similarity of the new movies offered with those the customer has already watched (Figure 5-7).

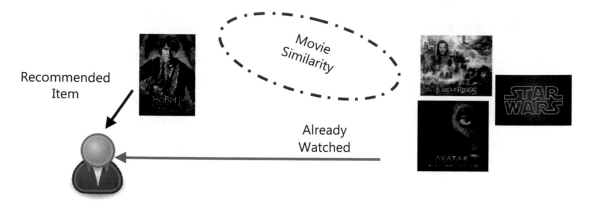

Figure 5-7. *Content-based filtering*

- *Collaborative filtering*: This is used to recommend items, based on how similar users liked the items (Figure 5-8).

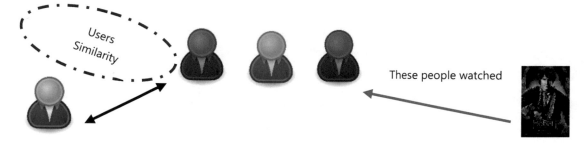

Figure 5-8. *Collaborative filtering [4]*

Business Understanding

As mentioned, business understanding is about identifying in what categories we can fit the business problem. It is important that identifying our problem fit into a particular category, such as predictive, descriptive, or prescriptive analysis. Business understanding requires interaction with the business experts and the business stakeholders. Moreover, the business problem we are going to solve can affect the algorithm selection process, data collection, and data cleaning. Chapters 6–8 provide some examples of machine learning for different business problems.

Summary

This chapter provided a brief introduction to the different data analytics and machine learning approaches, including descriptive, predictive, and prescriptive analytics. Power BI is a comprehensive tool for data-driven analysis that provides an infrustructure for doing any advanced analytics. In the next chapter, I will discuss how to use R in Power BI for data wrangling.

References

[1]   Michael Corcoran, "The Five Types Of Analytics. Michael Corcoran Sr Vice President &CMO", `https://docplayer.net/985643-The-five-types-of-analytics-michael-corcoran-sr-vice-president-cmo.html`.

[2]   Brian Lee Yung Rowe, "R for Quants, Part II (A)," Cartesian Faith, `https://cartesianfaith.com/2012/02/16/r-for-quants-part-ii-a/`, February 2012.

[3]   Pazzani M. J., Billsus D. "Content-based Recommendation Systems." In *The Adaptive Web. Lecture Notes in Computer Science*, vol 4321. Berlin, Heidelberg: Springer, 2007. Available online at `www.fxpal.com/publications/FXPAL-PR-06-383.pdf`.

[4]   Manojit Nandi, "Recommender Systems through Collaborative Filtering," Domino, `https://blog.dominodatalab.com/recommender-systems-collaborative-filtering/`, July 14, 2017.

CHAPTER 6

Data Wrangling for Predictive Analysis

In the machine learning process, after business understanding, the next step is collecting the right data, feature selection, and data wrangling. Data wrangling includes data cleaning, joining different data sources, quality control, data integration, data transformation, and data reduction processes (Figure 6-1).

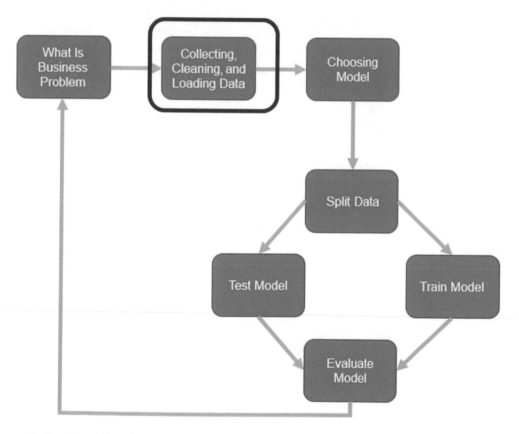

Figure 6-1. *Machine learning process*

© Leila Etaati 2019

L. Etaati, *Machine Learning with Microsoft Technologies*, https://doi.org/10.1007/978-1-4842-3658-1_6

In this chapter, I am going to show you how to perform data cleaning inside the Power BI Desktop Query Editor. A brief introduction to Power Query Editor will be provided, including how to import data from different resources, how to do data cleaning with Power Query Editor, and how to write R scripts inside it.

Power Query Editor

Power Query Editor is a data transformation tool for Power BI. It is a comprehensive tool for getting data, data cleaning, data modeling, and writing M, R, or Python scripts. To access the Power Query Editor in Power BI, you must click the Edit Queries icon (Figure 6-2).

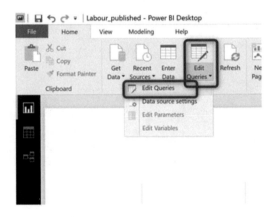

Figure 6-2. *Access Power Query Editor*

Power Query Editor has different options for data transformation. You can get data from such different resources as Excel, CSV, XML, JSON, Folder, SharePoint, SQL Server, SAP, MySQL, Oracle, Azure, Azure Blob, Azure SQL, Azure HDInsight, Google Analytics, Dynamics, Facebook, MailChimp, and more (Figure 6-3).

Figure 6-3. *Data resources available in Power Query Editor*

Power Query Editor has different components. The Home tab has a component for getting data from different resources, performing some simple data transformation, and an advanced editor for writing M language. Using Power Query, we are able to view in a small window the steps applied for data transformation (Figure 6-4).

Figure 6-4. *Home tab in Power Query*

Another component in Power Query is the Transformation tab. It provides some of the tools required for data transformation, such as changing date and time columns, statistic transformations, and so forth (Figure 6-5).

Figure 6-5. *Power Query Transformation*

In addition, there is a component named Run R scripts that allows users to write related R codes inside Power Query. In the next section, I am going to show you how we can do some data transformation with the aim of machine learning and data analysis, using Power Query.

Data Wrangling in Power Query

Before doing machine learning, we must go through two main processes: data preparation and data wrangling. Data preparation involves collecting data from resources, integrating it, and loading it into one resource, similar to the ETL (extract, transform, and load) process.

Data wrangling is loading the data and applying the data cleaning, formatting, and integration in the application layer.

The Python language includes some popular data wrangling processes, such as reshaping data, selecting data, and merging data.

Reshaping Data

One of the main approaches for reshaping data is pivoting. This involves converting column data to the column name, as illustrated in Figure 6-6.

Date	Type	Value
2nd March 2018	A	12.36
3rd March 2018	A	23.69
2nd March 2018	B	25.36
2nd March 2018	C	17.28
3rd March 2018	B	19.2

Type	A	B	C
Date			
2nd March	12.36	NaN	17.28
3rd March	23.69	19.2	NaN

Figure 6-6. *Pivoting data*

The related code to create data in Python (Figure 6-7) is

```
data=[["2nd March 2018","A",12.36],    ["3rd March 2018","A",23.69],
["2nd March 2018","B",25.36],       ["2nd March 2018","C",17.28],
["3rd March 2018","B",19.2]]
using package pandas
import pandas as pd
df=pd.DataFrame(data)
 pivot table
df=pd.pivot_table(df,index=[df[0]],columns=df[1])
```

```
                                2
1                               A       B       C
0
2nd March 2018   12.36   25.36   17.28
3rd March 2018   23.69   19.20     NaN
>>> █
```

Figure 6-7. *Pivoting using Python code*

In R, we can do this via the following code:

```
install.packages("tidyr")
date=c("2nd March 2018","2nd March 2018","2nd March 2018","2nd March
2018","2nd March 2018")
Type=c("A","A","B","C","B")
index=c(0,1,2,3,4)
Value=c(12.36,23.69,25.36,17.28,19.2)
df=data.frame(index,date,Type,Value)
library("tidyr")
spread(df,Type,Value)
and the result is the same (a bit different out put)
```

Now we are going to see how we can launch this process in Power Query without writing any code. To pivot data using Power Query, we must enter data, by using the Enter Data option (Figure 6-8).

Figure 6-8. *Entering data manually*

By clicking Enter Data, we are able to put data in Power Query manually (Figure 6-9).

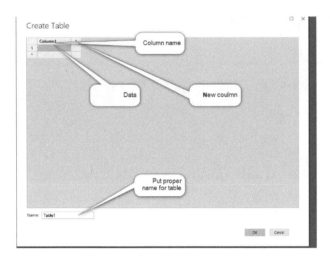

Figure 6-9. *Creating a data table*

We have the same data as we have in Python (Figure 6-10).

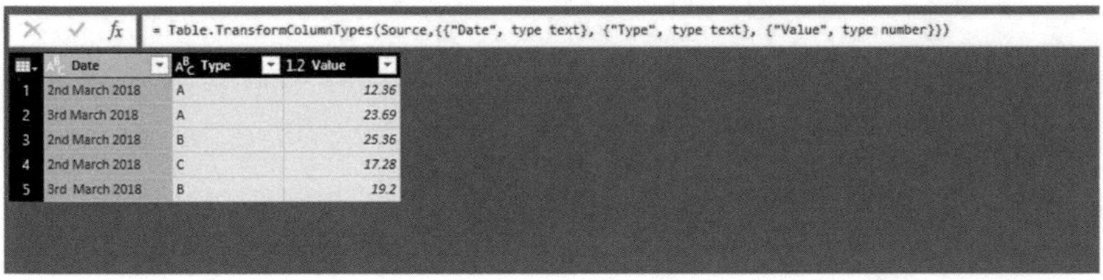

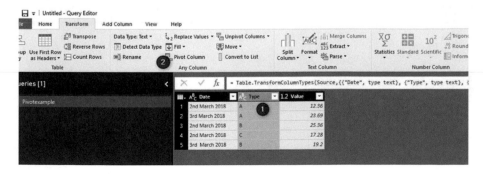

Figure 6-10. *Data set in Power BI*

Now we just click the Type column (Figure 6-11). Then we click Pivot Column under the Transform tab.

Figure 6-11. *Click the Type column and pivot option*

Next, we specify which column we are going to put a value and type to (Figure 6-12).

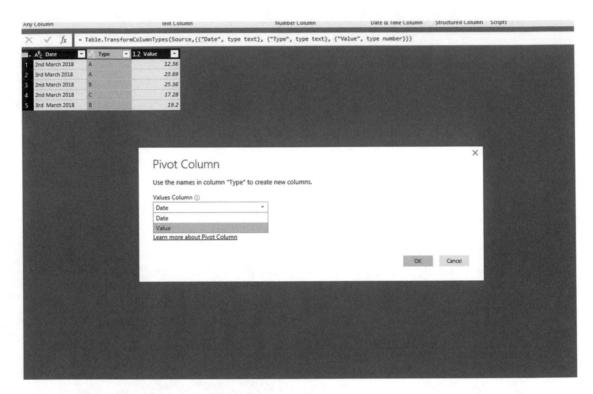

Figure 6-12. *Specifying type and values*

The result of pivoting is shown in Figure 6-13.

Date	1.2 A	1.2 B	1.2 C
1 2nd March 2018	12.36	25.36	17.28
2 3rd March 2018	null	19.2	null
3 3rd March 2018	23.69	null	null

Figure 6-13. *Pivot table*

There are other examples of reshaping, such as unpivoting, melting, and iteration, that all can be done in Power Query. In addition, the process of selecting and putting a condition to check data can be done quite easily in Power Query.

Selecting Data

For selecting a value with a condition in Python, we use the where function, as follows:

df.where(df[2]>17)

In the df data set, we are going to select values that are greater than 17 (Figure 6-14).

```
>>>  df.where(df[2]>17)
                      0    1      2
0                   NaN  NaN    NaN
1   3rd March 2018     A  23.69
2   2nd March 2018     B  25.36
3   2nd March 2018     C  17.28
4   3rd March 2018     B  19.20
```

Figure 6-14. *Selecting values using Python*

In Power Query, you must click the column you are going to filter, then choose the filter option, number of filters, and Greater Than Or Equal To option (Figure 6-15).

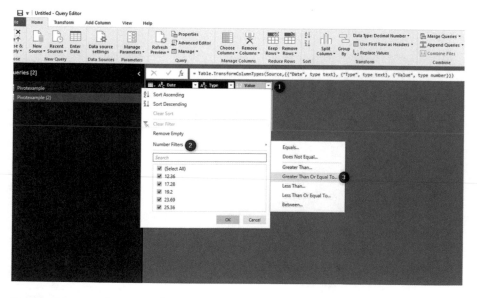

Figure 6-15. *Power Query select values*

Then, in Power Query, simply filter the column to 17 (Figure 6-16).

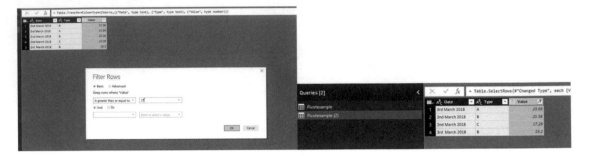

Figure 6-16. *Power Query filter value*

Merging Data

Another popular form of data preparation is merging data, for example, joining two tables, possibly from different data sources. In Python, if we want to do this, there is a merge function that we can use to connect two different data sets. For example, consider the following data set:

```
data1=[["a",11],["b",1],["c",99]]
data2=[["a",20],["b",0],["d",21]]
data1=pd.DataFrame(data1)
data1.columns=["Type","Value"]
data2.columns=["Type","Value"]
data2=pd.DataFrame(data2)
merg=pd.merge(data1,data2,how='left',on="Type")
```

As you can see in the preceding code, we can specify the join type and join column. We can change the how attribute to left, right, inner, and outer (Figure 6-17).

```
>>> merg
   Type  Value_x  Value_y
0    a       11     20.0
1    b        1      0.0
2    c       99      NaN
>>>
```

Figure 6-17. *Using Python to merge data*

The same process can be performed in Power Query. I have created two different data sets, Data1 and Data2, in Power Query (Figure 6-18).

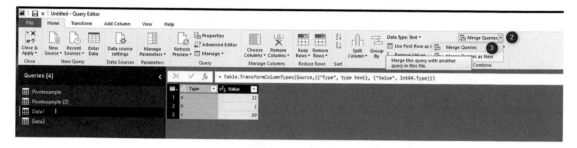

Figure 6-18. *Creating a data set in Power Query*

After creating a data set, you must click the Merge column, to merge Data1 with Data2 (Figure 6-18).

In the Merge window, we can specify which column we are going to merge, based on and what type of merge we are interested in (Figure 6-19).

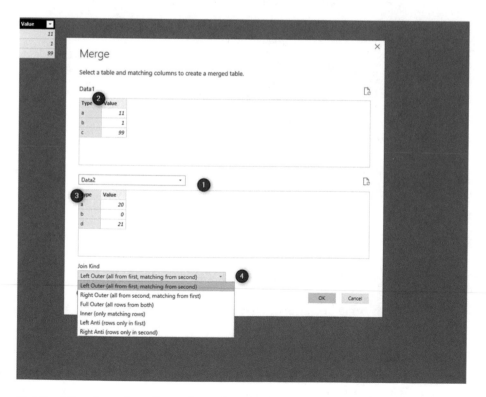

Figure 6-19. *Merging data based on the Type column and Left Outer join*

After merging, we must specify what columns we want to show to users (Figure 6-20).

Figure 6-20. *Column selection*

Then the output will be there, and we will be able to see the results (Figure 6-21).

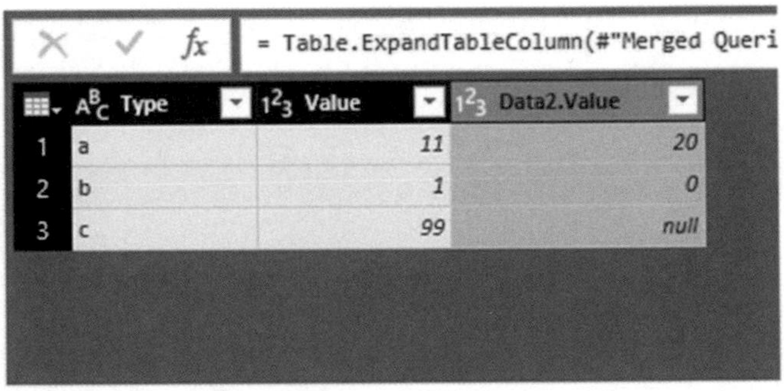

Figure 6-21. *Result of merging Data1 and Data2*

These are some basic data transformations that you can do in Power Query. There are more complex processes that you can do using the Power Query menu or M or R languages.

Data Transformation Using R Scripts

Not all data transformation is possible or easy using existing menus in Power Query. To improve our ability to transform data, we can use R inside Power Query. There is a data set about breast cancer in women available from the Kaggle web site (https://www.kaggle.com/lbronchal/breast-cancer-dataset-analysis). This data set is made up of 569 rows and 32 columns. The first column is patient ID, and the second is the diagnosis. The rest of the columns relate to the cancer cell's specification.

Columns 2 to 32 have some numeric values that are not within the same range. For example, the "radius_mean" column has values from 6.9 to 22, while the "compactness_mean" column has values from 0.019 to 0.34. There is another data preparation process, named normalization, to bring data into the same scale. This process is good for some algorithms, such as lKNN; however, it is not always recommended (see Figure 6-22).

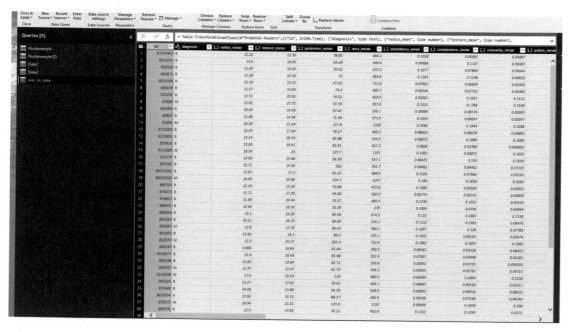

Figure 6-22. *Data set related to breast cancer in women*

Normalization

Normalizing data means bringing it within a specific range, such as 0 to 1. I am going to use a formula for normalizing names, following a "MinMax" approach. In this example, I will bring the data from all the columns in the cancer data set into the range of 0 to 1, except the patient ID and diagnosis columns (which consist of text).

First, for each column, we must find the minimum and maximum value. For each value, we must calculate the formula, as follows:

$$Normalize\ value = \left(\frac{\min(x) - x}{\max(x) - \min(x)} \right)$$

We can apply this transformation to data, using the R language in Power Query. In Power Query, there is an option for writing R code: Run R Script (Figure 6-23).

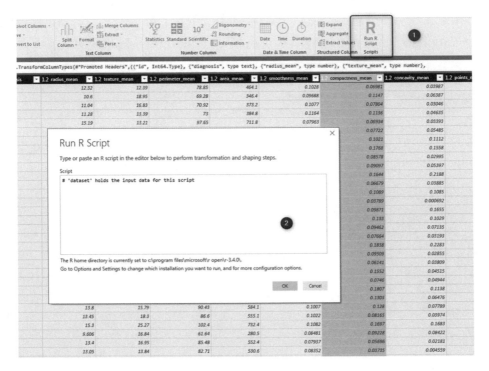

Figure 6-23. *Running R scripts in Power Query*

The Run R Script editor is not very advanced. The data you want to transform is stored under variable name dataset.

Hence, we are going to use the dataset variable and the formula for normalizing the data.

In R, I will write a function to put the MinMax formula there.

```
Normalize<- function (x)
{
  return ((x-min(x))/(max(x)-min(x)))
}
```

Then I must apply this function to the data set. For this, I must use another function in R, named lapply.

The `lapply` function gets the data set and the name of the normalized function. It then applies the function of the data set. In my example, you do not have to apply MinMax normalization on the first and second column, so you just use `dataset[3:32]` instead of `dataset`.

```
NormalizedData<-as.data.frame(lapply(dataset[3:32],Normalize))
```

As you can see in Figure 6-24, after writing the code, we need to press the OK button. Power Query will apply the normalization transformation to the data.

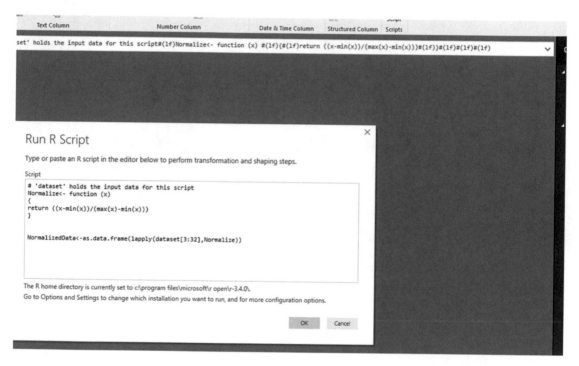

Figure 6-24. *R Script editor*

After running the codes, the result of the data transformation is shown in Figure 6-25. You can see the applied steps in Run R Script.

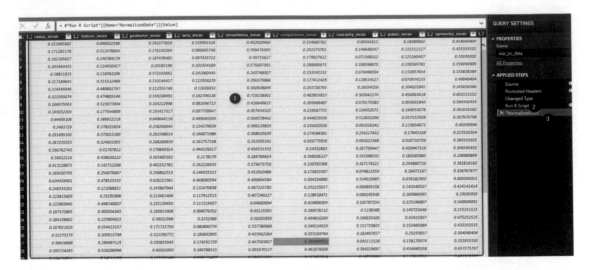

Figure 6-25. *Normalized data*

Other Data Transformation

There are other ways to transform data with Power Query.

Change Data Type

To change the data type in Power Query, click the Data Type option and choose the right data type. Likewise, you can change the data type by clicking the icon beside each column (Figure 6-26).

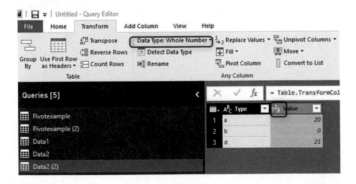

Figure 6-26. *Changing the data type*

Group By

In Power Query, we can also group data by specific aggregation options. First, we must click the column we want to group data by. Then we click the Group By icon in the menu (Figure 6-27). In the Group By window, we choose the Group by option we want and the aggregation type, under Operation. Next, we choose Sum as the aggregation option.

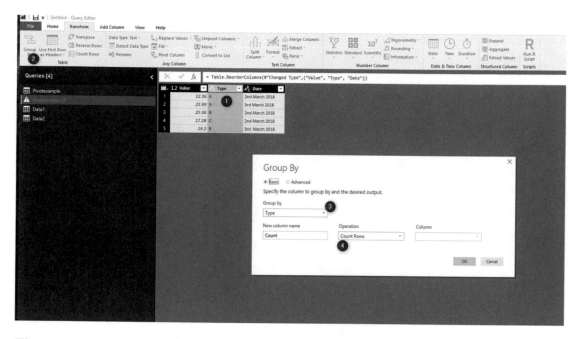

Figure 6-27. *Group by data with specific aggregation*

Finally, the data will be grouped by type value (Figure 6-28).

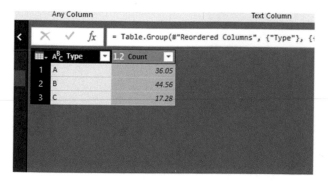

Figure 6-28. *The resulting aggregated data*

Many other kinds of data transformation, such as splitting columns based on the delimitator, transposing rows, changing the data type, adding date or time columns, including some statistical computation, merging columns, and so forth, are possible. Under the Add Column tab, it is possible to add custom columns, create columns from examples, create functions, format data columns, add columns for date, month, days, time, among other things. In addition, it is possible to transform data using the M language, although this is beyond the scope of this book.

Summary

This chapter offered a brief introduction to how to use R inside Power Query Editor. It explained how we can use it to reshape data, select data, write a mathematical function using R codes and apply it to a data set, and so forth. There are other uses for R or Python inside Power Query Editor, such as using R for regular expressions or using R and Python for machine learning. In the next chapter, more examples of using R in Power Query Editor will be presented.

CHAPTER 7

Predictive Analysis in Power Query with R

In this chapter, the process of doing machine learning inside Power BI Query Editor by writing R code will be explained. The main aim here is to provide some examples of how we can use R codes for predictive analysis (classification and regression). The concepts and codes related to some of the algorithms will be provided. In addition, the process of automating predictions via parameters inside Power BI Query Editor also will be discussed.

Neural Networks

What we expect from a computer is that we provide some inputs and then receive outputs that match our needs. Scientists try to mimic the human brain by creating an intelligence machine—a machine that does the same reasoning as humans.

The most important element of the human brain is neurons. Human brains consist of 75 million neurons. Each neuron is connected to others via synapses. So what we have in a neural network are some nodes that are connected to one another. In the human body, if a neuron is triggered by some external element, it will pass the message from the receiver node to other nodes, via synapsis. (Figure 7-1).

© Leila Etaati 2019
L. Etaati, *Machine Learning with Microsoft Technologies*, https://doi.org/10.1007/978-1-4842-3658-1_7

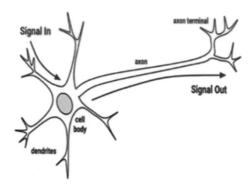

Figure 7-1. *Neural system*

Neural networks mimic the same concepts as the human brain. One node gets some input from the environment, and the neural network model creates outputs that produce the result just as a computer system would (Figure 7-2).

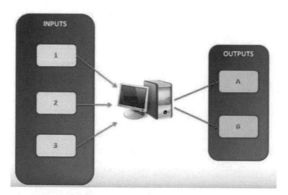

Figure 7-2. *Computer system architecture*

In a neural network there is a

- Set of inputs nodes

- Set of output nodes

- Some processing in the middle, to achieve a good result

- A flow of information

- A connection between nodes

Some of the connections are more important than others, meaning that they have a greater impact on the results than others. In neural networks, we refer to this importance as the connections' *weights*.

Another analogy that better expresses the goal of a neural network is the descent after climbing a mountain. When we reach the summit and the weather is foggy, we are only able to see one meter ahead. We must decide which direction to choose with only one meter of visibility. We take a first step based on the location, again deciding which direction to follow and taking other steps. So, with each step we are evaluating the course and choosing the best way to come down from the mountain (Figure 7-3).

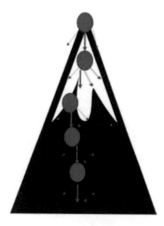

Figure 7-3. *Neural network comparison with mountain climbing*

Each decision can be viewed as a node that leads us to a better and faster resolution. In a neural network, there are some hidden nodes that perform the main task. They find the best value for the output while using a function called an activation function.

In this section, I am going to refer to an example from *Machine Learning with R* [1]. The example is about predicting the strength of concrete. The concrete has been used in many different structures, such as a bridge, apartment, roadways, and so on. For safety, the strength of the concrete is critical. The concrete's strength depends on the material used to create it, such as cement, slag, ash, water, and so forth. We have a data set of the ingredients of the concrete (Figure 7-4). You can download it from "Machine Learning with R datasets" [2].

cement	slag	ash	water	superplasti	coarseagg	fineagg	age	strength
141.3	212	0	203.5	0	971.8	748.5	28	29.89
168.9	42.2	124.3	158.3	10.8	1080.8	796.2	14	23.51
250	0	95.7	187.4	5.5	956.9	861.2	28	29.22
266	114	0	228	0	932	670	28	45.85
154.8	183.4	0	193.3	9.1	1047.4	696.7	28	18.29
255	0	0	192	0	889.8	945	90	21.86
166.8	250.2	0	203.5	0	975.6	692.6	7	15.75
251.4	0	118.3	188.5	6.4	1028.4	757.7	56	36.64
296	0	0	192	0	1085	765	28	21.65
155	184	143	194	9	880	699	28	28.99
151.8	178.1	138.7	167.5	18.3	944	694.6	28	36.35
173	116	0	192	0	946.8	856.8	3	6.94
385	0	0	186	0	966	763	14	27.92
237.5	237.5	0	228	0	932	594	7	26.26
167	187	195	185	7	898	636	28	23.89
213.8	98.1	24.5	181.7	6.7	1066	785.5	100	49.97
237.5	237.5	0	228	0	932	594	28	30.08
336	0	0	182	3	986	817	28	44.86
190.7	0	125.4	162.1	7.8	1090	804	3	15.04
312.7	0	0	178.1	8	999.7	822.2	28	25.1
229.7	0	118.2	195.2	6.1	1028.1	757.6	3	13.36
228	342.1	0	185.7	0	955.8	674.3	7	21.92
236	157	0	192	0	972.6	749.1	7	20.42
132	207	161	179	5	867	736	28	33.3
331	0	0	192	0	1025	821	28	31.74
310	143	0	168	10	914	804	28	45.3
304	76	0	228	0	932	670	90	49.19
425	106.3	0	153.5	16.5	852.1	887.1	91	65.2
166.1	0	163.3	176.5	4.5	1058.6	780.1	28	21.54
255	99	77	189	6	919	749	28	33.8
339	0	0	197	0	968	781	28	32.04
475	0	0	228	0	932	594	28	39.29
145.7	172.6	0	181.9	3.4	985.8	816.8	28	23.74
313	145	0	127	8	1000	822	28	44.52
331	0	0	192	0	1025	821	90	37.91
178	129.8	118.6	179.9	3.6	1007.3	746.8	28	39.16
165	0	143.6	163.8	0	1005.6	900.9	14	16.88
277.2	97.8	24.5	160.7	11.2	1061.7	782.5	14	47.71
325	0	0	184	0	1063	783	7	17.54

concrete ⊕

Figure 7-4. *Concrete data set*

A neural network can be used for predicting a value or class, or it can be used for predicting multiple things. In our example, we are going to predict a value, that is, the strength of concrete. First, we load the data in Power BI, and in Query Editor, we write some R codes. Then we must make some data transformations (Figure 7-5).

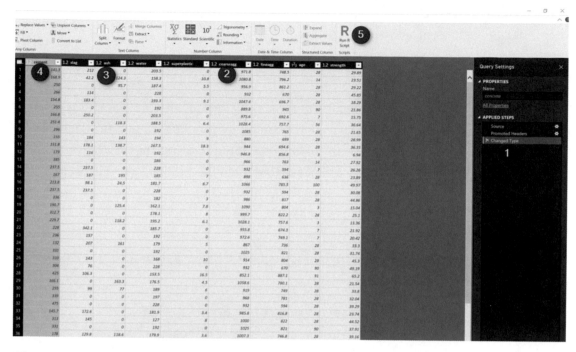

Figure 7-5. *Pivot using Python codes*

As you can see in Figure 7-5, in the sections labeled 2, 3, and 4 (circled in red), data is not on the same scale. We must impose some data normalization before applying any machine learning. The process of data normalization is explained in Chapter 6. The same code is used to normalize the data here.

```
normalize <- function(x) {
    return((x - min(x)) / (max(x) - min(x)))
}
concrete_norm <- as.data.frame(lapply(dataset, normalize))
```

After data cleaning and data transformation, we must separate in the data set some parts for training and some for testing. This process helps the model to learn from data and to mimic the data behavior. Therefore, we must devote more than 70% of the data for training and the rest for testing. To avoid bias, we must shuffle the data. A sample function in R has been used to create random row numbers for the data set. In addition, 80% of the data has been put in the training data set and the rest reserved for testing.

```
nrows<-nrow(dataset)
sampledata<-sample(nrows,0.8*nrows)
concrete_train <- concrete_norm[sampledata,]
concrete_test <- concrete_norm[-sampledata,]
```

There are many packages and algorithms for using neural network algorithms in R. One such package is `neuralnet`. This package contains a function for a neural network algorithm. To use this package, we must install it in RStudio, using `install.packages()` first. After installing the package, we only have to refer to the `vis` package `library` command.

```
library("neuralnet")
```

The next step is to create a training model using the training data set and identifying which column we are going to predict.

```
concrete_model <- neuralnet(strength ~ cement + slag
+ ash + water + superplastic + coarseagg + fineagg + age,
data = concrete_train)
```

Now that the model is created, we can test it for accuracy. We are going to run the model against the training data set for all eight attributes.

```
model_results <- compute(concrete_model, concrete_test[1:8])
predicted_strength <- model_results$net.result
```

And we must create an output data set to show to the user.

```
output<-dataset[-sampledata,]
output$Pred<-predicted_strength*100
```

The result will be stored in an output variable that is in a data frame structure. Another important consideration is that Power Query only recognizes the `data. Frame` format. So, other data structures, such as vectors, lists, and matrices cannot be shown in the Power Query editor (Figure 7-6).

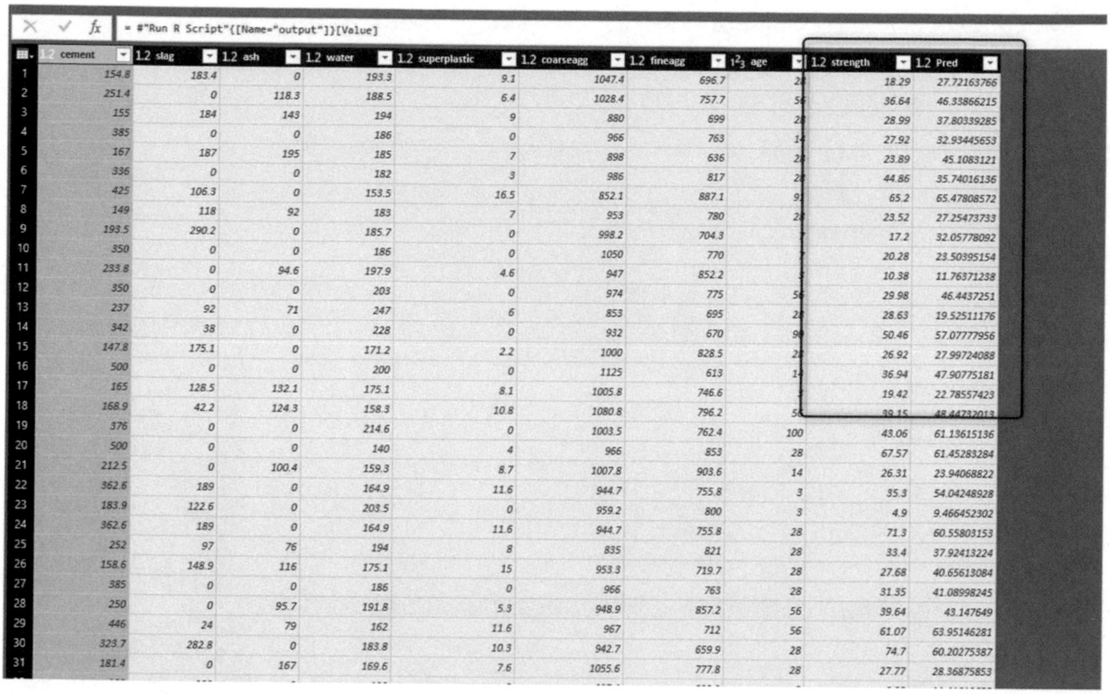

```
X  ✓  fx    = #"Run R Script"{[Name="output"]}[Value]
```

	cement	1.2 slag	1.2 ash	1.2 water	1.2 superplastic	1.2 coarseagg	1.2 fineagg	1²3 age	1.2 strength	1.2 Pred
1	154.8	183.4	0	193.3	9.1	1047.4	696.7	2	18.29	27.72163766
2	251.4	0	118.3	188.5	6.4	1028.4	757.7	5	36.64	46.33866215
3	155	184	143	194	9	880	699	2	28.99	37.80339285
4	385	0	0	186	0	966	763	14	27.92	32.93445653
5	167	187	195	185	7	898	636	2	23.89	45.1083121
6	336	0	0	182	3	986	817	2	44.86	35.74016136
7	425	106.3	0	153.5	16.5	852.1	887.1	9	65.2	65.47808572
8	149	118	92	183	7	953	780	2	23.52	27.25473733
9	193.5	290.2	0	185.7	0	998.2	704.3		17.2	32.05778092
10	350	0	0	186	0	1050	770		20.28	23.50395154
11	233.8	0	94.6	197.9	4.6	947	852.2		10.38	11.76371238
12	350	0	0	203	0	974	775	5	29.98	46.4437251
13	237	92	71	247	6	853	695	2	28.63	19.52511176
14	342	38	0	228	0	932	670	9	50.46	57.07777956
15	147.8	175.1	0	171.2	2.2	1000	828.5	2	26.92	27.99724088
16	500	0	0	200	0	1125	613	14	36.94	47.90775181
17	165	128.5	132.1	175.1	8.1	1005.8	746.6		19.42	22.78557423
18	168.9	42.2	124.3	158.3	10.8	1080.8	796.2	5	39.15	48.44732013
19	376	0	0	214.6	0	1003.5	762.4	100	43.06	61.13615136
20	500	0	0	140	4	966	853	28	67.57	61.45283284
21	212.5	0	100.4	159.3	8.7	1007.8	903.6	14	26.31	23.94068822
22	362.6	189	0	164.9	11.6	944.7	755.8	3	35.3	54.04248928
23	183.9	122.6	0	203.5	0	959.2	800	3	4.9	9.466452302
24	362.6	189	0	164.9	11.6	944.7	755.8	28	71.3	60.55803153
25	252	97	76	194	8	835	821	28	33.4	37.92413224
26	158.6	148.9	116	175.1	15	953.3	719.7	28	27.68	40.65613084
27	385	0	0	186	0	966	763	28	31.35	41.08998245
28	250	0	95.7	191.8	5.3	948.9	857.2	56	39.64	43.147649
29	446	24	79	162	11.6	967	712	56	61.07	63.95146281
30	323.7	282.8	0	183.8	10.3	942.7	659.9	28	74.7	60.20275387
31	181.4	0	167	169.6	7.6	1055.6	777.8	28	27.77	28.36875853

Figure 7-6. *Prediction result*

It is possible to see the neural network structure in the visualization area, to see the hidden node, layer, and so forth. Therefore, we must duplicate the data set for concrete in Power BI Report, using the R custom visual, as shown in Figure 7-7. Next, we must write the same codes for neural network prediction and add another line for plotting the model. Run the code, and you will see the neural network structure that has just appeared on the layer, and the error is 3.001.

```r
normalize <- function(x) {
    return((x - min(x)) / (max(x) - min(x)))
}
concrete_norm <- as.data.frame(lapply(dataset, normalize))
summary(concrete_norm$strength)
concrete_train <- concrete_norm[1:773,]
concrete_test <- concrete_norm[774:1030,]
library("neuralnet")
```

```
    concrete_model <- neuralnet(strength ~ cement + slag
    + ash + water + superplastic + coarseagg + fineagg + age,
    data = concrete_train)
plot(concrete_model)
```

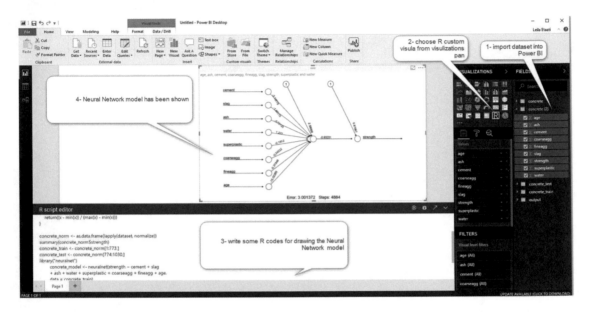

Figure 7-7. *Neural network model structure in Power BI Report*

We can mitigate the error by changing the number of hidden nodes and layers.

Decision Trees

A decision tree is a common approach for doing machine learning. This tool can be used
for prediction, descriptive analysis, and feature selection. A decision tree follows the way
that we reach decisions. Imagine a job seeker who wants to decide among a number of
different jobs. He or she has established some criteria for his/her selection, such as the
following: What are the responsibilities? What is the annual salary or hourly rate? Finally,
how many times a year is travel required? We can simulate the job seeker's decision-
making process, as shown in Figure 7-8. The root of the tree is the main decision point,
that is, saying yes or no to the job. Then the most important criterion is whether the job
title matches the searcher's expertise. The second most important criterion is salary.
Finally, if there is no leaf, the third criterion is to check the number of required travel

days per year. The decision tree uses information gain theory to identify what is the main criteria are for tree branching. Details on how this works are available at `http://radacad.com/decision-tree-conceps-part-1` [3].

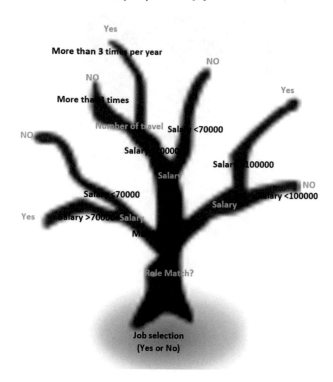

Figure 7-8. *Decision tree for job-seeking*

There are different ways of using decision trees in Power BI. One approach involves Power BI custom visualization.

To access this, you first must sign in to a Power BI account (Figure 7-9).

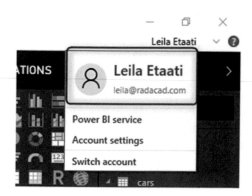

Figure 7-9. *Power BI account*

We must retrieve the visual from the Visualization panel by clicking the three dots and then choosing the Import from store option (Figure 7-10).

Figure 7-10. *Importing a Visual from the store*

On the Power BI custom visual page, there are different categories of visuals, including Filters, KPIs, Maps, Advanced Analytics, and more (Figure 7-11).

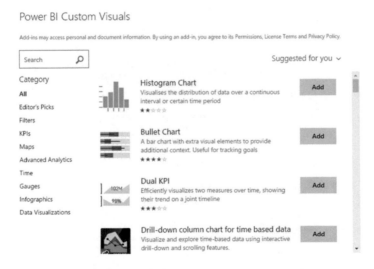

Figure 7-11. *Power BI custom visuals*

You need only click the Advanced Analytics option and then select Decision Tree Chart (Figure 7-12). Click the Add button to add the chart to Power BI visualization.

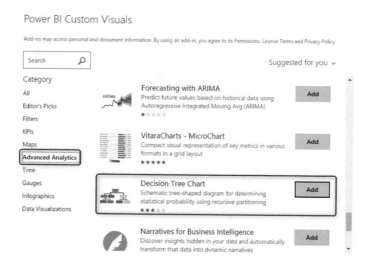

Figure 7-12. *Decision tree custom visual in the Power BI store*

Note   When you add this chart for the first time, you must be sure that you already have RStudio or any R version on your machine. Power BI will start to install some of the required packages, such as `rpart` into your local R version. Just allow Power BI install all the packages. In the next step, a new custom visual will appear in the Power BI Visualizations panel (Figure 7-13).

Figure 7-13. *Decision tree custom visual in the Visualizations panel*

To test the custom visual, we must import some data into Power BI Desktop for predictive analysis. The data is a free data set about the *Titanic* disaster [4]. We must choose the fields for decision making. The main aim (target) is to predict whether people survived. To do that, first we have to choose a couple of columns that may affect passenger survival, such as age, gender, and passenger class. Next, put the Survived column as the target variable, in the related data field (Figure 7-14).

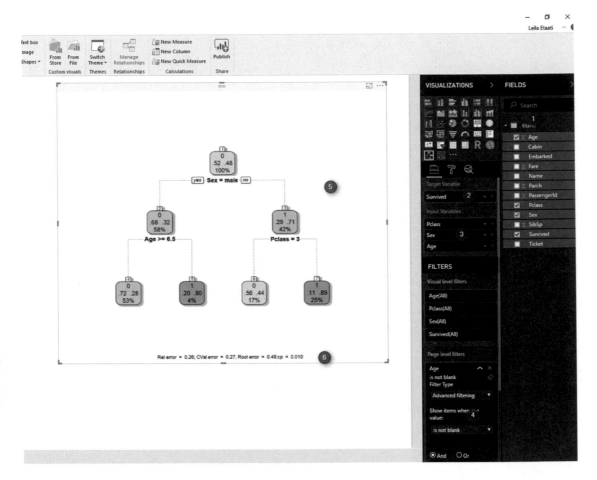

Figure 7-14. *Power Query filter value*

The next step is to remove the missing values ("blank") from the age column. Finally, the related decision tree chart appears in Power BI Report (Figure 7-14).

At the root of tree, there are four numbered tags. 0 stands for passengers who could not have survived. Also, these people are identified by a green tag. The "100%" means that all data is at the root. The "0.52" and "0.48" indicate that about 0.52 are men and 0.48 are women. In other words, the first attribute that the decision tree decided to analyze (based on entropy theory) is the gender of the passengers (Figure 7-15).

Figure 7-15. *The root node in the decision tree*

For the next level, on the left, the tag is in green, and it already branches to represent the male passengers. Based on that branch, we can summarize that most of the male passengers did not survive (0). However, as you can see in Figure 7-16, for women (the branch at the right side), the attribute that is going to be analyzed is passenger class.

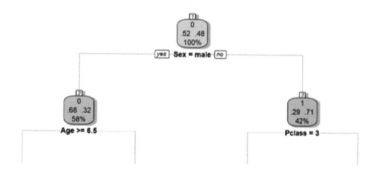

Figure 7-16. *The second Level of Tree Analysis*

For men (root) older than seven years of age (second node), there is a 58% possibility that they will not survive (green tag and 0) (Figure 7-17).

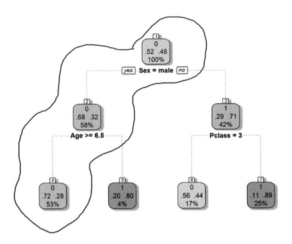

Figure 7-17. *The decision tree analysis for men*

Men (root) older than seven years old (second node) will not survive (green tag and 0), with the possibility of 53%. Also, males younger than seven will survive.

A decision tree inside Power Query can be used to do machine learning and show the result in Power BI Report (the same process that has been explained in the "Neural Networks" section).

In the next section, I am going to write R code for a decision tree inside Power Query and show how it is possible to pass parameters to it.

Automated Machine Learning Inside Power Query

In the previous section, I explained how decision trees can be used for prediction analysis. Now we are going to use it inside Power Query, for predictions without a specific chart.

First, we must click the Power Query Editor at the top of the page, to navigate to the Power Query environment. In Power Query, you must first download the data set for the *Titanic* from www.kaggle.com/c/titanic [4]. Then, click New Source, select the Text/CSV option to import the data set, and click OK (Figure 7-18).

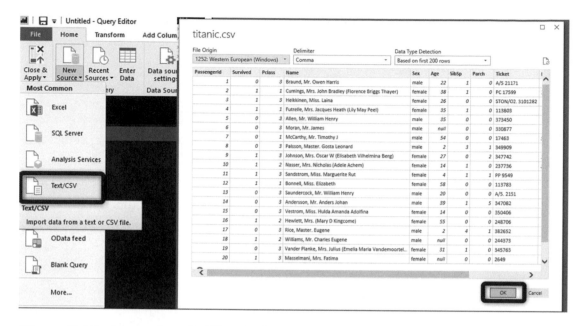

Figure 7-18. *Importing the Titanic data set into Power Query*

After importing the data set into Power Query, we must navigate to the Transform tab, then to Run R scripts. In the R editor, we will be able to write R codes. The first line of the code refers to a library named rpart. The rpart package first must be installed in your RStudio. Before installation, first make sure that you do not have it, by using the following command:

```
Library("rpart")
```

Otherwise, in RStudio, use the following code, to see what library is already installed on your machine.

```
packagematrix <- installed.packages();
NameOnly <- packagematrix[,1];
OutputDataSet <- as.data.frame(NameOnly);
OutputDataSet
```

First, we must ensure that rpart has been installed on our machine. Then we write the following code in the R editor (just as what we did earlier in this chapter for neural networks). We must now refer to the rpart library and divide the data either for training or testing.

```
library(rpart)
numrows<-nrow(dataset)
sampledata<-sample(numrows,0.8*numrows)
train<-dataset[sampledata,]
test<-dataset[-sampledata,]
```

Creating model is the next step. This pertains to the attributes we want to predict and create a model for, based on the training data set. In addition, we must have a formula for Survived ~. This indicates that we want to predict the survive column according to age, sex, and passenger class. The predict function will be used to predict the survival of the prediction analysis.

```
DT<-rpart(Survived~ Age+Pclass+Sex,data=train,method= ="class")
prediction<-predict (DT,test)
rpartresult<-data.frame(prediction,test)
```

So, the result of the prediction will be shown in Power Query, with the name rpartresult. The result will consist of two different additional columns. "X0" stands for the probability of passengers not surviving, and "x1" is the probability of passengers surviving. Now imagine that we want to use the rpart algorithm for classifying another data set, such as the cancer-related data discussed in Chapter 6. It is possible to parameterize the R code for passing the desired data set, prediction column, and so forth, to the R codes. To do this, we must duplicate the data set (Figure 7-19).

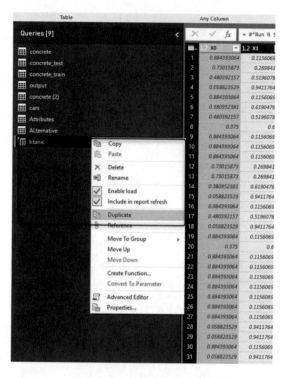

Figure 7-19. *Duplicating the Titanic data set*

Now just right-click the new data set, to create a function out of it. There is a need to create a function from the new duplicated data set (Figure 7-20).

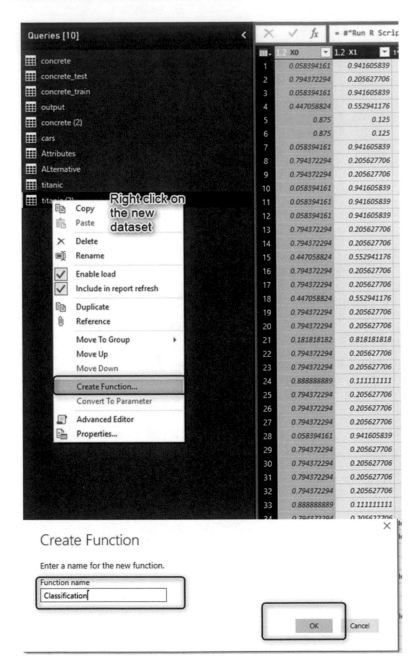

Figure 7-20. *Creating a function in Power Query*

After creating a function, we must customize it, by passing parameters. To do this, we must navigate to Advanced Editor (Figure 7-21).

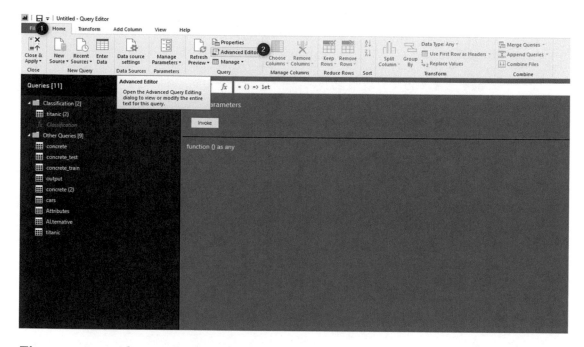

Figure 7-21. *Advanced Editor in Power Query*

In Advanced Editor, it is possible to see the steps previously applied to the Titanic data set in M language. As you can see in Figure 7-22, the source of the data set has been identified from my local machine.

Figure 7-22. *Advanced Editor for writing in M language*

The first three lines should be substituted with the following one:

```
(#"Source Table" as table) as table=>

    let

        Source = #"Source Table",
```

In the first line, we define a variable named Source Table, and in the third line, we assign it to the Source variable. In the next step, we will remove some of the lines starting with Promoted Headers and Changed Type. These lines are solely for the specific data set (titanic) transformation. Now we have the following lines, for which we must still make some transformation:

```
(#"Source Table" as table) as table=>

    let
         Source = #"Source Table",
         #"Run R Script" = R.Execute("# 'dataset' holds the input data for
         this script#(lf)library(rpart) #(lf)numrows<-nrow(dataset)#(lf)
         sampledata<-sample(numrows,0.8*numrows)#(lf)train<-
         dataset[sampledata,]#(lf)test<-dataset[-sampledata,]#(lf)DT<-
         rpart(Survived~ Age+Pclass+Sex,data=train,method=""class"")#(lf)
         prediction<-predict (DT,test)#(lf)rpartresult<-data.frame(predictio
         n,test)",[dataset=#"Changed Type"]),
         rpartresult = #"Run R Script"{[Name="rpartresult"]}[Value]
    in
         rpartresult
in
    Source
```

As you can see in preceding code, we have a header line #"Run R Script" = that contains a function R.Execute. This function contains all the R codes that we wrote. In M language, the output of one function will be passed to the next one. The previous function is for changing type Changed Type, which we already deleted. Now we must change the code in Run R Script, as follows:

```
         #"Run R Script" = R.Execute("# 'dataset' holds the input data for
this script#(lf)library(rpart) #(lf)numrows<-nrow(dataset)#(lf)sampledata<-
sample(numrows,0.8*numrows)#(lf)train<-dataset[sampledata,]#(lf)
test<-dataset[-sampledata,]#(lf)DT<-rpart(Survived~
Age+Pclass+Sex,data=train,method=""class"")#(lf)prediction<-predict
(DT,test)#(lf)rpartresult<-data.frame(prediction,test)",[dataset=#"Changed
Type"]),
```

The Changed Type should be substituted with Source, as shown in the following code:

```
let
    Source = #"Source Table",
    #"Run R Script" = R.Execute("# 'dataset' holds the input data for
    this script#(lf)library(rpart) #(lf)numrows<-nrow(dataset)#(lf)
    sampledata<-sample(numrows,0.8*numrows)#(lf)train<-
    dataset[sampledata,]#(lf)test<-dataset[-sampledata,]#(lf)DT<-
    rpart(Survived~ Age+Pclass+Sex,data=train,method=""class"")#(lf)
    prediction<-predict (DT,test)#(lf)rpartresult<-data.frame
    (prediction,test)",[dataset=Source]),
    rpartresult = #"Run R Script"{[Name="rpartresult"]}[Value]
in
    rpartresult
in
    Source
```

We still must make some additional changes. These are to be applied to the Name column that we want to predict. Currently, it is "Survived~ Age+Pclass+Sex," but we want to substitute the Survived column with a parameter that the user provided. Also, rather than another column for input, we want to consider all the columns. As a result, we must change the code, as follows:

```
(#"Source Table" as table, #"Prediction Column"as text) as table=>
    let
        Source = #"Source Table",
        #"Run R Script" = R.Execute("# 'dataset' holds the input data for
        this script#(lf)library(rpart) #(lf)numrows<-nrow(dataset)#(lf)
        sampledata<-sample(numrows,0.8*numrows)#(lf)train<-
        dataset[sampledata,]#(lf)test<-dataset[-sampledata,]#(lf)DT<-rpart(
        "&#"Prediction Column"&"~ .,data=train,method=""class"")#(lf)
        prediction<-predict (DT,test)#(lf)rpartresult<-data.frame(predictio
        n,test)",[dataset=Source]),
        rpartresult = #"Run R Script"{[Name="rpartresult"]}[Value]
    in
        rpartresult
in
    Source
```

We must refine the code a bit, by removing the last line in Source. So, the final code will be

```
(#"Source Table" as table,#"Prediction Column"as text) as table=>
    let
        Source = #"Source Table",
        #"Run R Script" = R.Execute("# 'dataset' holds the input data for
        this script#(lf)library(rpart) #(lf)numrows<-nrow(dataset)#(lf)
        sampledata<-sample(numrows,0.8*numrows)#(lf)train<-
        dataset[sampledata,]#(lf)test<-dataset[-sampledata,]#(lf)DT<-rpart(
        "&#"Prediction Column"&"~ .,data=train,method=""class"")#(lf)
        prediction<-predict (DT,test)#(lf)rpartresult<-data.frame(predictio
        n,test)",[dataset=Source]),
        rpartresult = #"Run R Script"{[Name="rpartresult"]}[Value]
    in
        rpartresult
```

After running the code, we will have a function with an input variable (Figure 7-23).

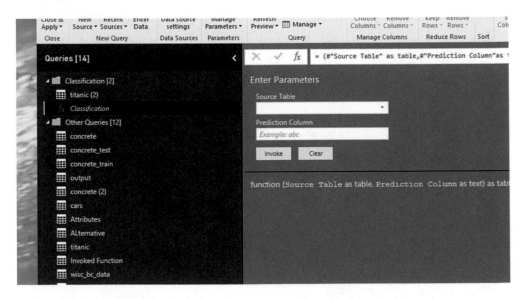

Figure 7-23. *Creating a function for classification with two inputs*

To test the function, we must create a data set to pass to the function. Import the new Titanic data set, then Ctrl+Click the four main columns: Survived, Pclass, Age, and Sex. Next, right-click and select the Remove Columns option (Figure 7-24).

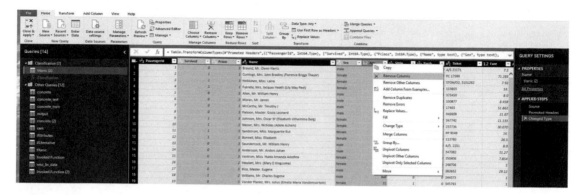

Figure 7-24. *Selecting the columns*

Finally, there is a data set with four columns now ready to pass to the function. In the function, for the first parameter, we must choose the Titanic data set, and for the second, the Prediction Column named Survived (Figure 7-25).

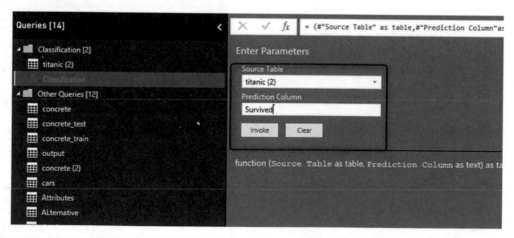

Figure 7-25. *Invoking the function*

Next, we may get a message for Edit Permission that is about providing permission to run external scripts on the query (Figure 7-26).

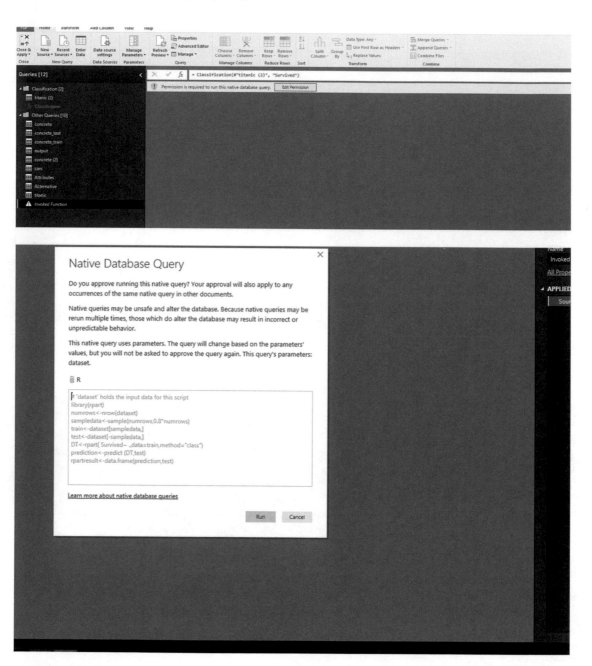

***Figure 7-26.** Permission request*

After accepting the permission, we can now see the result, as shown in Figure 7-27.

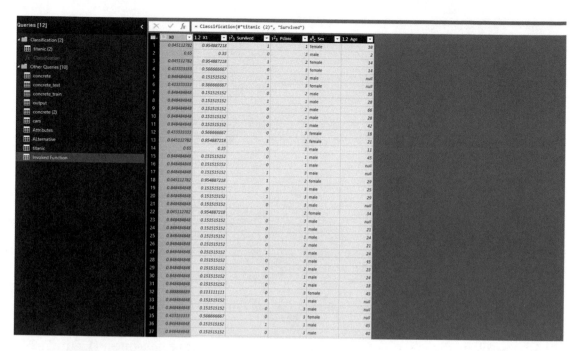

Figure 7-27. *Function result for Titanic data set*

To test the function, I imported another data set [5] that was introduced in Chapter 6. It is a data set related to breast cancer patients. I want to predict patient diagnosis: will a patient's cancer become malignant "M" or benign "B." We follow the same process as before for this new data set. First, we import it, then we pass the name and column of the data set to the function (Figure 7-28).

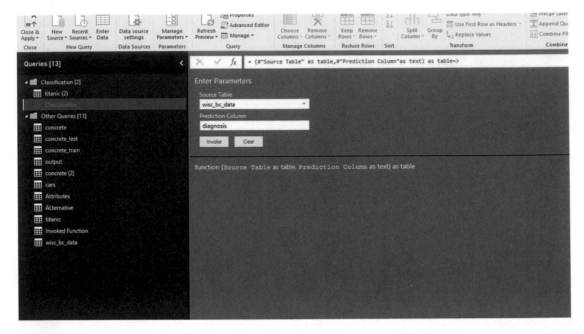

Figure 7-28. *Call classification function for the cancer data set*

After invoking the function, the prediction result appears as a new query (Figure 7-29).

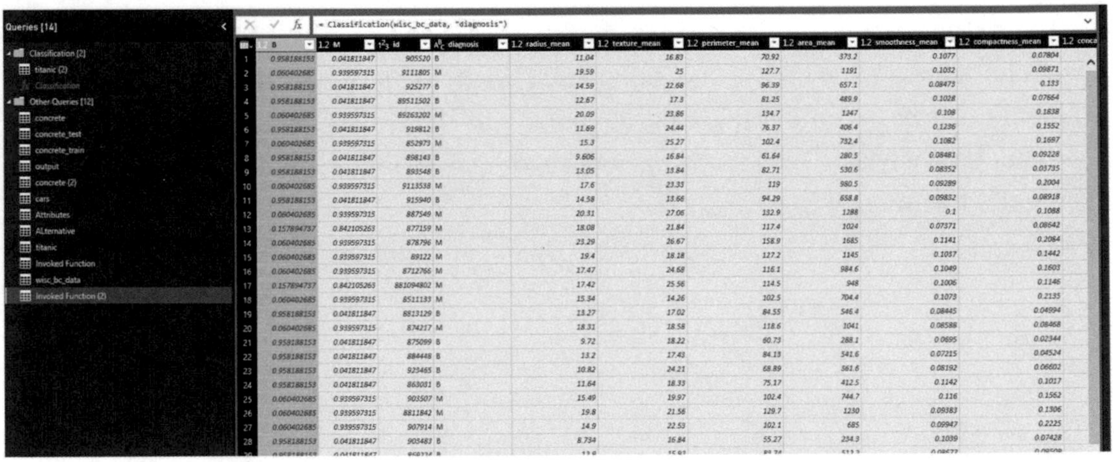

Figure 7-29. *Prediction result for cancer diagnosis data set*

Summary

The main aim of this chapter was to show how we can perform machine learning inside the Power Query Editor using R codes. Two different algorithms were introduced: neural networks and decision trees. I discussed how you can set parameters for making machine learning much more flexible. In the next chapter, I will discuss descriptive analysis using Power BI.

References

[1]   Lantz, Brett. *Machine Learning with R*. Birmingham, UK: Packt Publishing, 2015.

[2]   Zach Stednick, "Machine Learning with R datasets," GitHub, `https://github.com/stedy/Machine-Learning-with-R-datasets.git`, 2019.

[3]   Leila Etaati, "Decision Tree: Concepts—Part I," RADACAD, `http://radacad.com/decision-tree-conceps-part-1`, November 27, 2017.

[4]   Franck Sylla, "Titanic: Machine Learning from Disaster," Kaggle, `www.kaggle.com/c/titanic`, 2017.

[5]   Breast Cancer Wisconsin (Diagnostic) Data Set, Kaggle, `www.kaggle.com/uciml/breast-cancer-wisconsin-data/downloads/data.csv`, September 25, 2016.

CHAPTER 8

Descriptive Analysis in Power Query with R

This chapter focuses on descriptive analysis in Power BI. A brief introduction explains how we can use descriptive analysis to help decision making. Next comes a brief introduction to clustering, how clustering is performed in Power BI Report, and how we can do clustering in Power Query Editor. Finally, I will cover how to do market basket analysis in Power BI.

K-Means Clustering

Cluster analysis is the task of grouping similar objects in a same group or cluster. The clustered objects have more similarity to each other than other objects. For example, we may be interested in grouping our customers, based on their purchase behavior or demographic information [1]. Or, to cite an example in science, we may want to cluster the number and severity of earthquakes that occurred in New Zealand over the past ten years. For a medical purpose, we may want to classify patients with cancer, based on their laboratory results.

In machine learning, there are many different algorithms to help us do clustering. Some of these algorithms are centroid-based, such as k-means, GMM, Fuzzy c-means, and so forth. The others are based on connectivity [2], such as hierarchical clustering. There are some algorithms that are density-based or based on probability, dimensionality reduction, and neural networks/deep learning.

In this chapter, I am going to show you how we use k-means algorithms for classifying data. There is a data set for household power consumption that is available for free from the UCI Machine Learning Repository [3]. The data set is about the consumption of electric power in one household over a period of almost four years.

© Leila Etaati 2019

L. Etaati, *Machine Learning with Microsoft Technologies*, https://doi.org/10.1007/978-1-4842-3658-1_8

This data set has such attributes as date, time, global active minute active, and reactive power, average voltage, average current intensity, and watt hours for kitchen, dishwasher, oven, water heater, and so forth. You are going to see how we can naturally classify these data, using two different approaches in Power BI.

Clustering Custom Visuals

The first and easy way to cluster data is to use one of the custom visuals in the Power BI store: Clustering. To access it, you first must log in to a Power BI account. In the Visualizations panel, click the three dots, then choose the From Store option. Under Advanced Analytics, you will find the Clustering option for custom visuals (Figure 8-1).

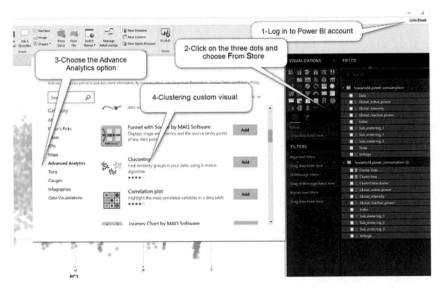

Figure 8-1. *Clustering custom visuals*

Add the custom visual to the Power BI environment. If it is your first time adding a Power BI custom visual, some of packages, such as Plotly, XML, and such will be installed. Next, you must choose four different columns from the filed area. As you can see in Figure 8-2, some columns, such as Voltage, Global intensity (household global minute-averaged current intensity), Submetering 3 and 1 (watt-hour activity energy for kitchen, dishwasher, water heater, and so forth) have been selected.

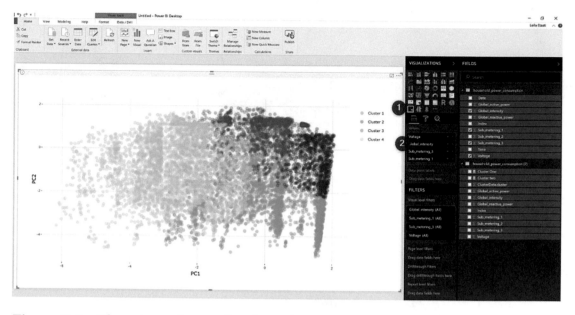

Figure 8-2. *Choosing columns for clustering*

After choosing the parameters, you must set them up. Click the format icon, then scale data to normalize it. Apply PCA, if you want to choose the number of clusters you can specify, or leave it as the default (clusters will be chosen automatically).

As you can see in Figure 8-3, the result of the clustering is shown in a clustering diagram. K-means clustering found out about four main clusters. As you can see in the picture cluster 4 has more items, while cluster 1 has fewer items than other clusters. However, the limitation of this visualization is that we cannot see the numbers and are not able to compare each cluster according to its attributes.

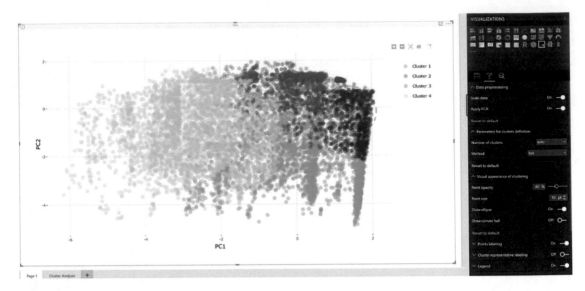

Figure 8-3. *Clustring parameters and results*

In the next section, the process of performing clustering analysis inside Power Query will be shown, as well as how we can use Power BI visual to demonstrate the result.

Clustering in Power Query

As explained in previous chapters, it is possible to do machine learning inside Power Query, using R code. In this section, the process of clustering data using R code inside Power Query will be explained, and you will see how we can use a Power BI visualization to better describe the data grouped by the relevant clusters.

First, we must go to the Query Editor, then we have to duplicate the data set that we have, by right-clicking the data set and choosing the Duplicate option (shown in Figure 8-4).

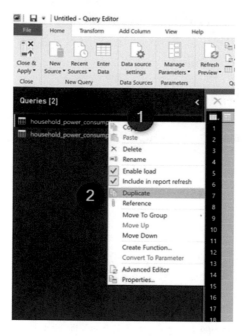

Figure 8-4. *Duplicating the household power consumption data set*

After duplicating the data set, you will have a copy of the power consumption for household data that you must transform before applying the R code.

1. Remove the date and time columns. Click each column, then right-click and select Remove.

2. Remove errors. You may have some errors, so you will have to set a rule for dealing with them, e.g., click the Remove rows and choose Remove Errors or Remove Blank Rows or Remove Missing Values (Figure 8-5).

Figure 8-5. *Data cleaning*

After data cleaning, you can run R scripts by clicking the Transform tab and selecting the Run R Script option. In R editor, first we must bring data in the same scale, using the normalization function in R, as follows:

```
normalize <- function(x) {
  return ((x - min(x)) / (max(x) - min(x))) }
NormalizedData <- as.data.frame(lapply(dataset, normalize))
```

The function kmeans clusters data using k-means clustering algorithms. This algorithm requires a data set and the number of clusters.

```
ClusterData<-kmeans(NormalizedData ,4)
```

After clustering the data, we must create an output data set. For this, we leverage the data.frame function, to create a data frame data set from the original data set and the number of clusters.

```
PowerConsumption<-data.frame(dataset,ClusterData$cluster)
```

After running the code, the data set now has original data, plus a new column that shows the cluster number. Moreover, we must add an index column to the current data set, to have a primary key for further analysis. To add a new column, click the Add Column tab in the top menu, then click Index Column, which starts from 0 by default, but you can change it to 1, by choosing another option.

As you can see in Figure 8-6, our data has now been prepared for visualization and further analysis. You now simply close and apply the changes.

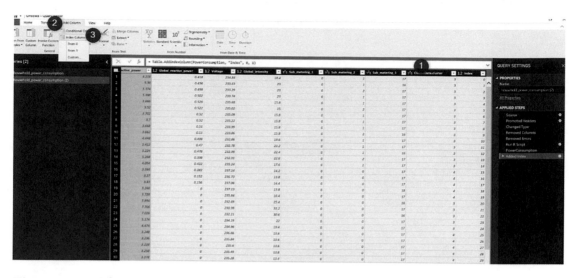

Figure 8-6. *Clustering data in Power Query*

In the Visualizations panel, we are going to use some simple visualization to compare the clusters (Figure 8-7). The first chart shows the number of items in each cluster. We can see how many items each cluster has.

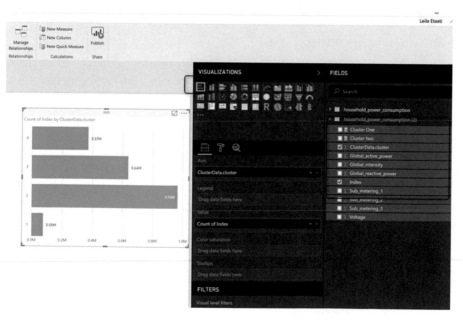

Figure 8-7. *Number of items in each cluster*

Also, you can use the Funnel chart option, to show the average of an attribute for a cluster (Figure 8-8).

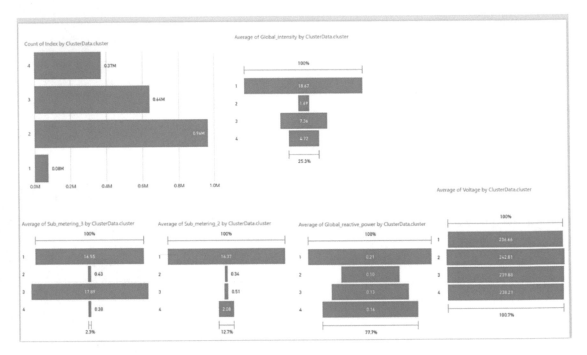

Figure 8-8. *Cluster comparison data*

It is also possible to do a what-if analysis. For example, if the voltage changes from 244 to 254, we can check what clusters mainly have that range and which other attributes have that subset in common. As you can see in Figure 8-9, clusters 2 and 3 mainly cover the 244 to 254 voltage range.

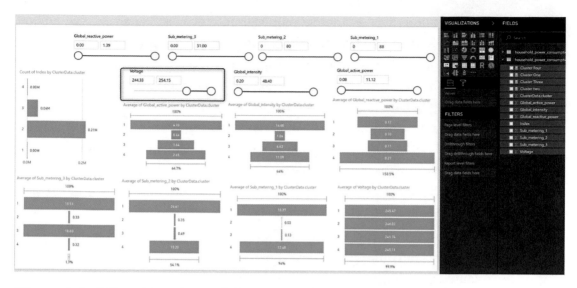

Figure 8-9. *What-if analysis of clustering results*

Market Basket Analysis (Association Rules)

Another approach for descriptive analysis and data mining is market basket analysis, or association rules. Market Basket (association rules) analysis is used to find customer purchasing behavior by stores, to determine the related items that have been purchased together. This approach is not only used for optimizing product placement and marketing investments but also for determining rules in health care, government policies, events management, and so forth [5].

In this section, I will explain how market basket analysis can be used, how to write it in R, and how to come up with good rules.

What Is Market Basket Analysis?

This analysis examines customer purchasing behavior. For example, for a beauty supply store, this analysis might reveal some association related to how frequently customers purchase shampoo and conditioner together. From a marketing perspective, perhaps promoting shampoo will lead customers to buying conditioner as well. From a sales perspective, placing shampoo beside conditioner on a store shelf will encourage customers to purchase both [4].

129

As stated, "association rules" is another name for market basket analysis. Association rules take the form if X then Y. For example, 60% of those who buy life insurance may then buy health insurance. To cite another example, 80% of those who buy books online may then also buy music online. Also, 50% of those who have high blood pressure and are overweight may then have high cholesterol [3].

Other examples of association rules include searching for interesting and frequently occurring patterns of DNA and protein sequences in cancer data, finding patterns in purchases or medical claims that occur in combination with fraudulent credit card or insurance claims, and identifying combinations of behavior that precede customers dropping their cellular phone service or upgrading their cable television package. You can see that association rules are not just about shopping but also can be applied in health care, insurance, and other industries. The main mathematical calculation of this method is explained here: `http://radacad.com/make-business-decisions-market-basket-analysis-part-1`.

There are three main attributes for market basket analysis.

> *Support*: The support of an item set or rule measures how frequently it occurs in the data.

> *Confidence*: Confidence is about the probability of a rule. For example, if a customer has purchased a flower, what is the probability that they are going to purchase a get-well-soon card.

> *Lifts*: Importance of the rules, that is, how much of the variance it explains

The first step in each analysis is to identify the main business problem. In this book, I have followed the examples provided in Lantz [6], which identify the most shopping list items that have been purchased together by customers. The second step is to import data into Power BI. You can download the data from GitHub [7]. This data set contains information about more than 9,000 customer transactions. For market basket analysis in R, we must install the `arules` package. In addition, we must install two other packages in RStudio related to `arules`: `Matrix` and `Methods`. To install these packages, you must have one R version in your machine, such as RStudio or Microsoft R Open. To install these packages, open R IDE, click New R Scripts, and type "Install.packages(<Package Name>)."

We follow the same procedure described in previous chapters for loading data and running the R scripts in Power Query (Figure 8-10).

Figure 8-10. *Importing a data set into Power BI and Run R Script*

You must then put the following code into the R scripts editor:

```
library(Matrix)
library(arules)
library(methods)
groceries <- read.transactions("[your local address]/groceries.csv",
sep = ",")
Temp<-apriori(groceries, parameter = list(support = 0.006, confidence =
0.25, minlen = 2))
output<-inspect(Temp[1:100])
```

In this code, the apriori function from arules is used.

The result of finding association rules in customer behavior is shown in Figure 8-11. The first column (lhs) lists the main item that people purchased; the third column (rhs) lists the items related to the lhs items. The support, confidence, and lift measures are shown in the fourth to sixth columns, respectively. A total 100 rules have been extracted. Finally, click Close and Apply at the top left side. Now we can create a visualization for showing an item and related items in Power BI.

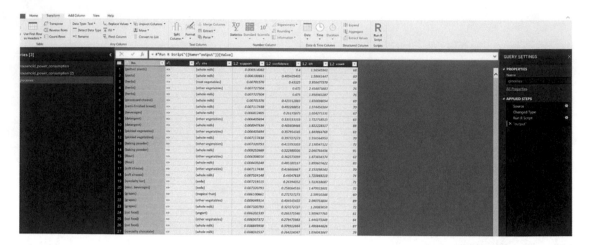

Figure 8-11. *Result of the market basket analysis*

Now we can create a visualization for showing an item and related items in Power BI. We use a specific custom visualization, "Forced-Directed Graph," from the Power BI web site, to show the relationships between items. To get this visual, click Market Place at the top of the Visualizations tab, then search for "Forced-Directed Graph."

After importing the custom visual, the related columns should also be imported (Figure 8-12). For the source, we put lh. For the target, rhs should be used. For the weight, we use the lift attribute.

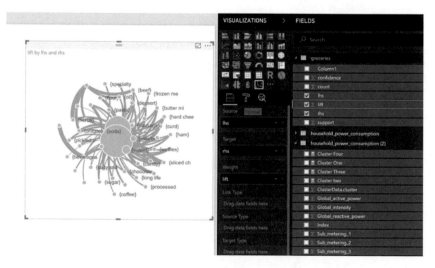

Figure 8-12. *Importing the custom visual and related columns*

Some of the visualization parameters, as shown in Figure 8-13, must be changed, to see the visualization better (Figure 8-14).

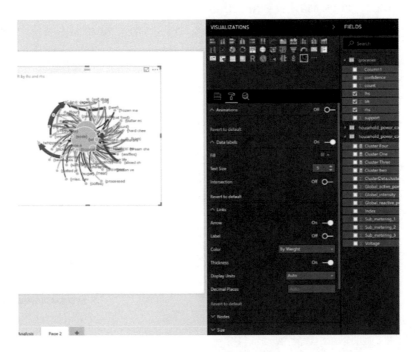

Figure 8-13. *Power Query filter value*

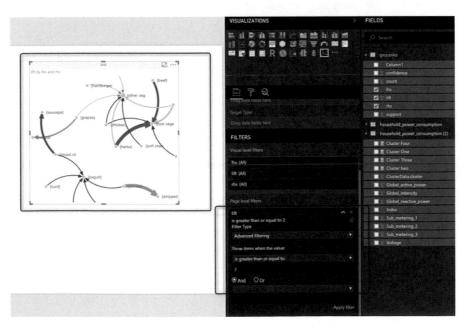

Figure 8-14. *Custom visual parameters setting*

We need another custom visual, Chiclet Slicer, from the Power BI store. This custom visual is a specific slicer that can be used to slice and dice the charts with a specific image. As previously, click Market Place, then search for Chiclet Slicer. After importing the visual, choose the value rhs, copy the slicer, and set the value lhs (Figure 8-15).

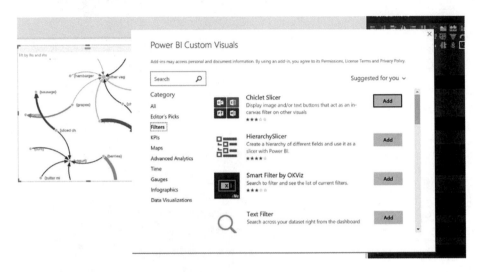

Figure 8-15. *Importing Chiclet Slicer*

You will see a report, as shown in Figure 8-16.

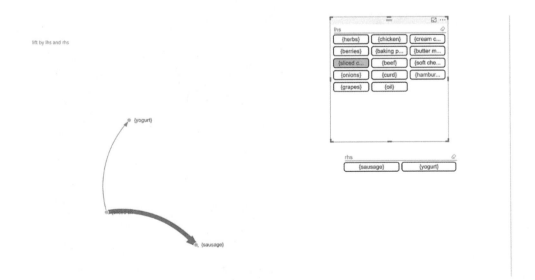

Figure 8-16. *Market basket analysis report*

By choosing an item, such as sliced cheese, with an rhs value in the slicer, a graph chart shows us the related items that people purchase most frequently with that item, such as sausage and yogurt.

Summary

This chapter gave a brief introduction to descriptive analytics. First, an explanation of the clustering was given. How to use k-mean clustering in Power BI visualization was then explained, as was the process of clustering in Power Query Editor. Finally, an explanation of market basket analysis was presented.

References

[1]   Ilknur Kaynar-Kabul, "Understanding data mining clustering methods," The SAS Data Science Blog, http://blogs.sas.com/content/subconsciousmusings/2016/05/26/data-mining-clustering/#prettyPhoto/0/, May 26, 2016.

[2]   Quora, "What are the best clustering algorithms used in machine learning?" www.quora.com/What-are-the-best-clustering-algorithms-used-in-machine-learning.

[3]   Georges Hebrail and Alice Berard, "Individual household electric power consumption Data Set," UCI Machine Learning Repository, https://archive.ics.uci.edu/ml/datasets/Individual+household+electric+power+consumption, August 30, 2012.

[4]   Leila Etaati, "Make Business Decisions: Market Basket Analysis Part 1," RADACAD, http://radacad.com/make-business-decisions-market-basket-analysis-part-1, February 14, 2017.

[5]   Association Rules: http://www.ms.unimelb.edu.au/~odj/Teaching/dm/1%20Association%20Rules%2008.pdf

[6]   Lantz, Brett. *Machine Learning with R*. Birmingham, UK: Packt Publishing, 2015.

[7]   Zach Sednick, "Machine Learning with R datasets," GitHub, https://github.com/stedy/Machine-Learning-with-R-datasets/blob/master/groceries.csv, 2019.

PART III

Machine Learning SQL Server

CHAPTER 9

Using R with SQL Server 2016 and 2017

In 2016, Microsoft announced the possibility of writing R codes inside SQL Server Management Studio. To be able to write R code in SQL Server 2016, we must install R Services first. In 2017, the ability to write Python codes inside SQL Server 2017 was provided. A developer can write the R and Python codes inside SQL Server Management Studio, using Machine Learning Server and accessing the different R or Python packages. In 2017, instead of R services, we have machine learning services, which allow us to embed R or Python codes in SQL scripts. In this chapter, the process of how we can set up SQL Server Management Studio to write R or Python scripts is explained. A brief explanation of some essential packages is also provided. In addition, best practices for how we can create a model and reuse it for another data set are explained.

SQL Server 2016 and 2017

The first step in using R in SQL Server 2016 is to install SQL Server 2016 [1]. You can choose one of SQL Server's editions, such as free Enterprise, Standard, or Express editions. To install, you must have an Admin account.

1. To start the setup wizard for SQL Server 2016, from the Installation tab, select New SQL Server stand-alone installation or add features to an existing installation (Figure 9-1).

© Leila Etaati 2019
L. Etaati, *Machine Learning with Microsoft Technologies*, https://doi.org/10.1007/978-1-4842-3658-1_9

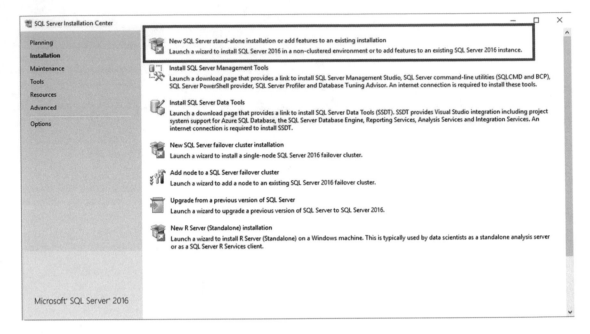

Figure 9-1. *SQL Server installation*

2. On the feature selection page, select R-Services (In-Database). As you can see in Figure 9-2, SQL Server Replication and R Services (In-Database) have been installed.

3. The final step is to consent to install Microsoft R Open. After installation is complete, you must restart your computer and run the SQL Server as Admin. For more information about the installation process, follow the Microsoft link on how to install R services in SQL Server 2016 [1].

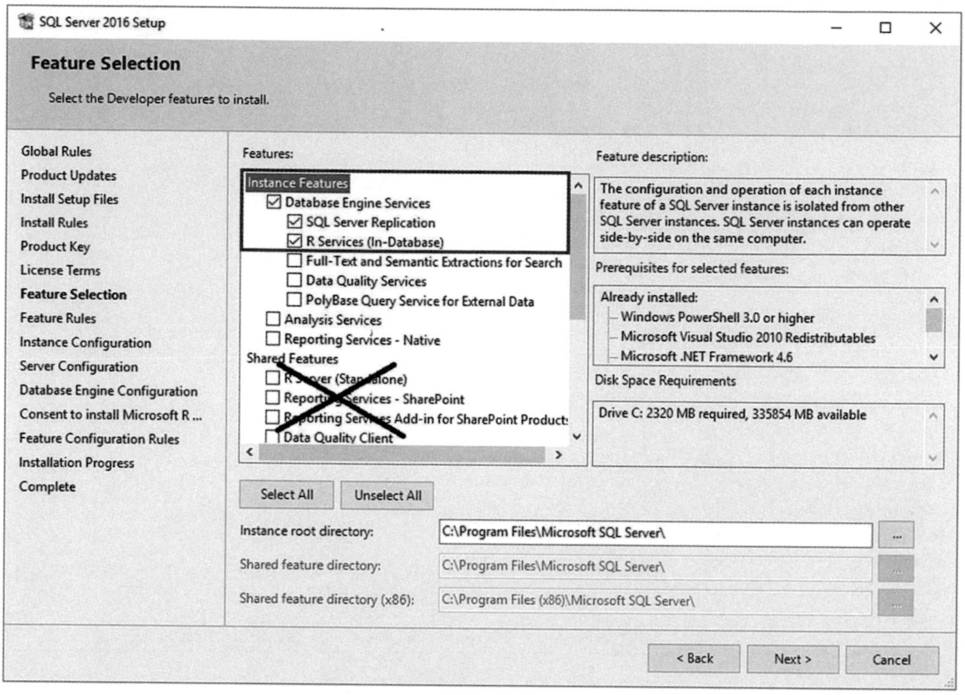

Figure 9-2. *SQL Server Feature Selection*

The process of setting up the machine learning services in SQL Server 2017 is the same as for the 2016 version. The only difference is that in feature selection, we have access to both R and Python languages. Moreover, we have to consent to install Microsoft R services and Python (Figure 9-3).

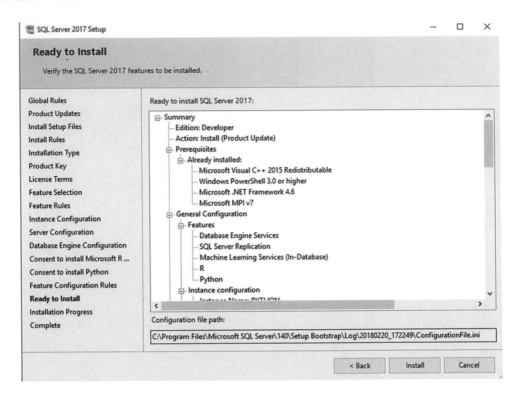

Figure 9-3. *Installing Machine Learning Services for SQL Server 2017*

Machine Learning Services in SQL Server 2017 runs on-premises and in the cloud. This service includes a rich set of algorithms, such as RevoScaleR, Revoscalepy, and MicrosoftML. Moreover, it supports a variety of Microsoft custom R and Python packages. In this chapter, I will explain how we can facilitate writing R scripts in SQL Server 2016 and 2017 (they are the same). In addition, how to use R for doing machine learning, what RevoScaleR is, and how specific algorithms are going to be supported are also explained. Some features, such as how to use pre-trained models for visual analysis and sentiment analysis and how to deploy the solution as a web service will be covered as well.

Running R Scripts

After installing the R services in SQL Server (2016 or 2017), you must enable writing an external script inside SQL Server Management Studio via a specific stored procedure. First, make sure you have already downloaded and installed SQL Server Management Studio [2].

Run Management Studio as Run as Admin and click New Query, to open a query window and run the following code:

```
sp_configure
```

By running the preceding code, you will get a list of stored procedures for configuration options (Figure 9-4).

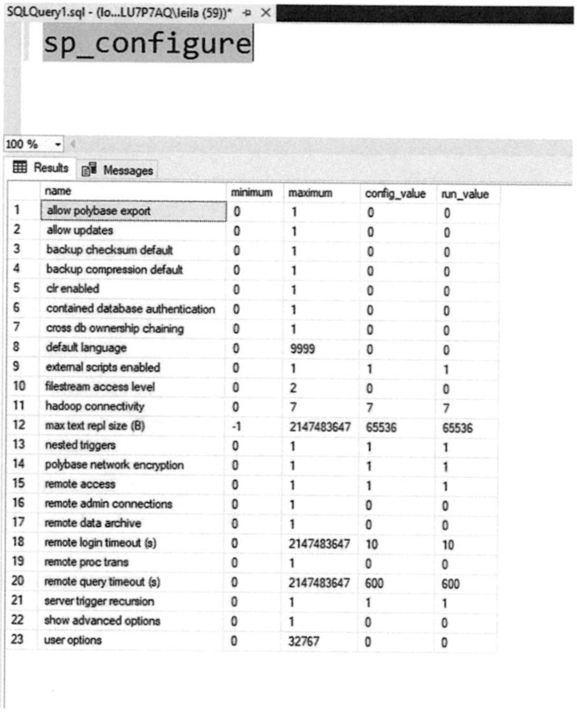

	name	minimum	maximum	config_value	run_value
1	allow polybase export	0	1	0	0
2	allow updates	0	1	0	0
3	backup checksum default	0	1	0	0
4	backup compression default	0	1	0	0
5	clr enabled	0	1	0	0
6	contained database authentication	0	1	0	0
7	cross db ownership chaining	0	1	0	0
8	default language	0	9999	0	0
9	external scripts enabled	0	1	1	1
10	filestream access level	0	2	0	0
11	hadoop connectivity	0	7	7	7
12	max text repl size (B)	-1	2147483647	65536	65536
13	nested triggers	0	1	1	1
14	polybase network encryption	0	1	1	1
15	remote access	0	1	1	1
16	remote admin connections	0	1	0	0
17	remote data archive	0	1	0	0
18	remote login timeout (s)	0	2147483647	10	10
19	remote proc trans	0	1	0	0
20	remote query timeout (s)	0	2147483647	600	600
21	server trigger recursion	0	1	1	1
22	show advanced options	0	1	0	0
23	user options	0	32767	0	0

Figure 9-4. *Configuration options available in SQL Server*

In line 9, there is a stored configuration procedure named external scripts enabled, with four columns. This stored procedure enables us to write R codes. It has two main attributes: `config_value` and `run_value`. When you run the following code:

```
sp_configure 'external scripts enabled'.
```

the initial value for `config` and `run` is zero (Figure 9-5).

	name	minimum	maximum	config_value	run_value
1	external scripts enabled	0	1	0	0

Figure 9-5. *Running the external scripts store procedure*

To run R code in SQL Server 2017/2016, we must change the run_value to 1.

```
Exec sp_configure 'external scripts enabled' ,1 Reconfigure with override
```

Now, if we run the code in Figure 9-5, we will get another result (Figure 9-6).

Results	Messages				
	name	minimum	maximum	config_value	run_value
1	external scripts enabled	0	1	1	1

Figure 9-6. *Enabling the running of R scripts in SQL Server*

It is possible that the run_value has not changed to 1, so you must restart SQL Server Management Studio.

After the run_value changes to 1, it is possible to check if R script has been enabled. We execute a stored procedure that has three main inputs:

@language gets the name of scripting language.

@script stores the related R scripts. In the following example, we assign the input variable to output one OutputDataSet<-InputDataSet'.

@input_data_1 stores the related data for consumption of R scripts. In the following example, it is a very simple SQL Code: select 1 as hello.

```
exec sp_execute_external_script  @language =N'R',
@script=N'OutputDataSet<-InputDataSet',
@input_data_1 =N'select 1 as hello'
with result sets (([hello] int not null));
go
```

If you run the preceding code, you will see that the output is hello and the value is 1 (Figure 9-7). The output of a stored procedure can be identified by "with result sets." The column name to be shown in the output is hello, and the output value is an integer number (1), and it should not be null. As a result, we have [hello] int not null.

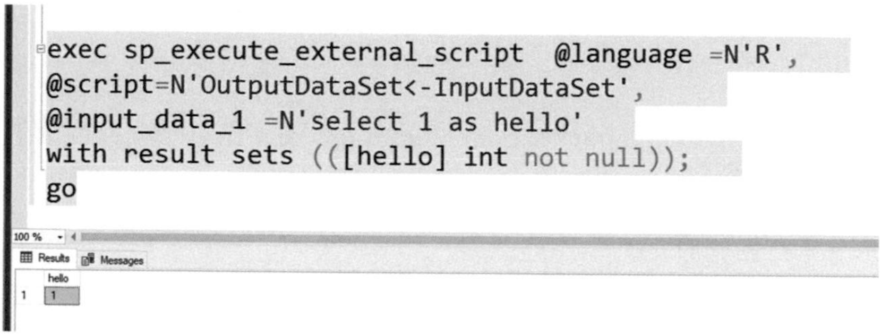

Figure 9-7. Enabling R scripts

Packages in R

It is possible to check the path for R-services. The code for getting the library path for R is

```
OutputDataSet <- data.frame(.libPaths())
```

To run the stored procedure, we set the language parameter to R.

```
@language = N'R'
```

The input R scripts is

```
@script = N'OutputDataSet <- data.frame(.libPaths());'.
```

So, the whole code would be

```
EXECUTE sp_execute_external_script  @language = N'R'
, @script = N'OutputDataSet <- data.frame(.libPaths());'
WITH RESULT SETS (([DefaultLibraryName] VARCHAR(MAX) NOT NULL));
GO
```

After running the code, the library path of R will be shown in the output window (Figure 9-8).

```
EXECUTE sp_execute_external_script  @language = N'R'
, @script = N'OutputDataSet <- data.frame(.libPaths());'
WITH RESULT SETS (([DefaultLibraryName] VARCHAR(MAX) NOT NULL));
GO
```

```
Results    Messages
DefaultLibraryName
C:/Program Files/Microsoft SQL Server/MSSQL13.MSSQLSERVER/R_SERVICES/library
```

Figure 9-8. *R library path*

You can check the installed packages in Machine Learning Services. The R code for checking the installed packages is

```
packagematrix <- installed.packages();
 NameOnly <- packagematrix[,1];
OutputDataSet <- as.data.frame(NameOnly)
```

As we are not getting any input value from the user, we do not have any input for the stored procedure (Figure 9-9).

```
EXECUTE sp_execute_external_script @language=N'R'
 ,@script = N'str(OutputDataSet); packagematrix <- installed.packages();
 NameOnly <- packagematrix[,1]; OutputDataSet <- as.data.frame(NameOnly);'
  ,@input_data_1 = N'SELECT 1 as col'
  WITH RESULT SETS ((PackageName nvarchar(250) ))
```

After running the code, you can see the existing R packages in SQL Server.

As you can see in Figure 9-9, the list of R packages is shown. There is a variety of libraries available from Microsoft and some other open source or third-party packages. In the next section, I will explain two of them.

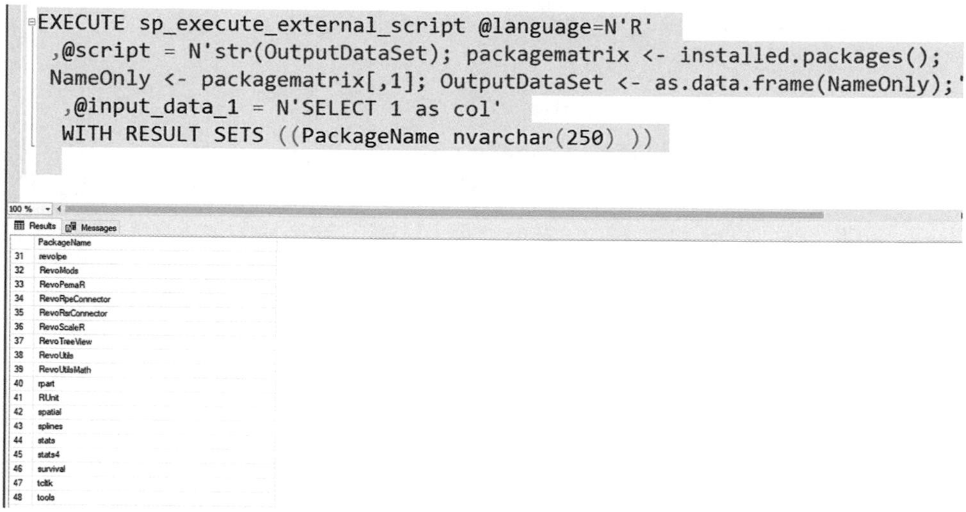

```
EXECUTE sp_execute_external_script @language=N'R'
  ,@script = N'str(OutputDataSet); packagematrix <- installed.packages();
 NameOnly <- packagematrix[,1]; OutputDataSet <- as.data.frame(NameOnly);'
   ,@input_data_1 = N'SELECT 1 as col'
   WITH RESULT SETS ((PackageName nvarchar(250) ))
```

100 %   ▾ ◂

▦ Results ▓ Messages

	PackageName
31	revolpe
32	RevoMods
33	RevoPemaR
34	RevoRpeConnector
35	RevoRsrConnector
36	RevoScaleR
37	RevoTreeView
38	RevoUtils
39	RevoUtilsMath
40	rpart
41	RUnit
42	spatial
43	splines
44	stats
45	stats4
46	survival
47	tcltk
48	tools

Figure 9-9. *R Packages in SQL Server Machine Learning Services*

RevoScaleR Package

RevoScaleR is a package created by Revolutionary Analytics (now owned by Microsoft), with the aim of importing, transforming, and analyzing data at scale. There are different categories of functions available from the data store, imports and save as, data transformation, draw some charts such as histogram, line, and so forth, descriptive analysis, predictive analysis, package management and so forth [3].

In this section, I will introduce some of the functions that you may use for machine learning purpose. The examples will be shown in SQL Server 2017.

rxLinMod

rxLinMode fits a linear model to data. In the following example, I will show you how to use this function to create a model for predicting the strength of concrete in relation to such input variables as the amount of water, cement, ash, and age. The rxLinMode function creates a model based on a formula and a training data set.

As you can see in following code, the first line is EXECUTE sp_execute_external_ script @language=N'R', which calls a stored procedure that allows the user to write an R script inside SQL Server. This stored procesure is responsible for using external scripts such as R or Python inside SQL Server Code.

```
EXECUTE sp_execute_external_script @language=N'R'
 ,@script = N'require("RevoScaleR")
 formula=strength~cement+ash+age+water
Model_1=rxLinMod(formula,data=inputDataSet)
Model=data.frame(payload = as.raw(serialize(Model_1, connection=NULL)))'
  ,@input_data_1 = N'Select strength,cement,ash,age,water from [dbo].
  [concrete]; '
 , @output_data_1_name = N'Model'
 ,@input_data_1_name = N'inputDataSet'
  WITH RESULT SETS (([concreteModel] varbinary(max) NOT NULL  ));
```

The second line in the code, contains the relevant R code stored in the "@script" parameter. The code refers to the RevoScaleR package by using the function require. There is no need to install this package, as it already exists in Machine Learning/R services. The second R code line is about creating a formula. Our mission is to predict the strength of concrete according to some other variables such as amounth of water, cement and so forth. The formula that allows us to do this is strength~cement+ash+age+ water, which stores the formula in a "formula" variable. The third line contains the rxLinMod function, which creates a linear model from the formula. Finally, the last line of the code stores the formula in an output variable named "Model".

@input_data_1 stores the data collected from the SQL database, using SQL query N'Select strength,cement,ash,age,water from [dbo].[concrete]. Finally, the output variable Model will store the linear model.

After creating the model, I want to store it, for predicting the new series of data. To store the model, the following code is used:

```
IF NOT EXISTS (SELECT 1 FROM sys.objects
                        WHERE object_id = OBJECT_ID(N'[dbo].[LinearModel]')
                            AND [type] IN (N'U'))
BEGIN
      CREATE TABLE [dbo].[LinearModel](
            [Model] [varbinary](MAX) NULL
      );
END
```

Next, we ,must insert the model into a table. The following code inserts the model into a LinearModel table.

```
Insert into [dbo].[LinearModel]
EXECUTE sp_execute_external_script @language=N'R'
 ,@script = N'require("RevoScaleR")
 formula=strength~cement+ash+age+water
Model_1=rxLinMod(formula,data=inputDataSet)
Model=data.frame(payload = as.raw(serialize(Model_1, connection=NULL)))'
  ,@input_data_1 = N'Select strength,cement,ash,age,water from [dbo].
  [concrete]; '
 , @output_data_1_name = N'Model'
 ,@input_data_1_name = N'inputDataSet'
```

The model is already stored in the database. Now, in another stored procedure, we are going to use the model, to predict the data.

```
declare @rx_model varbinary(max) = (select [Model] from [dbo].[LinearModel] );
  exec sp_execute_external_script
                          @language = N'R'
                        , @script = N'
                        require("RevoScaleR");
                        cdr_model<-unserialize(rx_model);
                        predictions <- rxPredict(modelObject = cdr_model,
                        data = PredictionData)
                        prediction <-as.data.frame(predictions);'
    , @input_data_1 = N'Select strength,cement,ash,age,water from [dbo].
    [concrete]'
    , @input_data_1_name = N'PredictionData'
    , @output_data_1_name=N'prediction'
    , @params = N'@rx_model varbinary(max)'
    , @rx_model = @rx_model
    with result sets (("prediction" float not null ))  ;
```

There is another input for a stored procedure that is not just a data set. It contains input for models that we have already stored in a database.

By running the stored procedure, the following prediction results are shown (Figure 9-10).

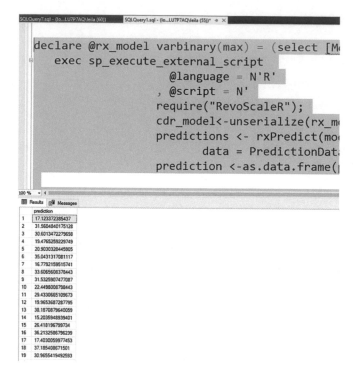

Figure 9-10. *Linear model for concrete strength prediction*

There are other models for regression analysis. These include `rxLogit`, used for logistic regression; `rxGlm`, for generalizing the linear model to data; and others. In addition, for other types of analysis, such as group prediction (classification), there are such algorithms as `rxDTree`, `rxBTree`, `rxDForest`, and `rxNaiveBayes` [3].

Azure ML Package

Azure ML is another package to manage an experiment created in Azure ML Studio (see Chapter 12). This package has some popular functions and allows users to create a web service from R functions. This package also allows R users to explore the Azure ML data set, explore existing data sets, and so forth. Details of how to use this package are provided in Chapter 12, following an explanation of Azure Machine Learning Studio.

Creating R Visuals in SQL Server Reporting Services

It is possible to generate R charts in SQL Server and show the chart in SQL Server Reporting Services (SSRS). The first step is to install the required package into Machine Learning Services. To do this, we can use the `install.packages()` command in an external scripts stored procedure, as follows:

```
EXECUTE sp_execute_external_script @language=N'R'
 ,@script = N' install.packages("ggplot2");'
  ,@input_data_1 = N'SELECT 1 as col'
  WITH RESULT SETS ((PackageName nvarchar(250) ))
```

The preceding code may work, but sometimes it doesn't, because of the administrator permission. You may receive a message such as the following warning in `install.packages("arules")`:

```
'lib = "C:/Program Files/Microsoft SQL Server/MSSQL14.ML2017/R_SERVICES/
library"' is not writable
Error in install.packages("ggplot2") : unable to install packages
Calls: source -> withVisible -> eval -> eval -> install.packages
```

To address this problem, we must run `Rugi.exe` as admin, to install the package. In addition, we must specify where to install the packages. As a result, the path of the Machine Learning Services for R in SQL Server is required. There is a function in R, `.libPaths()`, that shows the location of installed packages. So, we must run this code in SQL Server 2017, to find out the R library path.

```
EXECUTE sp_execute_external_script  @language = N'R'
, @script = N'OutputDataSet <- data.frame(.libPaths());'
WITH RESULT SETS ((([DefaultLibraryName] VARCHAR(MAX) NOT NULL));
GO
```

By running the code, the Machine Learning Services library path will be shown in SQL Server output windows (Figure 9-11).

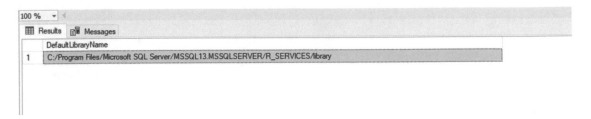

Figure 9-11. *The library path for Machine Learning Services*

By installing ggplot2, there may be another message requesting installation of other packages. After installing the ggplot2 library, we can write R code to create a chart and store it in SQL Server. I am going to draw a chart using the following SQL codes:

```
exec sp_execute_external_script @language =N'R', @script=N'library("ggplot2")
fields<-inputDataSet fields<-na.omit(fields) image_file = tempfile();
jpeg(filename = image_file, width=1000, height=1000); print(ggplot
(fields,aes(x=fields$TaxAmt,y=fields$TaxAmt))+geom_boxplot()+facet_
grid(fields$Color~.) ) dev.off(); OutputDataset <- data.frame(data=
readBin(file(image_file,"rb"),what=raw(),n=1e6)) ',@input_data_1 =N'select
Color,Size,class,TaxAmt,SalesAmount from [dbo].[FactInternetSales] FIS inner
join [dbo].[DimProduct] DP on FIS.ProductKey=dp.ProductKey' ,@input_data_1_
name = N'inputDataSet' ,@output_data_1_name = N'OutputDataset' WITH RESULT
SETS ((plot varbinary(max)));
```

R Code Section

```
library("ggplot2")
fields<-inputDataSet
fields<-na.omit(fields)
image_file = tempfile();
jpeg(filename = image_file, width=1000, height=1000);
print(ggplot(fields,aes(x=fields$TaxAmt,y=fields$TaxAmt))+geom_
boxplot()+facet_grid(fields$Color~.)
)
dev.off();
OutputDataset <- data.frame(data=readBin(file(image_
file,"rb"),what=raw(),n=1e6
```

Some brief explanation about the preceding code follows:

`library("ggplot2")`: refers to the package.

`fields<-inputDataSet`: gets the data.

```
image_file = tempfile();
```

`jpeg(filename = image_file, width=500, height=500)`; creates the image file from the ggplot2 package.

`ggplot(fields,aes(x=fields$TaxAmt,y=fields$TaxAmt))+geom_boxplot()+facet_grid(fields$Color~.)` refers to code that has been explained in previous posts.

```
dev.off();
OutputDataset <- data.frame(data=readBin(file(image_file,"rb"),what=raw(),
n=1e6
```

This code creates a Var binary variable to convert the plot into a variable of binary type. The preceding code creates a table chart with a box plot.

The next step is to get the data from SQL Server.

Input Data

```
@input_data_1 =N'select Color,Size,class,TaxAmt,SalesAmount from [dbo].
[FactInternetSales] FIS inner join [dbo].[DimProduct] DP on FIS.
ProductKey=dp.ProductKey' ,@input_data_1_name = N'inputDataSet' ,@output_
data_1_name = N'OutputDataset'
```

The relevant data set, AdventureWorks, can be downloaded from www.microsoft.com/en-us/download/details.aspx?id=49502 [4].

Return Data

```
WITH RESULT SETS ((plot varbinary(max)));
```

Finally, we must return the plot, in the form of a binary variable.

By running the code, we may get the result shown in Figure 9-12.

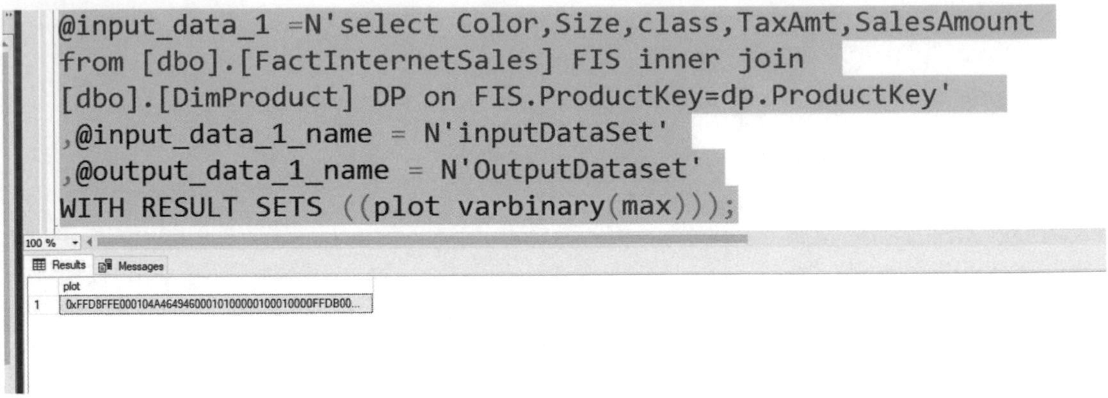

```
@input_data_1 =N'select Color,Size,class,TaxAmt,SalesAmount
from [dbo].[FactInternetSales] FIS inner join
[dbo].[DimProduct] DP on FIS.ProductKey=dp.ProductKey'
,@input_data_1_name = N'inputDataSet'
,@output_data_1_name = N'OutputDataset'
WITH RESULT SETS ((plot varbinary(max)));
```

```
100 %    ▾ ◀
▦ Results  ▨ Messages
     plot
1    0xFFD8FFE000104A464946000101000001000100000FFDB00...
```

Figure 9-12. *Creating a binary value for the chart*

Now we must store the data in a table. First, we create a table with the name ggplot inside SQL Server, using the following code:

```
IF NOT EXISTS (SELECT 1 FROM sys.objects WHERE object_id = OBJECT_
ID(N'[dbo].[ggplot]') AND [type] IN (N'U')) BEGIN alter TABLE [dbo].
[ggplot]( [plot] [varbinary](MAX) NULL ); END
```

Then we enter the plot into the table, by inserting the following command:

```
insert into [dbo].[ggplot] exec sp_execute_external_script @language =N'R',
@script=N'library("ggplot2") fields<-inputDataSet fields<-na.omit(fields)
image_file = tempfile(); jpeg(filename = image_file, width=1000,
height=1000); print(ggplot(fields,aes(x=fields$TaxAmt,y=fields$TaxAmt))
+geom_boxplot()+facet_grid(fields$Color~.) ) dev.off(); OutputDataset
<- data.frame(data=readBin(file(image_file,"rb"),what=raw(),n=1e6)) ',
@input_data_1 =N'select Color,Size,class,TaxAmt,SalesAmount from [dbo].
[FactInternetSales] FIS inner join [dbo].[DimProduct] DP on FIS.
ProductKey=dp.ProductKey' ,@input_data_1_name = N'inputDataSet' ,@output_
data_1_name = N'OutputDataset'
```

Now we have a chart that has been created and stored in our database.

Showing the Chart in SSRS

To show the chart in SQL Server data tools, we must create a new SSRS project (Figure 9-13).

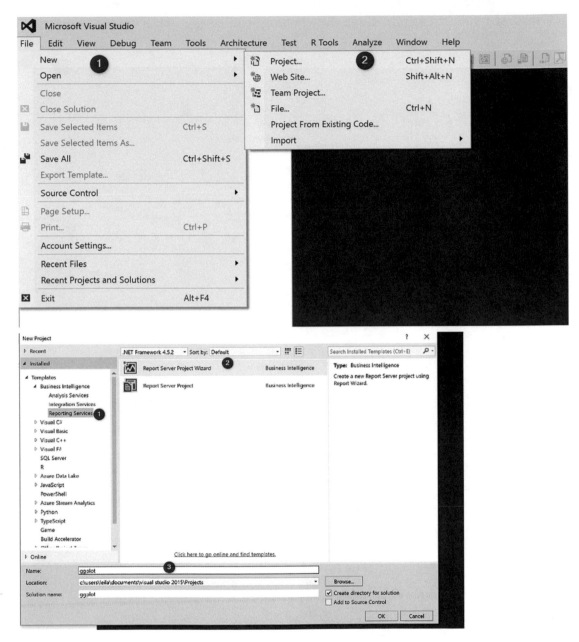

Figure 9-13. *Create a SSRS project in SQL Server data tools*

Next, we follow the required steps for creating an SSRS report (Figure 9-14).

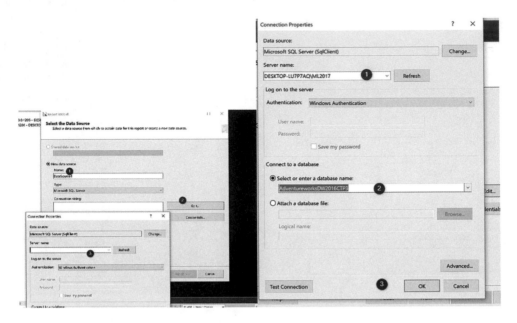

Figure 9-14. *Creating an SSRS project with data tools*

Then must create a query to get the plot from the ggplot table (Figure 9-15).

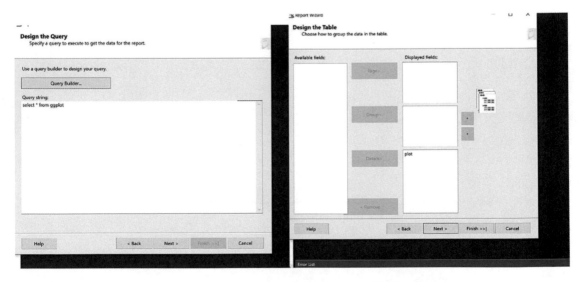

Figure 9-15. *Getting the data from the SQL Server table in SSRS*

Next, we must insert an image into the report area and view the preview tabs (Figure 9-16) to check the charts.

Figure 9-16. *Box plot chart in SSRS*

Summary

This chapter gave a brief explanation of how to run R scripts in SQL Server 2016 and 2017. It outlined how to run the necessary code via external scripts and stored procedures. In addition, it discussed how with packages such as RevoScaleR and Azure ML, we can access additional machine learning and R services. Furthermore, the process of how we can perform predictive analytics was explained via an example. The next chapter offers an overview of how to do machine learning in Azure Databricks.

References

[1]   Microsoft, "Install SQL Server 2016 R Services," SQL Docs, https://docs.microsoft.com/en-us/sql/advanced-analytics/install/sql-r-services-windows-install, September 30, 2028.

[2]   Microsoft, "Download SQL Server Management Studio (SSMS),"
       Download SMSS, `https://docs.microsoft.com/en-nz/sql/`
       `ssms/download-sql-server-management-studio-ssms`, March
       28, 2019.

[3]   Microsoft, "RevoScaleR package," Docs, `https://docs.`
       `microsoft.com/en-us/machine-learning-server/r-reference/`
       `revoscaler/revoscaler`, January 28, 2018.

[4]   Microsoft, "AdventureWorks Databases and Scripts for SQL Server
       2016 CTP3," Download Center, `www.microsoft.com/en-us/`
       `download/details.aspx?id=49502`, 2019.

[5]   Buck Woody, Danielle Dean, Debraj GuhaThakurta, Gagan
       Bansal, Matt Conners, Wee-Hyong Tok, *Data Science with
       Microsoft SQL Server 2016*, `https://download.microsoft.`
       `com/download/C/7/4/C744F71B-BE31-4EE7-887A-`
       `FF525B026B3C/9781509304318_Data%20Science%20with%20`
       `Microsoft%20SQL%20Server%202016_pdf.pdf`, 2016.

CHAPTER 10

Azure Databricks

Databricks is an analytics service based on the Apache Spark open source project. Apache Spark is a batch processing and real time processing environment. Apache Spark is quite popular among data scientists because of its ability to analyze huge amounts of data, its streaming capabilities, graph computation, machine learning, and interactive queries engine. Spark provides in-memory cluster computing. One of the popular tools for big data analytics on Spark is Databricks. Databricks has been used for ingesting a significant amount of data, cleaning data, applying machine learning, and so forth. In February 2018, there was an integration between Microsoft Azure and Databricks that provides a better collaboration between data engineers, data scientists, and data analytics. This integration provides data science and data engineering teams with a fast, easy, and collaborative Spark-based platform in Azure [1]. Azure Databricks is a new platform for big data analytics and machine learning. The notebook in Azure Databricks enables data engineers, data scientists, and business analysts to collaborate using a single tool. This chapter gives an overview of what Azure Databricks is, the environment it inhabits, and its use in data science.

Databricks Environment

To create Azure Databricks in an Azure environment, log in to one of your Azure accounts. From there, create an Azure Databricks module (Figure 10-1).

© Leila Etaati 2019
L. Etaati, *Machine Learning with Microsoft Technologies*, https://doi.org/10.1007/978-1-4842-3658-1_10

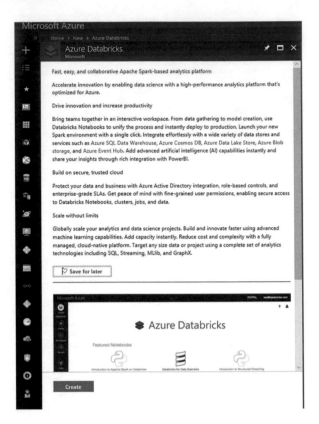

Figure 10-1. *Azure Databricks environment*

After creating the Azure Databricks module, Azure will navigate to a new page. To access Azure Databricks, click Launch Workspace (Figure 10-2).

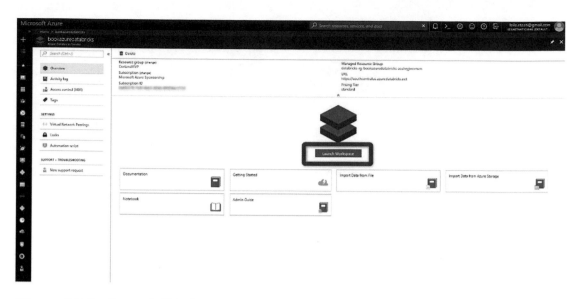

Figure 10-2. *Launch Workspace*

As you can see in Figure 10-3, the Azure Databricks environment has different components. The main components are Workspace and Clusters. The first step after launch is to create a cluster. Clusters in Databricks provide a unified platform for ETL (extract, transform, and load), stream analytics, and machine learning. Clusters are of two types: interactive and job. Notebook clusters are used to analyze data collaboratively. However, job clusters are used to run fast and robustly automated workloads, using APIs. Cluster pages may contain both cluster types. Each cluster can have different nodes. To start, you must create a cluster. Click the Create Cluster option (Figure 10-3).

Figure 10-3. *Creating clusters in Databricks*

On the Create Cluster page (Figure 10-4), enter the relevant information, such as cluster name, version (default), Python version, minimum and maximum workers, and so forth.

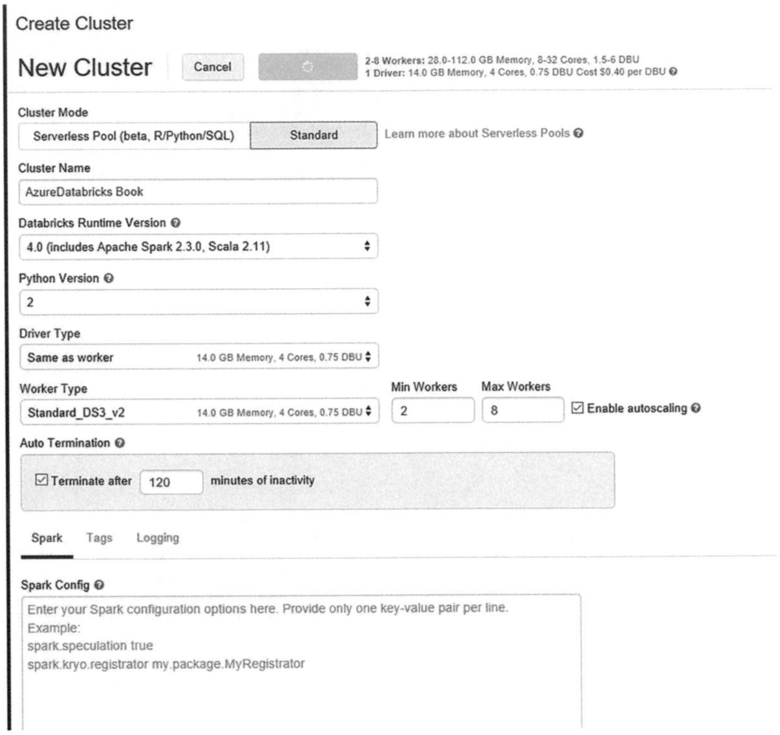

Figure 10-4. *Create Cluster page in Azure Databricks*

As you can see in Figure 10-4, we a have driver node and a worker node. The worker node is for distributing your workload. The driver node is responsible for maintaining the SparkContext. It is possible to resize automatically and autoscale the size of the cluster. By enabling autoscale, the minimum and maximum number of workers can be limited during a cluster's lifetime.

To use Clusters, you should wait till State changes to Running (Figure 10-5). By creating an interactive cluster, you can create a notebook in which to write codes and from which to get results quickly.

Figure 10-5. *Running Clusters*

To create a notebook, click the Workspace option and create a new notebook (Figure 10-6).

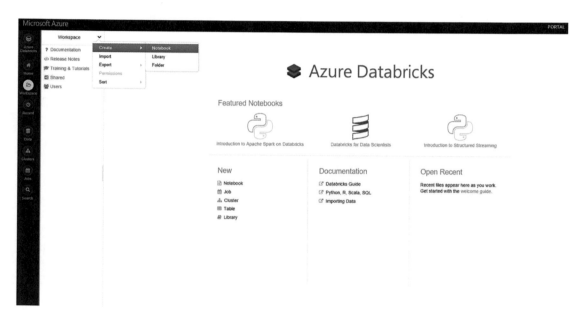

Figure 10-6. *Creating a notebook in Databricks*

By creating a new notebook, you can specify which notebook belongs to which cluster and what the main language for the Notebook (Python, Scala, R, and SQL) is. In this example, the R language has been selected as the default. However, you can still write in the notebook in other languages, by writing: %scala, %python, %sql, or %r before the scripts (Figure 10-7).

Figure 10-7. *Creating an R notebook in Databricks*

By default, in the notebook, there is a place to write code. As you can see in Figure 10-8, there an editor with name Cmd1 as a node in which to write the codes and run them all. In our example, there is only one node, and the primary language in which to write the code is R. In addition, we use the existing data set in the gpplot2 package named mpg, by writing the following code:

```
library(ggplot2)
display(mpg)
```

The display command shows the data set in Databricks. To run the code, click the arrow at the right side of the node and select Run Cell (Figure 10-8).

Figure 10-8. *Writing an R notebook in Databricks*

After running the code, the result will appear at the end of the cell in table style. As you can see in Figure 10-9, the initial result is shown as a table; however, it is possible to show the result in the same format as other charts.

Figure 10-9. *Running the R*

To show the chart, you must click the chart icon at the bottom of the cell (Figure 10-10).

Figure 10-10. *Show the chart in Databricks*

You can change the item that you want to show in the chart, by clicking the Plot Options (Figure 10-11).

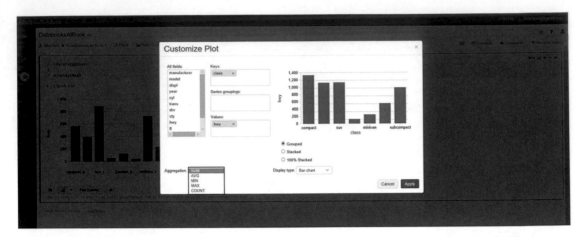

Figure 10-11. *Chart Option in Databricks*

It is possible to create a new cell to write more codes in R or Scala. For our example, we must upload a data set named Titanic into Azure Databricks.

To import data, click the Data option at the left side of the window (Figure 10-12), Then click Add Data. This navigates to a new page (Figure 10-12). Then click Upload File. Just browse and upload the `titanic` file. If you need this file, you can access it from `www.kaggle.com/c/titanic`.

Figure 10-12. *Importing data with the Data option*

As you can see in the Figure 10-13, we must create a table with a user interface (UI) and choose the related cluster to be uploaded there.

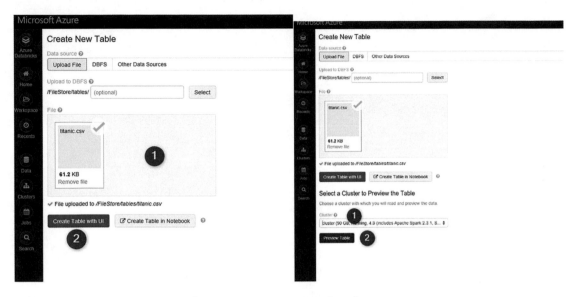

Figure 10-13. *Importing data into Azure Databricks*

We now create a new workspace named

```
val titanic = spark.table("titanic")
display(titanic.select("*"))
```

To work with the Titanic data set, we only have to select the Survived, Sex, Age, and PClass columns (see Figure 10-14).

```
val specificColumnsDf = titanic.select("Survived", "Pclass", "Sex", "Age")
val renamedColumnsDF = specificColumnsDf.withColumnRenamed("Sex", "Gender")
display(renamedColumnsDF)
```

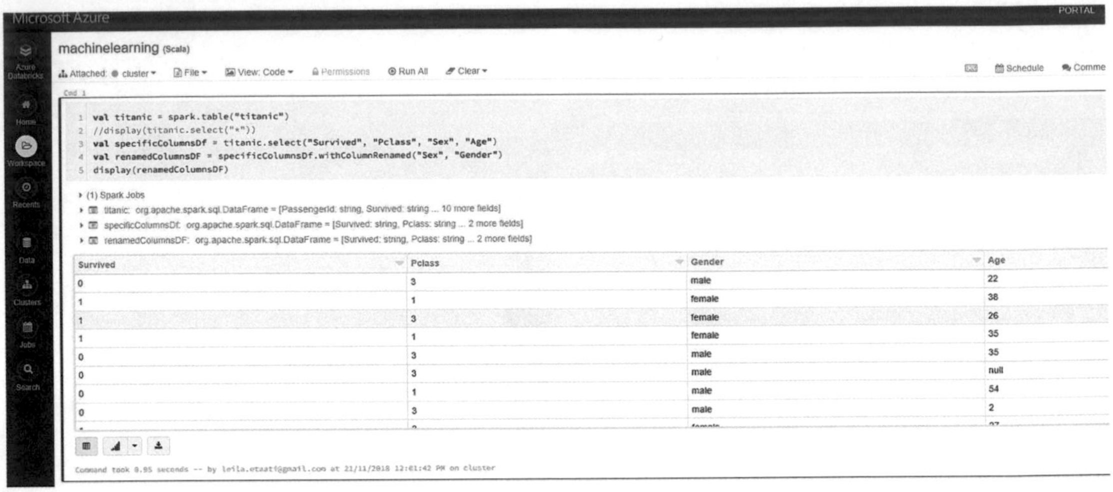

Figure 10-14. *Running the Scala language to get data from Azure Data Lake Store*

Now, for the purpose of machine learning, we are going to predict if a new passenger of a specific age, gender, and passenger class will survive or not. For this, we must run the R codes to this data in another cell, to create a model and predict whether a passenger of a specific age, gender, and passenger class will survive. We must pass the data from Scala to R. To do this, we must create a temporary table to give the table to the R code, using the following code:

```
renamedColumnsDF.createOrReplaceTempView("TempTable")
```

We add a new cell by clicking the plus sign under the latest cell. In the new cell, we must write R codes. Therefore, we must mention the language by putting %r at the start of the code. Also, we are using some packages from SparkR, so we use the function SQL, to fetch data from the last Scala cell. Finally, we store the data with a dataset variable.

```
%r
library(SparkR)
sql("REFRESH TABLE TempTable")
df <- sql("SELECT * FROM TempTable")
dataset<-as.data.frame(df)
display(df)
```

In the same cell or the new one, you can write some code for machine learning. In our example, we are looking to check whether a passenger of a specific passenger class, age, and gender is going to survive. The *rpart* package can be used to create a decision tree. This package helps us to predict the probability of survival.

```r
%r
library(SparkR)
sql("REFRESH TABLE TempTable")
df <- sql("SELECT * FROM TempTable")
dataset<-as.data.frame(df)
library(rpart)
DT<-rpart(Survived~.,data=dataset,method="class")
test<-dataset[,2:4]
Prediction<-predict(DT,test)
output<-data.frame(test,Prediction)
display(output)
```

By running the cell, the output will be displayed (Figure 10-15).

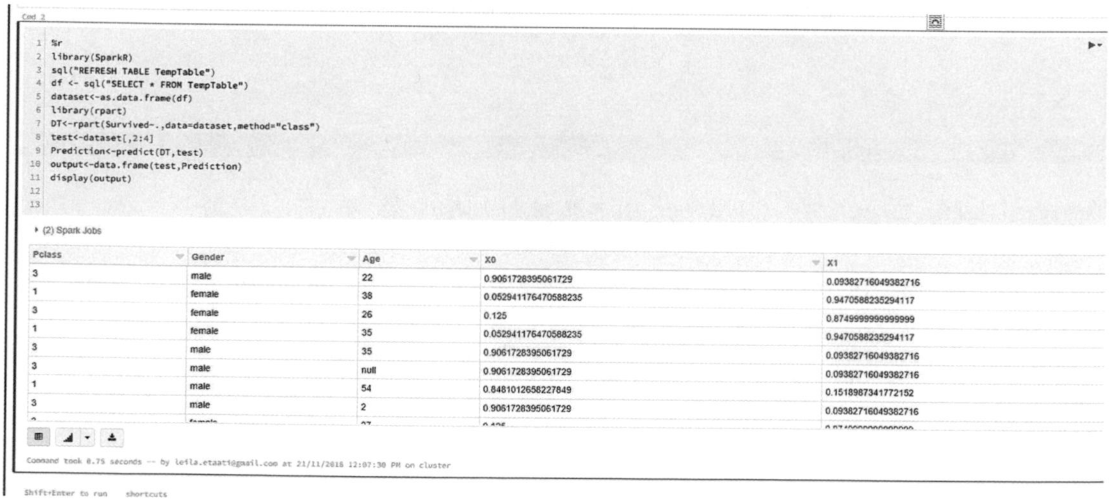

Figure 10-15. *Creating a new cell in Azure Databricks*

It is possible to draw charts using such R packages as ggplot2 as well. For example, if we want to see the Pclass, age, and gender in a scatter chart with a specific legend, we can leverage the following code.

```r
%r
display(output)
library(ggplot2)
ggplot(output,aes(x=output$Age,y=output$Pclass,
color=output$Gender))+geom_jitter()
```

As you can see in Figure 10-16, a scatter chart with the legend output$Gender will result.

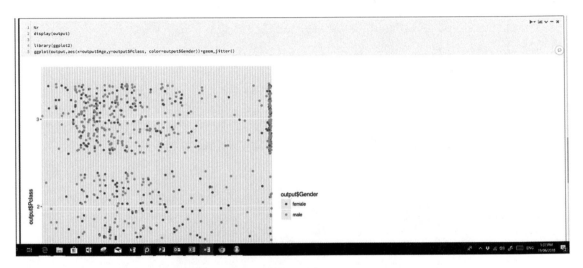

Figure 10-16. *Creatiing a new cell in Azure Databricks*

Azure Databricks is not only for machine learning. It can also retrieve data from different resources on which to apply changes and then shows the result in some visualization tool, such as Power BI. In addition, it is possible to schedule the process (Figure 10-17).

Figure 10-17. *Scheduling a process using Databricks*

There are different ways to get data from SQL database, including such Azure services as Azure Blob, Data Lake Store, Azure Cosmos, among others [2].

Summary

This chapter provided a concise overview of how we can use Azure Databricks for machine learning. It discussed how we can use the Databricks environment for writing R and Scala scripts and how we can pass data from one cell in a Databricks environment to another. Finally, you saw how we are able to apply R codes to train a model and use it for predicting. The processes of how to import data and how to do machine learning was explained as well. The next chapter will provide an overview of how to do machine learning in Azure Data Lake.

References

[1] Ali Ghodsi, "Introducing Azure Databricks," Databricks, `https://databricks.com/blog/2017/11/15/introducing-azure-databricks.html`, posted November15, 2017.

[2] Azure Databricks, "Data Sources," `https://docs.azuredatabricks.net/spark/latest/data-sources/index.html`, 2019.

PART IV

Machine Learning in Azure

CHAPTER 11

R in Azure Data Lake

Azure Data Lake Store is one of the components in Microsoft Cloud that helps developers, data scientists, and analysts to store data of any size and shape. Azure Data Lake is optimized for processing large amounts of data. It provides parallel processing with optimum performance. In Azure Data Lake, we can create a hierarchical data folder structure. Because of these capabilities, Azure Data Lake makes it easy for data scientists to apply advanced analytics and machine learning modeling with high scalability cost-effectiveness. Azure Data Lake Analytics includes U-SQL, which is a language like SQL that enables you to process unstructured data [1]. It is possible to perform machine learning inside Azure Data Lake and explore the Azure Data Lake from RStudio to create models inside the RStudio environment. Moreover, it is possible to get data from Azure Data Lake with Hive query and to use that data inside Azure Machine Learning. In this chapter, you will see how we can write and work with data, using U-SQL language with R in Azure Data Lake, and how we can import data from Azure Data Lake to RStudio or import data from RStudio into Azure Data Lake.

Azure Data Lake Environment

Azure Data Lake is one of the components of Microsoft Cloud with the aim of storing data. As you can see in Figure 11-1, the second component in Azure Portal is about storing data. Azure Data Lake Store can store data of any size or format (structured and unstructured). It is also used for doing analytics (third component). Azure Data Lake Analytics can be used for data analytics (using U-SQL) and machine learning.

© Leila Etaati 2019
L. Etaati, *Machine Learning with Microsoft Technologies*, https://doi.org/10.1007/978-1-4842-3658-1_11

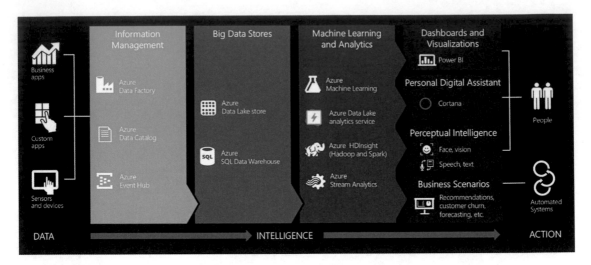

Figure 11-1. *Microsoft Cloud components*

To access the Azure Data Lake Store and Data Lake Analytics, you must have an Azure account. You can create one, by accessing the following link: `https://tsmatz.wordpress.com/2017/06/08/azure-data-lake-r-extension/`. Sign in "Portal.Azure.com," then, click the Create a resource icon on the left side of the portal (Figure 11-2). By typing "data lake," two different components for Azure Data Lake will appear. To begin, we first are going to create Azure Data Lake Store.

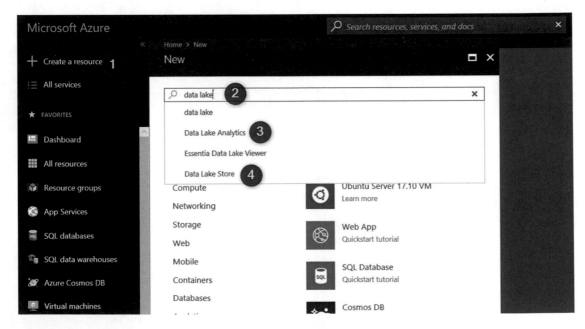

Figure 11-2. *Creating Azure Data Lake Store and Data Lake Analytics*

By clicking the Create option, first you will have to provide some information, such as the name of the service, subscription, resource group, and the server location (Figure 11-3).

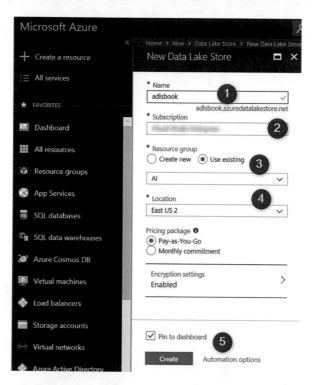

Figure 11-3. *Creating Azure Data Lake Store*

It takes a while to create components. As you can see in Figure 11-4, Azure Data Lake Store has been created. After the creation of Azure Data Lake store, we can upload new data there.

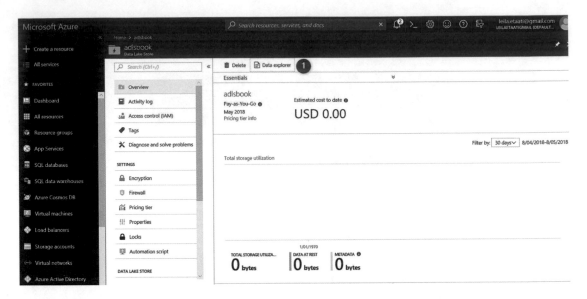

Figure 11-4. *Creating Azure Data Lake Store*

By clicking the Data Explorer option, you can view the data and structure. From here, as you can see in Figure 11-5, it is possible to upload data, create folders, define the access level, and so forth.

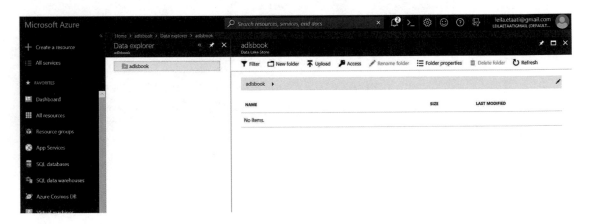

Figure 11-5. *Data Explorer in Azure Data Lake Store*

Currently, there is no data in Azure Data Lake Store. It is possible to import data from other Azure components to Data Lake Store. In this session, with the aim of machine learning, first we are going to create a sample of data via Azure Data Lake Analytics.

For this, we must create a Data Lake Analytics resource (Figure 11-6). We follow the same process as we did for Data Lake Store. However, we must specify what Data Lake Store we are going to use. Please note: You must always create Data Lake Store first, then Data Lake Analytics.

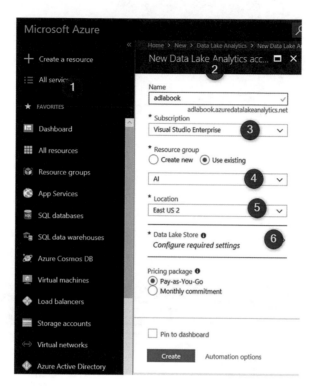

Figure 11-6. *Creating the Azure Data Lake Analytics resource*

After specifying the name, location, related Data Lake Store, subscriptions, and so forth, you must wait until the component is created and shown on the Azure Dashboard (Figure 11-7).

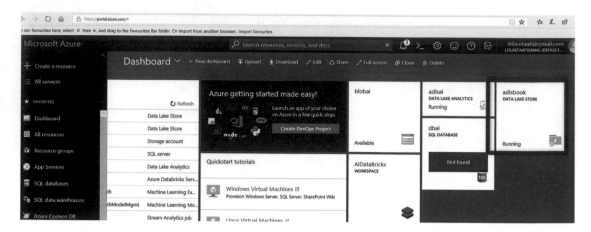

Figure 11-7. *Created Data Lake Store on Azure Dashboard*

Just click the created Azure Data Lake Analytics. Data Lake Analytics can be useful for developing and running massive parallel data and transforming and processing data in U-SQL, R, Python, and .NET. To start, we are going to import some sample data and codes. At the top of the page, click on the Sample scripts option (Figure 11-8).

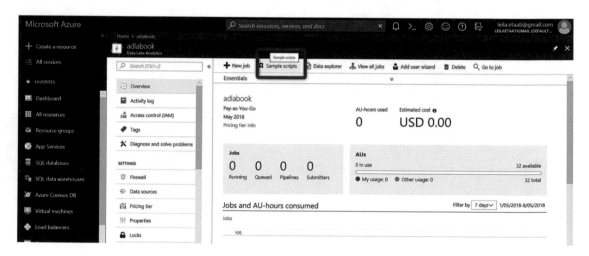

Figure 11-8. *Data Lake Analytics Sample scripts*

In the Sample scripts page, there are two main sample data: Sample data missing and U-SQL Advanced Analytic…. We need the latter, to access the sample data and codes. The sample data will be stored in Data Lake Store (Figure 11-9).

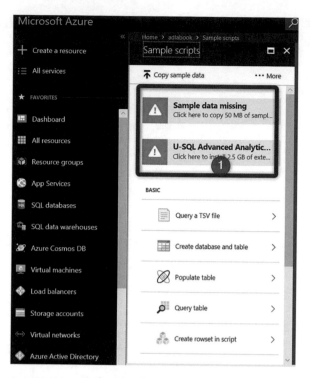

Figure 11-9. *Sample data in Data Lake Analytics*

To write the U-SQL and import some sample data and codes, click the U-SQL Advanced Analytics option. Following, about 2.5GB will be downloaded into Azure Data Lake Store. After the download starts, you will see the process of enabling U-SQL and importing data on the Install U-SQL Extensions page. The installation process is shown as a pipeline, which may take about two minutes to run (Figure 11-10).

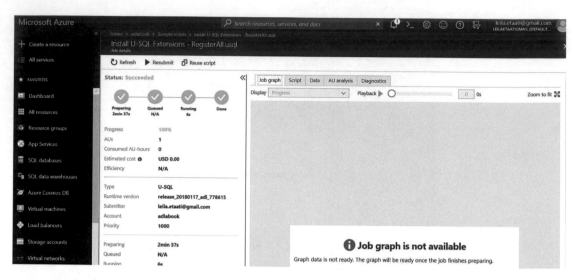

Figure 11-10. *The process of installing the U-SQL extensions*

Next, close the page and click adlsbook and then Data explorer, at the top of the page (Figure 11-11).

Figure 11-11. *Imported data in Azure Data Lake Store*

You can browse the Data Lake Store folders. Under adlsbook, among the folders listed, there are two named R and Python. Click the R folder, to see the combined data, U-SQL files, zip files, and so forth (Figure 11-12).

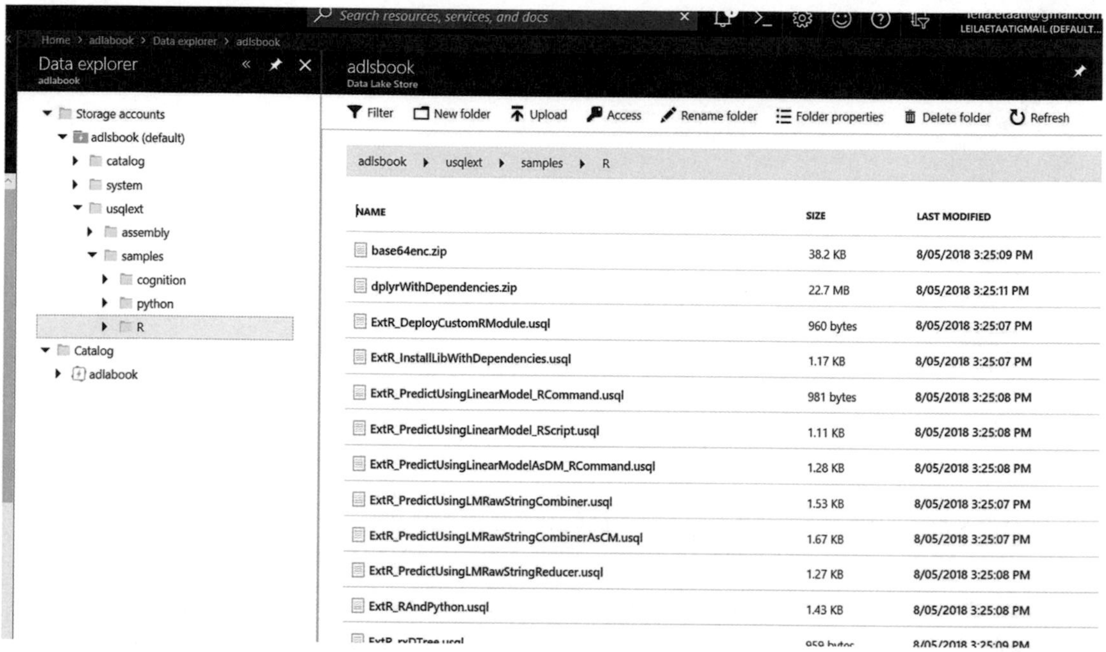

Figure 11-12. *Data Explorer—R and Python sample files*

Click one of the U-SQL files in the R folder, such as `ExtR_PredictUsingLinearModel_RScript.usql`. By clicking the files, you can see the related U-SQL files content in a separate page, as shown in Figure 11-13. As you can see in the figure, the U-SQL scripts are similar to the SQL language. It is possible to check the file format, download the codes, rename the files, revoke or grant access to files via Access, and so forth. In the next section, I will explain U-SQL language and how to write R codes or Python in it.

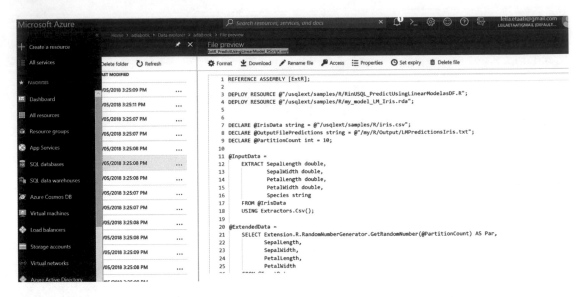

Figure 11-13. *U-SQL files for predictive models in R scripts*

Running R Scripts in U-SQL

To see how the U-SQL language works, click one of the code samples in the R folder. Then click `ExtR_rxDTree.usql`. In this example, we are going to predict a flower species, based on its sepal length. First, we must obtain the data from some resource. In the code, the data has been extracted from `/usqlext/samples/R/iris.csv`. The data set location is in Azure Data Lake Store in folder usqlext, samples, under the R codes. Copy the entire code and return to the Azure Data Lake Analytics main page and click New job, at the top of the page (Figure 11-14).

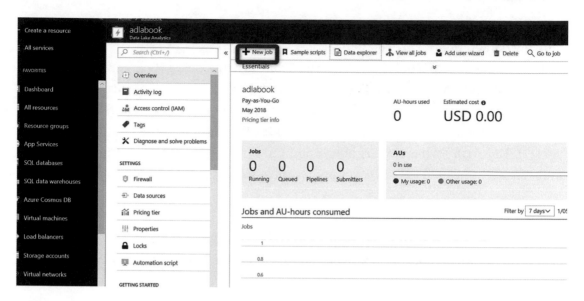

Figure 11-14.   *Copy the code and click New job*

In the New job page, there is an editor that allows you to put the code there (Figure 11-15).

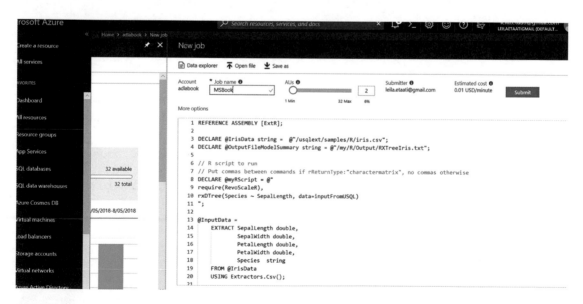

Figure 11-15.   *Passing the U-SQL code from New job page in Azure Data Analytics*

After inserting the code in the editor, at the top of the page, you can insert "MSBook" in the Job name box.

We can submit the code to run it, but we are going to change the code. In the following paragraphs, I will explain the code.

This code is a simple predictive analysis. There is a free data set named iris that is about the flower's specification. This data set has five columns: the species type and the sepal and petal length and width. Our analysis is going to predict the species of a flower based on its sepal length. The first step is to identify how to access the input data (iris data set). This data set has already been imported to the Data Lake Store under the R folder. To consume data in U-SQL scripts, we must store it in a variable.

```
DECLARE @IrisData string =  @"/usqlext/samples/R/iris.csv";
```

In addition, we want to write back the result of the prediction in another location. So, in the path, we define a new path and store the output link in a separate variable, as follows:

```
DECLARE @OutputFileModelSummary string = @"/usqlext/MSBook/RXTreeIris.txt";
```

The next part, about the R scripts definition, uses the following code:

```
DECLARE @myRScript = @"
require(RevoScaleR),
rxDTree(Species ~ SepalLength, data=inputFromUSQL)
";
```

The @myRScript variable will store the related R code that we are going to run in the next step. The preceding code uses the RevoScaleR package in R. This package contains an rxDTree function that is a decision tree algorithm to predict the flower's species, based on the sepal length.

Now we are able to employ some U-SQL language, to extract the data from the input link into a variable named @InputData, using the following code:

```
@InputData =
    EXTRACT SepalLength double,
            SepalWidth double,
            PetalLength double,
            PetalWidth double,
            Species  string
    FROM @IrisData
    USING Extractors.Csv();
```

```
@ExtendedData =
    SELECT 0 AS Par,
            *
    FROM @InputData;
```

The U-SQL code uses the `Extractors.Csv()` function to get the data from a CSV file. In the next step, we are going to run the code, using the `Extension.R.Reducer()` function.

```
@RScriptOutput = REDUCE @ExtendedData ON Par
PRODUCE Par, RowId int, ROutput string
READONLY Par
USING new Extension.R.Reducer(command:@myRScript,
rReturnType:"charactermatrix", stringsAsFactors:true);

OUTPUT @RScriptOutput TO @OutputFileModelSummary USING Outputters.Tsv();
```

Now you can submit the code, using the Submit button. After submitting the code, the MSBook job will run (Figure 11-16).

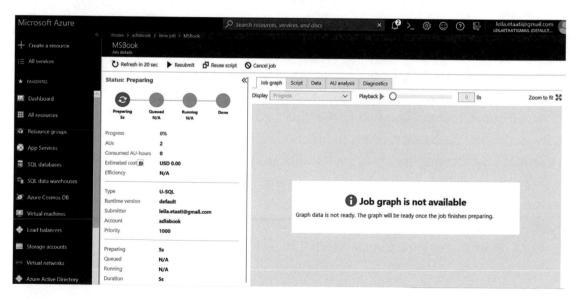

Figure 11-16. *Process of running the MSBook job*

After running the code, you must check the output folder, to see if the model is stored there as a text file (Figure 11-17).

Figure 11-17. *The output folder holding the decision tree model*

The same process that we followed in Chapter 9 for machine learning, we can apply here. We can create a model and store it in Azure Data Lake Store as a text file. Then we can consume the model for another job to evaluate the model or use it to predict a new series of data. The created model in last phase can be consumed in another job.

Managing Folders via RStudio

It is possible to load the data from Azure Data Lake Store (ADLS) into RStudio for the purpose of machine learning. Moreover, we can manage ADLS from the RStudio environment, using R scripts. So, without accessing ADLS, we are able to manage the portal, bring data from ADLS to RStudio to practice machine learning. However, after we ensure that our codes are good enough, we can use U-SQL inside ADLS, to embed R codes in the ADLS environment (as mentioned in the preceding section). In this section, the process of accessing files from the RStudio environment will be explained.

From the last section, we have already created an ADLS. However, we must create a connection from Azure to an external application (in this case, RStudio). For this purpose, we must create an Azure Active Directory for service-to-service authentication.

Click Azure Active Directory, on the left side of the Azure portal page (Figure 11-18).

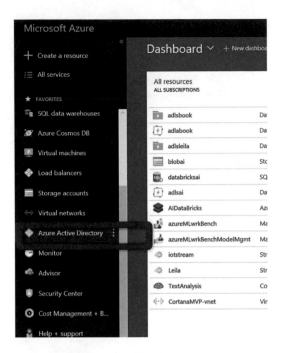

Figure 11-18. *Azure Active Application in Azure*

Next click App registrations and then New application registration (Figure 11-19).

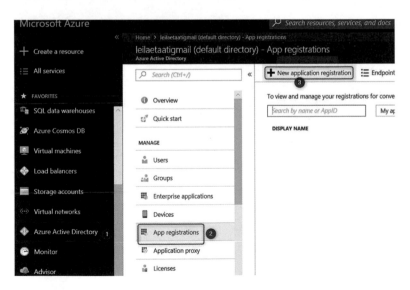

Figure 11-19. *Application Registration in Azure Active Directory*

Now you need only provide some general information, such as name, application type, and sign-on URL.

The sign-on URL can be changed later, so for now, I have entered a random URL (the web site address `http://radacad.com`) (Figure 11-20).

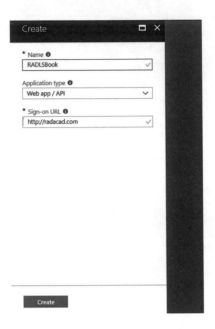

Figure 11-20. *Application registration in Azure Active Directory*

After creation, the create application is not shown on the page, so you must click View all applications (Figure 11-21). This will refresh the page and show you the application registration list.

Figure 11-21. *Application registration*

Now you are able to see the application registration list on the page (Figure 11-22).

Figure 11-22. *Application ID from application registration*

To access the ADLS, we require three different identifications, such as application ID (Client ID), Tenant ID, and Client Secret ID.

Client ID, which is the application ID, can be retrieved from App registrations (Figure 11-22). For a Tenant ID, you must return to Active Directory and click Properties, then copy the Directory ID as Tenant ID (Figure 11-23).

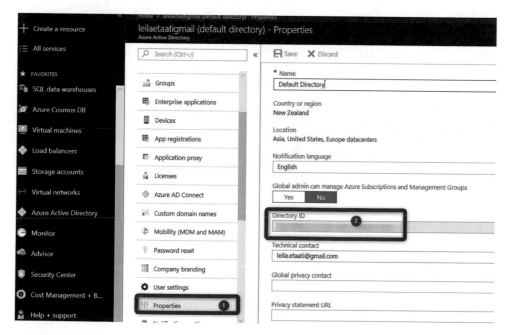

Figure 11-23. *Directory ID (Tenant ID)*

The last token that we need to get from Azure is the Client Secret ID. To get the Secret ID, you must go to Azure Active Directory, then to App registrations, and choose the app you created. Now just click the created app (Figure 11-24).

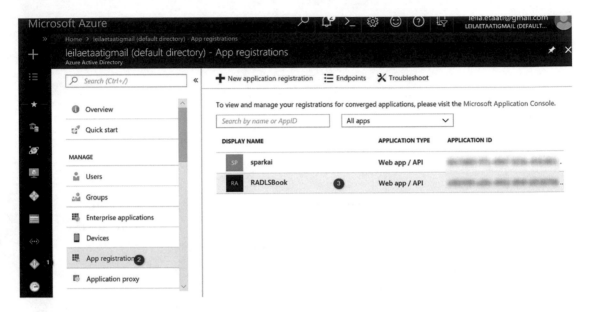

Figure 11-24. *Getting Client Secret ID from Azure Active Directory—Part 1*

Now you must click RADLSBook, to go to the main page. In RADLSBook click Settings (Figure 11-25).

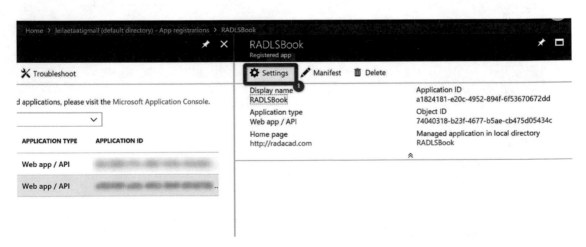

Figure 11-25. *Getting Client Secret ID from Azure Active Directory—Part 2*

On the Settings page, click the Key option. On the Key page, you will be able to create a password. We must create a new password. Click Key description and enter a name (Figure 11-26).

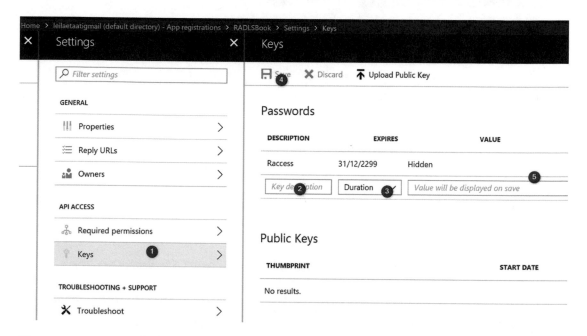

Figure 11-26. *Getting Client Secret ID from Azure Active Directory—Part 3*

Next, you must specify the duration of the password. Finally, save the key, to be able to see the code. After you have saved the code, you will receive a message indicating that you have to copy the code, and if you leave the page, the code will become hidden. So, as soon as you create the code, you will have to copy it (Figure 11-27).

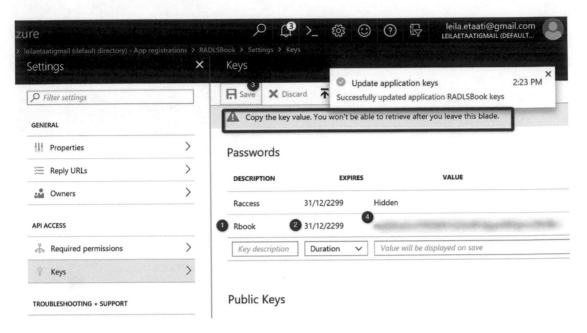

Figure 11-27. *Getting Client Secret ID from Azure Active Directory—Part 4*

Now you have the authentication tokens. The next step is to open RStudio, to write some R scripts to get the data from Azure Data Lake, upload data into Azure Data Lake, list the folder, and so forth. This can help to debug our R code easily first, then use the codes in U-SQL.

Open RStudio in your machine, then open an empty R script. To work with the data in Azure, we must install some library, as listed following:

```
install.packages("httr")
install.packages("jsonlite")
install.packages("curl")
```

After installing the libraries, to make sure they are already installed and check the package dependencies, write the following code:

```
library(httr)
library(jsonlite)
library(curl)
```

Now we must create some connection to Azure Active Directory via the following code:

```
h <- new_handle()
handle_setform(h,
                "grant_type"="client_credentials",
                "resource"="https://management.core.windows.net/",
                "client_id"="<Your Client ID (Application ID) Figure 11-22>",
                "client_secret"="<Client Secret   Figure11-27>"
)
```

Then, to get the list folder you have in Azure Data Lake Store, use the following codes. You must use the Tenant ID (Figure 11-22) and your Azure Data Lake Store name (e.g., adlsbook).

```
req <- curl_fetch_memory("https://login.windows.net/<Tenant ID from
Figure 11-22>/oauth2/token", handle = h)

res <- fromJSON(rawToChar(req$content))
r <- httr::GET("https://<Your Azure Data Lake
Store>.azuredatalakestore.net/webhdfs/v1/?op=LISTSTATUS",

add_headers(Authorization = paste(res$token_type, res$access_token)))
```

Now we can browse the folders in the main Azure Data Lake Store, using the following code:

```
nlite::toJSON(jsonlite::fromJSON(content(r,"text")), pretty = TRUE)
```

Just make sure you do not have any typos and that you properly copied and pasted the codes. As shown in Figure 11-28, there are already three folders in adlsbook: catalog, system, and usqlext. The folders are shown in the R output console.

Figure 11-28. *Folders listed in Azure Data Lake Store (adlsbook)*

Figure 11-28 shows the list of folders, the directory type, the access time, created time, owner, and so forth.

To access the data, we must provide the path of the file that we want to access. For example, we want to get the data in *adlsbook,* from usqlext, samples, R, and iris.csv (Figure 11-29).

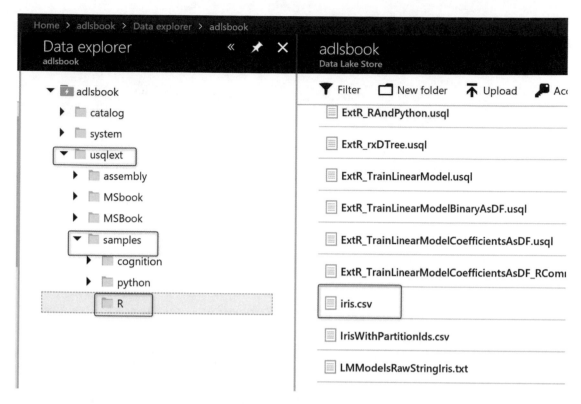

Figure 11-29. *The iris data in adlsbook*

The path will be as follows: `https://adlsbook.azuredatalakestore.net/webhdfs/v1/usqlext/samples/R/iris.csv?op=OPEN&read=true`

Note: The connection may get lost, so you must run the codes we used for creating a connection.

```
h <- new_handle()

handle_setform(h,

            "grant_type"="client_credentials",

            "resource"="https://management.core.windows.net/",

            "client_id"="<Your Client ID (Application ID) Figure 11-22>",

            "client_secret"="<Client Secret  Figure11-27>"

)
```

```
req <- curl_fetch_memory("https://login.windows.net/<Tenant ID from
Figure 11-22>/oauth2/token", handle = h)
res <- fromJSON(rawToChar(req$content))

r <- httr::GET("https://adlsbook.azuredatalakestore.net/webhdfs/v1/usqlext/
samples/R/iris.csv?op=OPEN&read=true",

                add_headers(Authorization = paste(res$token_
                type,res$access_token)))
```

To access the data, you can easily download the following and access to data.

```
writeBin(content(r), "C:/pbi/iris.csv")
 irisDownloaded <- read.csv("C:/pbi/iris.csv")
  head(irisDownloaded)
```

It is also possible to upload data from RStudio to Azure Data Lake or create a folder. Go to https://blogs.msdn.microsoft.com/microsoftrservertigerteam/2017/03/14/ using-r-to-perform-filesystem-operations-on-azure-data-lake-store/ to see all the possibilities.

You can run the U-SQL inside Visual Studio as well. To do this, you must have Visual Studio 2015 or 2017 on your machine. There are lots of weblog posts on how to run the U-SQL language in Visual Studio [2].

Summary

This chapter explained how you can apply Azure Data Lake for practicing machine learning. You saw how we are able to run R codes inside Azure Data Lake Analytics and store the results inside it. In addition, a brief explanation was provided of how to access the Azure Data Lake Store data via R Studio, how to use the U-SQL language. How to run the U-SQL language inside Visual Studio is outside the scope of this book.

References

[1] Mark Tab, et al., "Scalable Data Science with Azure Data Lake,"
     Microsoft Azure, `https://docs.microsoft.com/en-us/azure/`
     `machine-learning/team-data-science-process/data-lake-`
     `walkthrough`, November 12, 2017.

[2] Saveen Reddy, et al., "Develop U-SQL scripts by using Data
     Lake Tools for Visual Studio," Microsoft Azure, `https://docs.`
     `microsoft.com/en-us/azure/data-lake-analytics/data-lake-`
     `analytics-data-lake-tools-get-started`, August 12, 2018.

CHAPTER 12

Azure Machine Learning Studio

Azure Machine Learning (ML) Studio is a cloud machine learning platform. It features a drag-and-drop environment that is easy to use. It contains more than 20 predefined machine learning algorithms. With Azure ML Studio, it is possible to import data from different resources, devise machine learning experiments, and create a web service from the model. Moreover, it is possible to run the R or Python codes inside the Azure ML Studio environment. In this chapter, first I will explain the environment and how to formulate an experiment in it, how to create a simple machine learning model, how to test and evaluate the model, and how to import data from the local machine from other Azure components. Also, I will discuss the process of creating a web service from the model. The process of how to run R codes inside the Azure ML Studio will be explored. In addition, the process of exploring an Azure ML experiment in R Studio will be elaborated.

Azure Machine Learning Environment

To use Azure ML Studio, you must log in to `https://studio.azureml.net/`. To log in, you can use any account from Google, Yahoo, or a company account (Figure 12-1). There are two subscriptions for Azure ML; one is free, and the other is the standard version.

© Leila Etaati 2019
L. Etaati, *Machine Learning with Microsoft Technologies*, https://doi.org/10.1007/978-1-4842-3658-1_12

Figure 12-1. *Machine Learning Studio login*

After logging in to the portal, there is an empty environment. As you can see in Figure 12-2, on the left side of the screen, there are seven different options: Projects, Experiments, Web Services, Notebooks, Datasets, Trained Models, and Settings. Experiments is the main place to create the models. As you can see in the figure, Experiments is empty on first use.

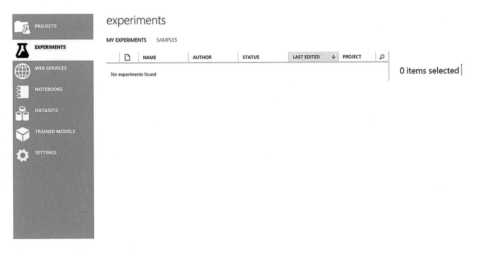

Figure 12-2. *Azure ML Studio environment*

It is possible to have many different workspaces, combining free or standard subscriptions. As shown Figure 12-3, the user can switch between these environments.

Figure 12-3. *Azure ML workspace*

In the following sections, different components of Azure ML will be explained briefly.

Azure Machine Learning Experiment

An experiment is the primary vehicle for creating machine learning models. As you can see in Figure 12-3, we have two main experiments: My Experiments and Samples. My Experiments is a place to create new machine learning models and storage to save all user-created experiments. The Samples experiments contain predefined examples by Microsoft.

To create a new experiment, click Experiments on the left side of the screen, then click the New option at the bottom left of the page and then Blank Experiment (Figure 12-4).

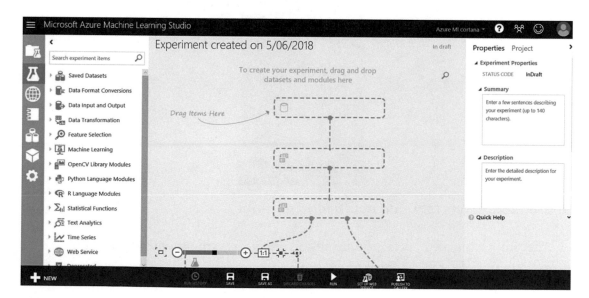

Figure 12-4. *Setting up an experiment*

As you can see in Figure 12-4, the experiment is in a drag-and-drop environment. On the left side of the screen, there are components that help us create an ML model, such as Saved Datasets, Data Transformation, Machine Learning, and so forth.

To create an experiment, you must get data. There are two main ways to import data: importing data from the local machine (Figure 12-5) or using built-in data components. For our example, first I am going to import data from the local machine. The data set is the Titanic data set available at `http://web.stanford.edu/class/archive/cs/cs109/cs109.1166/stuff/titanic.csv` [1]. To import data, we must click the Datasets option at the left side of the screen and then click the New option.

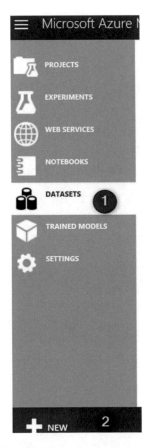

Figure 12-5. *Importing data from a local machine*

After importing the data set, we are able to create an experiment with the aim of predicting whether a passenger of a specific age, gender, and passenger class will survive. To create a new experiment, you must first click the Experiments option at the left side of the screen. Azure ML consists of different modules (nodes), with each activity shown as separate nodes. In the search area, type "Titanic." Then drag and drop the node into the white design surface area, as shown in Figure 12-6. As you can see in Figure 12-6, the Titanic data set has been shown as a separate node with only one output. To view the data set, you must right-click the output node and click the Visualize option. This allows you to see the data and some additional useful information, under such columns as PassengerID, Survived, Pclass, Name, and others.

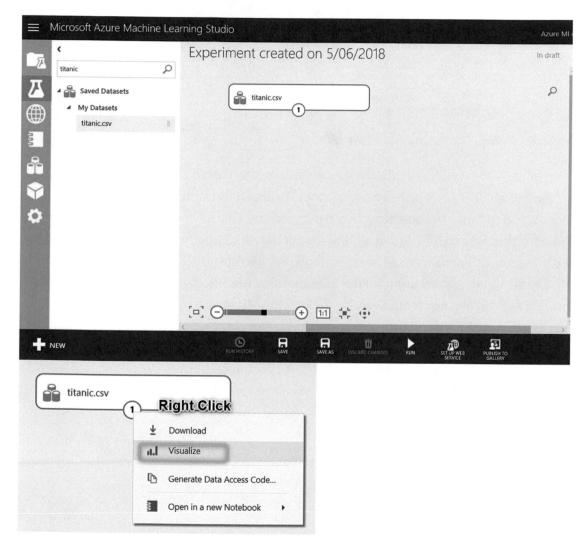

Figure 12-6. *Importing and visualizing data*

Moreover, there is a small histogram chart under the name of each column that indicates the value frequency of each column (Figure 12-7). Also, by clicking each column, you can see a statistical summary on the right side of the page, as shown in Figure 12-7.

Experiment created on 5/06/2018 ❯ titanic.csv ❯ dataset   ×

rows	columns
891	12

	PassengerId	Survived	Pclass	Name	Sex	Age	SibSp			◢ Statistics	
view as										Mean	29.6991
										Median	28
	1	0	3	Braund, Mr. Owen Harris	male	22	1			Min	0.42
										Max	80
	2	1	1	Cumings, Mrs. John Bradley (Florence Briggs Thayer)	female	38	1			Standard Deviation	14.5265
										Unique Values	88
										Missing Values	177
	3	1	3	Heikkinen, Miss. Laina	female	26	0			Feature Type	Numeric Feature
	4	1	1	Futrelle, Mrs. Jacques Heath (Lily May Peel)	female	35	1			◢ Visualizations	
										Age	
	5	0	3	Allen, Mr. William Henry	male	35	0			Histogram	
										compare to None	

Figure 12-7. *Visualizing the data set*

The next step is to clean the data. As you can see in Figure 12-7, for the age of people on the *Titanic*, 177 rows have a missing value. One of main activities before creating models is to remove or substitute the missing values. There is a module, Clean Missing Data, for this. Search for it and drag and drop it into the Experiments area. As you can see in Figure 12-8, this module has one input and two outputs. Connect the output from the Titanic data set to the input of the missing value module. Then specify how you want to solve the missing value problem, by clicking the Missing value module. There is a Properties page for this module, from which you can choose the column(s) you want to remove missing values from. Then specify the cleaning mode, such as substitute with a mean, median, or a custom value. It is possible to remove the entire missing data row or substitute it using a PCA algorithm [2]. As you can see in Figure 12-8, Age has been selected, and the Cleaning mode is Remove entire row.

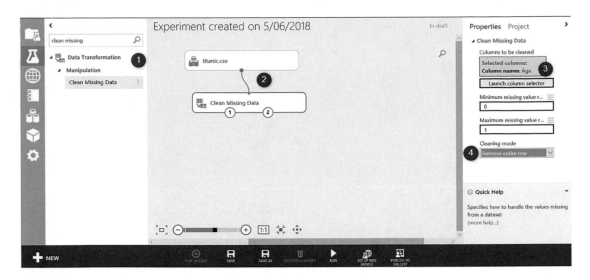

Figure 12-8. *Removing a missing value from data*

Another data transformation that we should perform is to remove columns that have no impact on the Survived column, such as PassengerID, Name, and so forth. The only columns that we need to run machine learning on are Age, Sex, Pclass, and Survived. There is another module, named Select Columns, in Dataset. Drag and drop this module into Experiments, then connect the first output of Clean Missing Data to the input of Select Columns in Dataset. Then, in the Properties panel, choose the desired columns (Figure 12-9). Now the main data cleaning and wrangling for this data set has been done. The next step is to choose the related algorithms.

The main purpose for machine learning here is to predict whether a new passenger will survive. According to the discussion in Chapter 4, we are predicting a class, not a continuous value. Predictive analytics using a classification approach can solve this problem. In Azure ML, there are about 25 main algorithms that have been grouped into four main scenarios: Anomaly detection, Classification, Clustering, and Regression. For our scenario, we must use classification algorithms. If you expand the classification algorithm list, there is another grouping based on the number of classes you are going to predict. If there is a two-class problem, you must use algorithms with Two-Class. The problem concerns predicting a situation in which people survived or not.

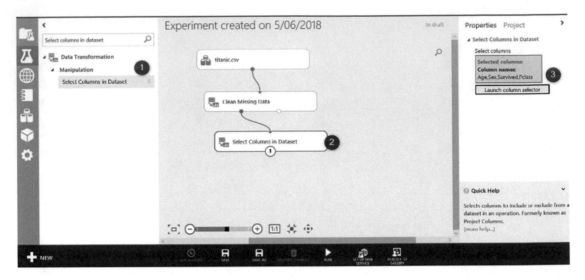

Figure 12-9. *Selecting columns in a data set*

As you can see in Figure 12-10, under Classification, we have nine different algorithms for predicting those who survived or did not. Each of these algorithms can be used in a different situation, with different data types. There is a cheat sheet for choosing the best algorithms provided by Microsoft [3]. For the *Titanic* problem, we don't have more than 100 columns, the data is not linear, and we need high accuracy and fast training. As a result, I am choosing the Two-Class Boosted Decision Tree algorithm. However, the best practice is to select different algorithms and then compare their accuracy.

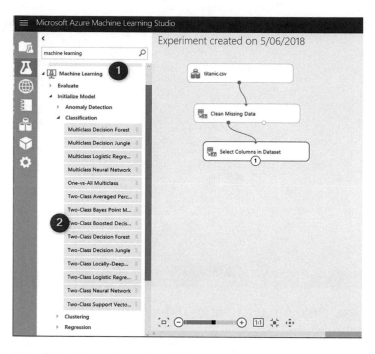

Figure 12-10. *Machine learning algorithms in Azure ML*

Following the machine learning life cycle introduced in Chapter 4, we have to split the data, some for the purpose of training and the rest for testing. In Azure ML, there are three different modules that are used for splitting data, training models, and testing models: Split Data, Train Model, and Score Model. First, I drag and drop the Split Data (Figure 12-11). Split Data allows us to specify how much data should go into training and how much into testing. As you can see in Figure 12-11, the Split Data has been connected to the output of the Select Columns in Dataset. The split percentage has been set to 0.7 (30% for testing and 70% for training). One of the output nodes is for training, and the other is for testing.

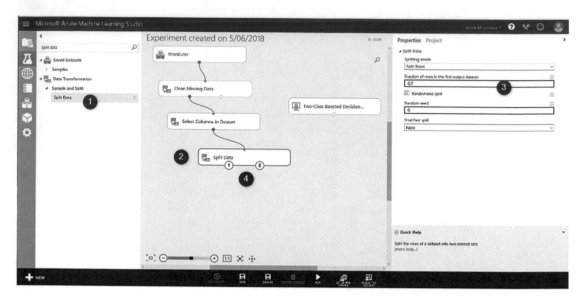

Figure 12-11. *Split Data for machine learning purposes*

We must drag and drop the relevant module for training and testing into Experiments. As you can see in Figure 12-12, the right output from the split module has been connected to Train Model, and the other output from the Split Data has been connected to Score Model. Moreover, under the Train Model properties, the Survived column has been selected.

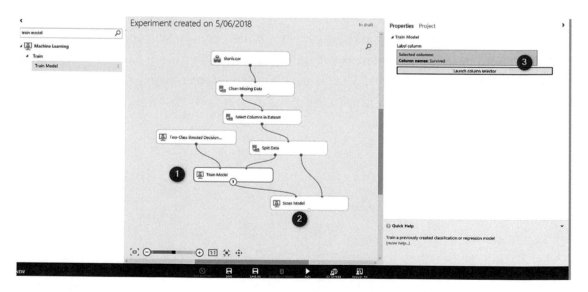

Figure 12-12. *Dragging and dropping the Train Model and Score Model into Experiments*

Now we are able to run the code, to see the result of the prediction from the Score Model output. To run it, click the Run button at the bottom of the page. After running the experiments, we will be able to see the result of the test data prediction in the output of the Score Model module. Right-click the output and visualize the data (Figure 12-13).

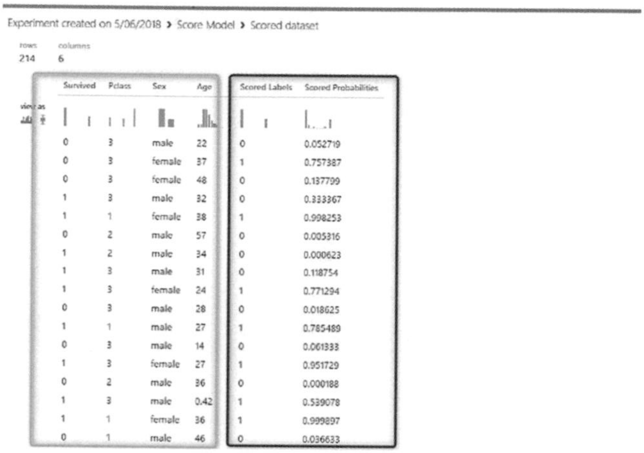
Experiment created on 5/06/2018 › Score Model › Scored dataset

rows 214 columns 6

Survived	Pclass	Sex	Age	Scored Labels	Scored Probabilities
0	3	male	22	0	0.052719
0	3	female	37	1	0.757387
0	3	female	48	0	0.137799
1	3	male	32	0	0.333367
1	1	female	38	1	0.998253
0	2	male	57	0	0.005316
1	2	male	34	0	0.000623
1	3	male	31	0	0.118754
1	3	female	24	1	0.771294
0	3	male	28	0	0.018625
1	1	male	27	1	0.785489
0	3	male	14	0	0.061333
1	3	female	27	1	0.951729
0	2	male	36	0	0.000188
1	3	male	0.42	1	0.539078
1	1	female	36	1	0.999897
0	1	male	46	0	0.036633

Figure 12-13. *The prediction result for Titanic example*

It is possible to evaluate the model using Evaluate Model, to check the accuracy of the created model. In the next section, the process of creating an application programming interface (API) will be explained.

Creating a Web Service

The next step after evaluating the model is optionally to create an API so everyone is able to use the model by providing the data. To create the web service, you must run the experiment first, then click Setup Web Service (Predictive Web Service recommended). An input and output link for web services has been created, as you can see in Figure 12-14.

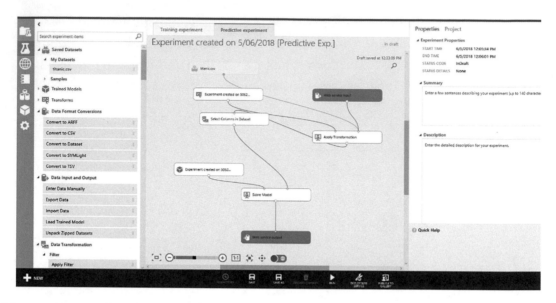

Figure 12-14. *Creating a web service from a machine learning model*

Run the experiment again, then click Deploy Web Service at the bottom of the page. By deploying the web service, a new page will be shown. On this page, you can see details of the API, both for single processing and batch processing of data.

As you can see in Figure 12-15, there is an API key that you can share to allow others to use the ML model. Moreover, for API URLs, there are two main ways to use the API: a request and response approach and batch processing.

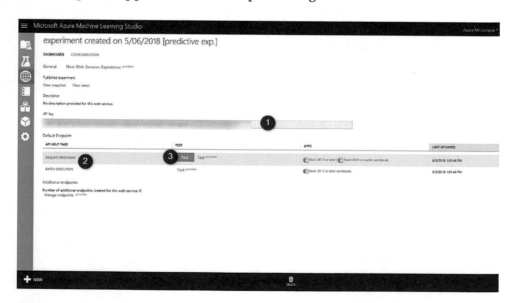

Figure 12-15. *Creating a web service for the Titanic problem*

Click the Batch Execution option and navigate to the new page that contains the API information (Figure 12-16). As you can see in the figure, the web service URL is shown for request information.

Figure 12-16. *Web service information page*

In addition, it is possible to embed the created model in other applications, such as web applications, reports, and so forth, leveraging any language, such as C#, Python, and R. On the web service information page, go to the Sample Code section. As you can see in Figure 12-17, there are sample codes in C#, Python, and R that enable users to embed the code into applications. However, you must change the input and output of the web service, so end users are able to provide proper information and get the related prediction. For example, in the web service created in Figure 12-15, the input for the service also gets the passenger ID, name, and other irrelevant data from users that we must refine in order to receive such information as age, gender, and passenger class. In another example, regarding output, a user may only be interested in obtaining the prediction and the probability, not all the other input columns.

Pclass	Numeric
Sex	String
Age	Numeric
Scored Labels	Numeric
Scored Probabilities	Numeric

Figure 12-17. *Web service sample code*

In the next step, I am going to refine the web service input and output, by adding Select Columns in Dataset modules for output, and change the select column for web service input (Figure 12-18).

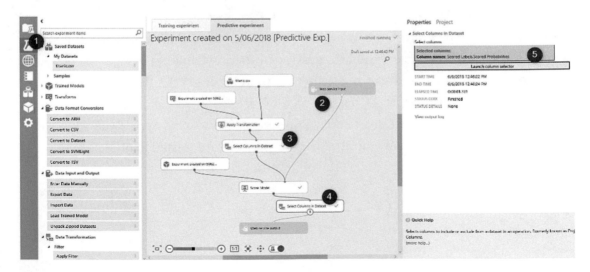

Figure 12-18. *Change input and output for web service*

As you can see in Figure 12-18, for the web service input, we disconnect the link and connect it to the input of the Score Model, and in the Select Column in Dataset module (Figure 12-18, 3), only age, gender, and passenger class have been selected. Similarly, for the web service output, the Select Columns in Dataset module has been dragged and dropped to select only the Scored Label and Scored Probability. Next, we connect the web service output to the Select Columns in Dataset modules. Finally, we run the experiment and deploy it again. There is a message about overwriting the web service, which we must confirm. After deploying again, on the web service page, click the Test button (Figure 12-19, 1). After, we can test the API.

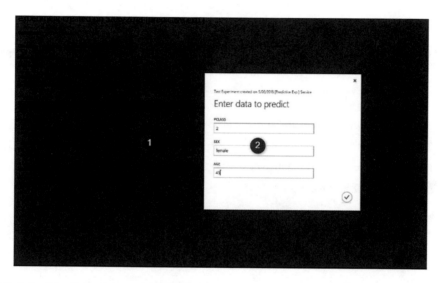

Figure 12-19. *Testing the web service*

As you can see in Figure 12-19, by entering three inputs, Age, Gender(Sex), and Passenger Class (Pclass), into API, the result of the machine learning will be shown for this specific row at the bottom of the page (Figure 12-20, 1).

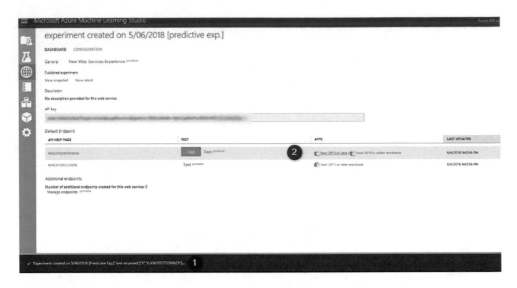

Figure 12-20. *Result of the API and call to Excel*

The next step allows us to analyze the API in Excel. We just have to navigate to Apps (Figure 12-20) and click Excel 2013 or Later (Figure 12-20, 2). After clicking the Excel icon, a message to Download the Sample Data appears. Save the Excel file and open it, then enable the Excel (Figure 12-21).

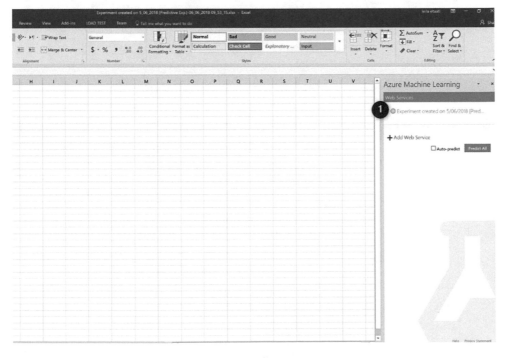

Figure 12-21. *Enabling the Azure ML API in Excel*

Next, a new window will appear. Use the sample data (Figure 12-22, 1), then, under the Input field, choose the input data range (Figure 12-22, 2). Then, under the Output field, write the output cell number (Figure 12-22, 3). Then click the Predict option.

Figure 12-22. *Enabling the Azure ML API in Excel*

By running the code and choosing the Auto Predict option, the result of the prediction will be shown in output cells (Figure 12-23).

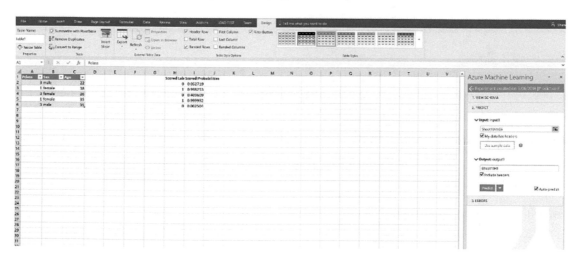

Figure 12-23. *API call in Excel*

It is possible to add more input rows for more predictions.

R and Azure ML Studio

In Azure ML Studio, there are 25 algorithms. However, in some cases, users may want to use their own algorithms. It is possible to write R or Python code inside the Azure ML Studio. In this section, you will see how we can visualize the charts and see the output of the data there.

Create a new experiment in Azure ML Studio. Use the same data set (Titanic). Drag and drop "Titanic" into the Experiments area. Then, in the Search area, type "Execute R Scripts." Drag and drop the module into the Experiments area (Figure 12-24).

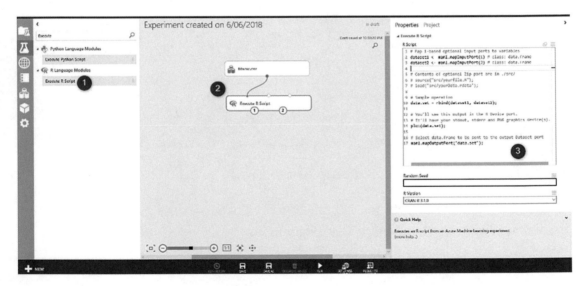

Figure 12-24. *Executing R scripts in Azure ML*

As you can see in Figure 12-24, there is an editor for writing R scripts. The Execute R Scripts module has three input nodes. The first two at the left are for data sets, and the last one is for zip files. By clicking this module, we can write the codes. As you can see in Figure 12-24, the input data from node 1 has been retrieved with the following code and stored in dataset1.

```
dataset1 <- maml.mapInputPort(1) # class: data.frame
```

In this example, the input node contains the Titanic data set (Figure 12-24). So, I will change the code, as follows:

```
Titanic<- maml.mapInputPort(1) # class: data.frame
```

In next step, we are going to create a box plot from the age of the *Titanic* passengers, using the following code:

```
boxplot(titanic$Age)
```

Next, we create a statistical summary of the data.

```
output<-data.frame(titanic$Age,titanic$Pclass,titanic$Sex)
summary(output)
```

Finally, we want to show only age, sex, and passenger class in the output node. The final code would look as in Figure 12-25.

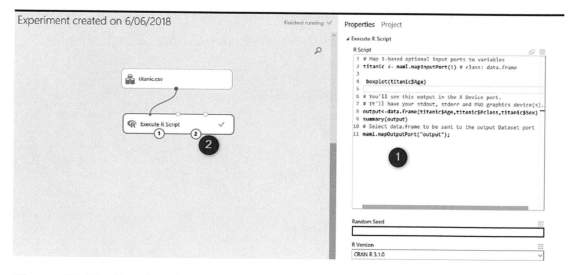

Figure 12-25. *R scripts in Azure ML Studio*

Now we have to run the experiment. There are two output nodes for Execute R Script. The output node on the left side holds the output variable that has three main columns (Figure 12-26).

Experiment created on 6/06/2018 › Execute R Script › Result Da

rows	columns		
891	3		
	titanic.Age	titanic.Pclass	titanic.Sex
view as			
	22	3	male
	38	1	female
	26	3	female
	35	1	female
	35	3	male
		3	male
	54	1	male
	2	3	male
	27	3	female
	14	2	female
	4	3	female
	58	1	female
	20	3	male
	39	3	male
	14	3	female
	55	2	female
	2	3	male

Figure 12-26. *First output of Execute R Scripts in Azure ML Studio*

The other output contains some information about the R chart and the statistical summary of it. To view the output, right-click the right output node and visualize the node (Figure 12-27).

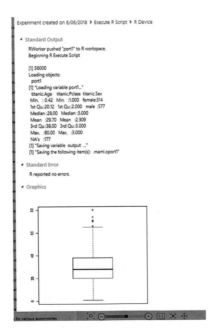

Experiment created on 6/06/2018 › Execute R Script › R Device

▲ Standard Output

RWorker pushed "port1" to R workspace.
Beginning R Execute Script

[1] 56000
Loading objects:
  port1
[1] "Loading variable port1..."
 titanic.Age   titanic.Pclass titanic.Sex
 Min.   : 0.42   Min.   :1.000   female:314
 1st Qu.:20.12   1st Qu.:2.000   male :577
 Median :28.00   Median :3.000
 Mean   :29.70   Mean   :2.309
 3rd Qu.:38.00   3rd Qu.:3.000
 Max.   :80.00   Max.   :3.000
 NA's   :177
[1] "Saving variable output ..."
[1] "Saving the following item(s): .maml.oport1"

▲ Standard Error

R reported no errors.

▲ Graphics

Figure 12-27. *Second output of Execute R Scripts*

It is possible to explore the Azure ML data sets and experiments from RStudio. Moreover, R users can write a function in RStudio and then create an API from it.

For this, first, you must install the Azure ML package in RStudio, using the following command:

```
install.package("AzureML")
```

The second step is to get some identifications keys from Azure ML Studio. Navigate to studio.azureml.net, in your Azure ML environment, click Settings, copy the Workspace ID (Figure 12-28), and store it in a variable in RStudio, as follows:

```
id<- "your workspace ID"
```

Figure 12-28. *Workspace ID from Azure ML environment*

Navigate to another tab in the Settings menu and choose Authentication tokens. Copy the primary authentication token and allocate it to a variable in RStudio.

```
auth<-"your authorization token"
```

There is a workspace function in the Azure ML package that creates a reference to an Azure ML Studio workspace, by getting the authentication token and Workspace ID.

```
ws <- workspace( id , auth  )
```

It is possible to receive an error for missing R tools software. Therefore, you must install the latest version of R tools from [4] and store it in the same root of the RStudio.

Finally, for exploring all the experiments in Azure ML, there is an `experiments` function that gets the `ws` object as input to connect to the Azure ML environment.

```
experiments(ws, filter = "all")
```

Using the `experiments` function allows you to filter which experiment from Azure ML you want to check the details of. You can set the filter values to `all`, `samples`, and `my datasets`. In this example, I set the filter to `all`. By applying the name function in RStudio to check the detail information, you can see the columns, such as the experiment's name, versions, owner, and so forth (Figure 12-29).

```
> e <- experiments(ws, filter = "all")
> View(e)
> names(e)
 [1] "ExperimentId"                         "Description"
 [3] "Etag"                                 "Creator"
 [5] "IsArchived"                           "JobId"
 [7] "VersionId"                            "RunId"
 [9] "OriginalExperimentDocumentationLink"  "Summary"
[11] "Category"                             "Tags"
[13] "IsPartialRun"                         "StatusCode"
[15] "StatusDetail"                         "CreationTime"
[17] "StartTime"                            "EndTime"
[19] "Metadata"
```

Figure 12-29. *Exploring the attributes we are able to see from Azure ML Experiments*

It is possible to upload a data set from RStudio into Azure ML with the `upload.dataset` command.

There is a data set in the `ggplot2` package that I am going to upload to the Azure ML Studio.

```
library(ggplot2)
upload.dataset(mpg,ws,"mpg")
```

You must to provide the data set, workstation objects (`ws`), and a name with which you want to save the data set in the Azure ML environment. Now, if you explore the data sets in Azure ML, you will be able to see the newly uploaded data set there.

Summary

This chapter presented a brief introduction to Azure ML Studio. First, a simple machine learning model for predicting the survival of *Titanic* passengers was implemented. The next step was to create an API from the model, analyze it, and show the result in Excel. In addition, how to write R codes inside Azure ML using the Execute R Scripts module was explained. The chapter's final section explained how to explore Azure ML Studio via R code and upload data sets from RStudio into Azure ML datasets.

References

[1]   Stanford University, "A Titanic Probability," Data set, `http://web.stanford.edu/class/archive/cs/cs109/cs109.1166/stuff/titanic.csv`, 2016.

[2]   Sebastian Raschka, "Implementing a Principal Component Analysis (PCA)," SebastianRaschka, `https://sebastianraschka.com/Articles/2014_pca_step_by_step.html`, April 13, 2014.

[3]   Xiao Zhang et al., "Machine learning algorithm cheat sheet for Azure Machine Learning Studio," Microsoft Azure, `https://docs.microsoft.com/en-us/azure/machine-learning/studio/algorithm-cheat-sheet`, March 3, 2019.

[4]   Brian Ripley, Duncan Murdoch et al., "Building R for Windows," CRAN—R Project, `https://cran.r-project.org/bin/windows/Rtools/`.

CHAPTER 13

Machine Learning in Azure Stream Analytics

Azure Stream Analytics is an event-processing engine that allows users to analyze high volumes of data streaming from devices, sensors, and applications. Azure Stream Analytics can be used for Internet of Things (IoT) real-time analytics, remote monitoring and data inventory controls. However, Azure Stream Analytics is another component in Azure on which we could run machine learning. It is possible to use a machine learning model API created in Azure ML Studio inside Azure Stream Analytics for applying machine learning to streaming data from sensors, applications, and live databases. In this chapter, I will explain how to use machine learning inside Azure Stream Analytics. First, a general introduction to Azure Stream Analytics is given, then, a simple example of an Azure ML Studio API that is going to be applied to the stream data is presented.

Azure Stream Analytics Environment

Azure Stream Analytics is an event-processing component in the Azure environment. To create Azure Stream Analytics, you must log in to an Azure account and create a Stream Analytics job (Figure 13-1).

© Leila Etaati 2019
L. Etaati, *Machine Learning with Microsoft Technologies*, https://doi.org/10.1007/978-1-4842-3658-1_13

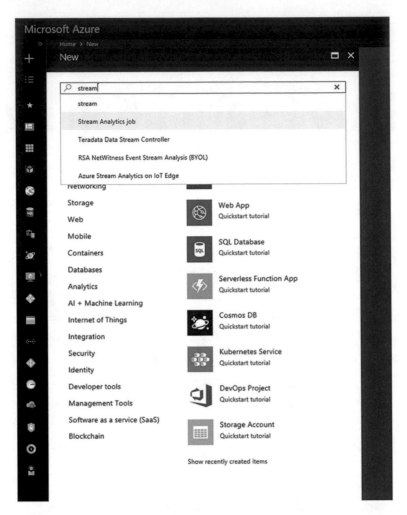

Figure 13-1. *Creating an Azure Stream Analytics job in an Azure environment*

After creating a Stream Analytics job in Azure, you must set up some predefined parameters, such as the job name, subscription, resource group, and so forth (Figure 13-2).

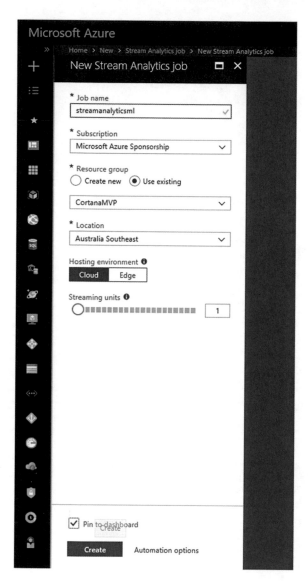

Figure 13-2. *Stream Analytics job initialization*

Stream Analytics is like a service bus inside Azure, able to fetch data from some components and apply some analytics on received data and pass it to other components. As a result, the Stream Analytics environment contains three main components: Inputs, Outputs, and Query. Stream Analytics is able to fetch data from just three main components: Event Hub, IoT Hub, and Blob storage. These three components are used mainly for collecting data from external sensors, applications, and live APIs. Stream Analytics can pass data to some other Azure components, such as Blob storage, Azure SQL database, Power BI, and so forth (Figure 13-3).

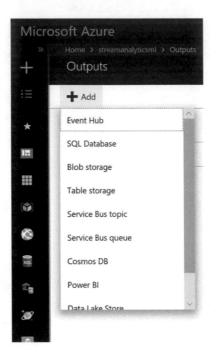

Figure 13-3. *Stream Analytics Outputs*

Finally, the last important component is Query Editor, which helps users to apply some analytics on received data before sending them to output (Figure 13-4).

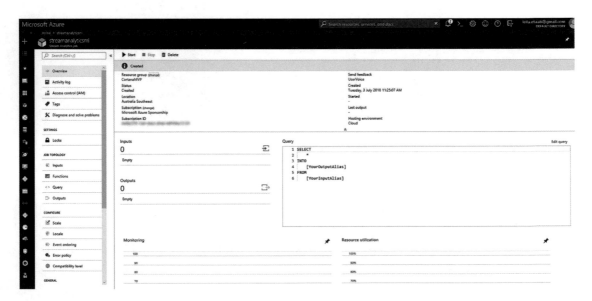

Figure 13-4. *Stream Analytics main components (Inputs, Outputs, and Query)*

The language used in Stream Analytics is the Stream Analytics Query Language, which is very to the SQL scripting language.

Case Study

For our case study, I will show how to get data from an application via Event Hub, then pass the collected data into Stream Analytics, apply machine learning and then show the live result in Power BI Services.

The process is explained in Figure 13-5. As you can see in the figure, there is an application that sends live data to Event Hub. Stream Analytics receives the live data, applies an Azure ML API model on the received data, and then sends it to Power BI. In Power BI Report, the end user can see the live data in addition to the result of the machine learning that was applied to it.

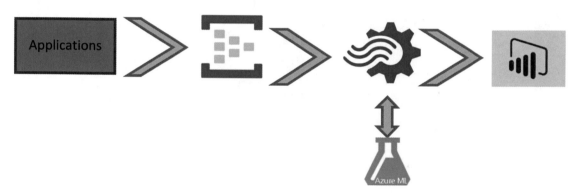

Figure 13-5. *Case study for fetching data, applying machine learning, and then showing the result in Power BI*

Event Hub

The first step is to create an Event Hub service in the cloud. To create an Event Hub service, follow the same procedures for creating Stream Analytics. Create a new service and provide the relevant information (Figure 13-6).

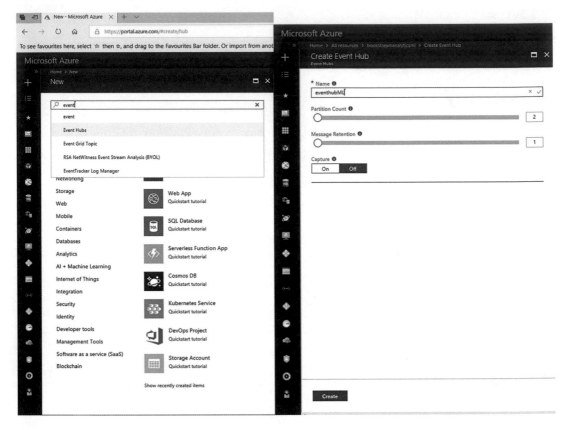

Figure 13-6. *Creating an Event Hub in Azure*

With an Event Hub service, you can add a new Event Hub to your service
(Figure 13-7).

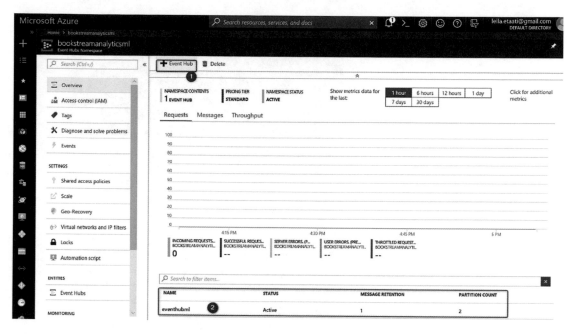

Figure 13-7. *Creating a new Event Hub*

Application

The second step is to create an application that generates some sample data. The application is a sample .NET framework application that auto-generates some random data. (The application has been included in the book materials for Chapter 13.) Open the folder containing the application (Figure 13-8).

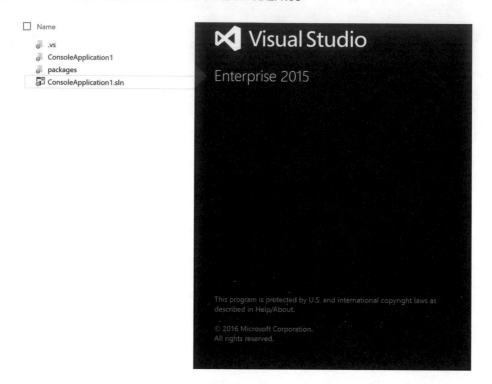

Figure 13-8. *Application creating random live number*

As I mentioned earlier in this chapter, I'll be using a .NET C# console application to pass the data to Event Hub. This application has been created by Reza Rad [1]. In his blog post, in the "Push Data Application" section, Rad explains the process of creating this application step by step.

However, for the application that has been included in the related materials for this chapter, you must open it with Visual Studio, then open the Solution Explorer, go to References, right-click and select Manage NuGet Packages. Next, click Browse, select WindowsAzure.ServiceBus, and install it (Figure 13-9).

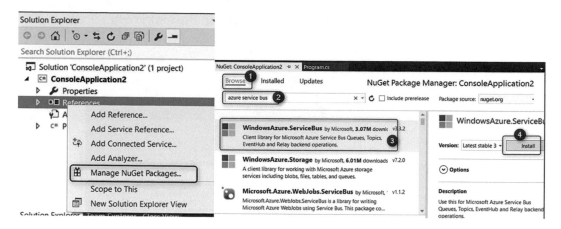

Figure 13-9. *Install Azure Service Bus in Visual Studio*

After installing Azure Service Bus, you must set up the configuration. Click App. config, then in the code for the key section (Figure 13-10), change the end point URL name and keys (from the created Stream Analytics in the next section).

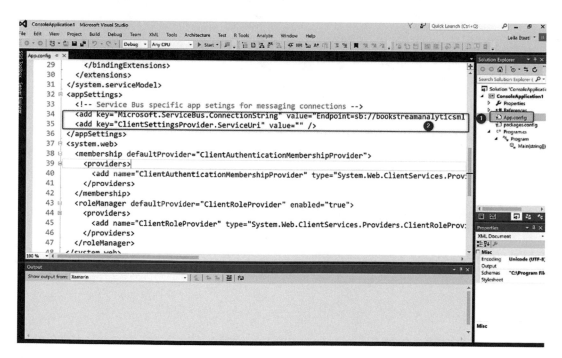

Figure 13-10. *Setting up the configuration*

Finally, you must enter the name of your Event Hub in the main code section under the program (Figure 13-11).

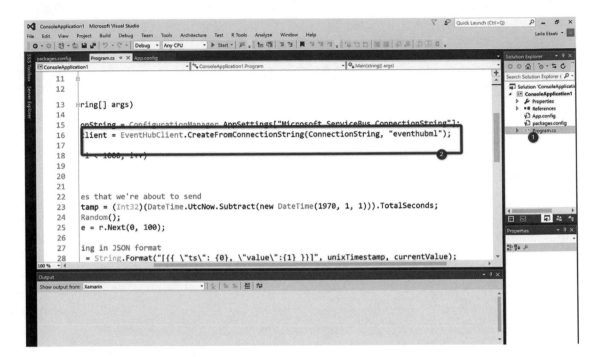

Figure 13-11. *Changing the Event Hub name in the code*

Now the code is ready. Before running the code, you must set up the Stream Analytics.

Azure Stream Analytics

The first step is to create a Stream Analytics job in Azure (Figure 13-12).

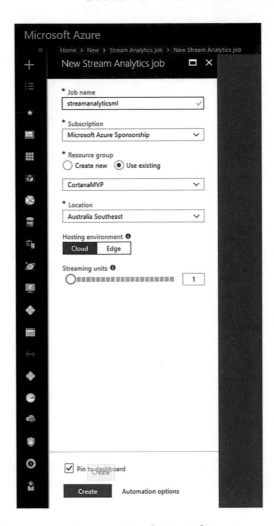

Figure 13-12. *Creating a new Stream Analytics job in Azure*

After creating Stream Analytics, you must set up the Inputs, Outputs, and Query. As mentioned, Stream Analytics is able to retrieve data from other Azure components. As you can see in Figure 13-13, Stream Analytics can get data from the three main Azure components and then pass stream data to other resources, such as Power BI, SQL Database, and so forth. The transformation query leverages an SQL-like query language that is used to filter, sort, aggregate, and join streaming data over a period [2].

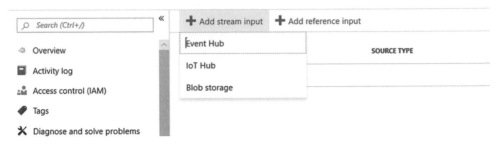

Figure 13-13. *Inputting data for Stream Analytics*

In our case study, we are going to get data from the Event Hub, apply machine learning to it, and then pass it to Power BI, to see the live data with applied analytics.

To create input, click the Inputs option on the main Stream Analytics page (Figure 13-14).

Figure 13-14. *Creating Input for Azure Stream Analytics*

After creating input for Stream Analytics, we must create output, following the same process for input (Figure 13-15).

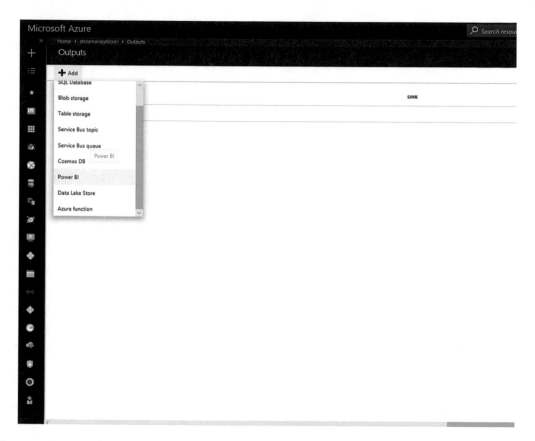

Figure 13-15. *Creating output for Power BI in Stream Analytics*

After creating Stream Analytics input and output and before creating the query, we must set up some keys and names in the .NET code. Click the Stream Analytics components, then Shared access policies. Click RootManageSharedAccessKey, then copy the Primary Key (Figure 13-16).

Figure 13-16. *Key for shared access*

Copy the data and then paste it in the main code section shown in Figure 13-11.

Azure ML

In Azure ML Studio, I have created a simple model for grouping data. The main aim of this model is to fetch data from the application, then group it into four main groups. Next, I create an API, so that Stream Analytics is able to pass data to it and get the group number and the real value. Import the sample data that the application is going to generate (Figure 13-17). The sample data has been included in the book materials for Chapter 13. Then drag and drop the Select Columns in Dataset component to the selected value column. Finally, leverage another component named Group Data into Bins.

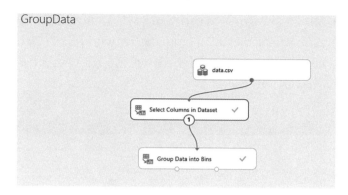

Figure 13-17. *Azure ML model*

Take the following steps, to generate an API for this model.

1. Run the model using the Run option at the bottom of the page.

2. Click Setup Page, to create input and output for the API (Figure 13-18).

3. Then, run the model again and click Deploy Web Service.

After creating a web service, a new page will be shown. On the new page, in the middle of the page, the API key for the web service appears.

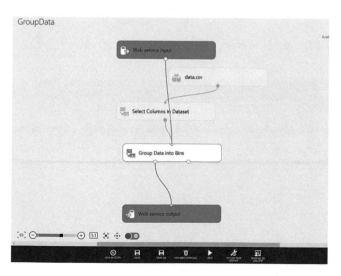

Figure 13-18. *Azure ML web service creation*

To connect from Stream Analytics to the Azure ML API, we must click APPs (at the bottom of the page), then click Excel 2010 or an earlier workbook (Figure 13-19). A new Excel workbook will be downloaded. Open the Excel file, then, at the top of the page, you will see the web service URL and access key.

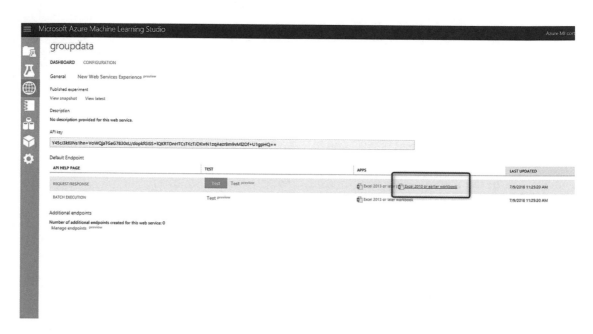

Figure 13-19.   *Azure ML web service creation*

Copy the code for the web service URL and the access key (Figure 13-20).

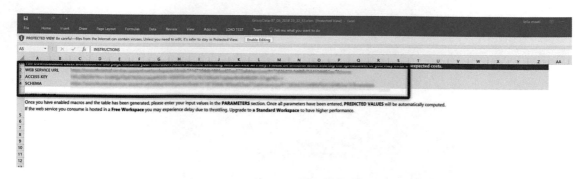

Figure 13-20.   *Access key and URL in Excel file*

Now that we have the keys and URL, we must set up a function in Stream Analytics, to access the created model in Azure ML Studio.

Stream Analytics Function

At this stage, we have created an Event Hub application to generate a random number, Stream Analytics, and an Azure ML model and API to group the streamed data.

In this section, we must create a function inside Stream Analytics to call the created API in Azure ML. Click Azure Stream Analytics job, then click Functions (Figure 13-21).

Figure 13-21. *Creating a function in Azure Stream Analytics*

On the Functions page, select the subscription name, the key, and URL extracted from the Excel file (Figure 13-22).

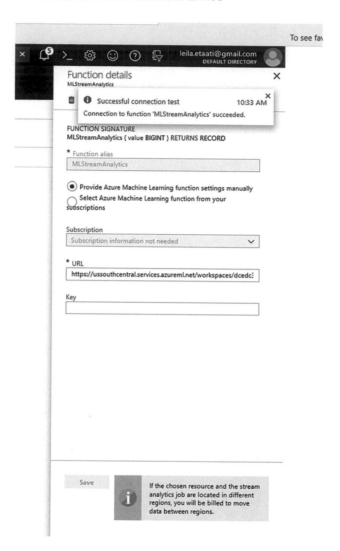

Figure 13-22. *Creating a function*

On theStream Analytics main page, we must add some code in Query Editor, to call the function. Click Edit Query, then in the editor, paste the following code:

```
WITH MLStreamAnalytics AS (
SELECT value, MLStreamAnalytics(value) as result
FROM azureml
)
```

```
SELECT
  value, result.[value_quantized]
INTO
    MLoutput
FROM
   MLStreamAnalytics
```

The first part of the code is for calling the function and getting the result from it. As you can see in Figure 13-23, the first part of the code is about creating a temporary table to call the MLStreamAnalytics(value). The next step is about getting the data from the Event Hub component (from Azure ML).

The second part of the code gets the data from a function in Azure Stream Analytics and passes the data to the Power BI component (MLoutput).

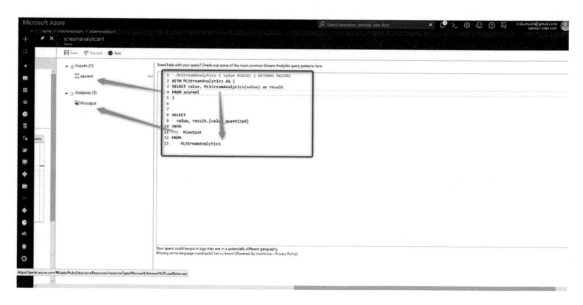

Figure 13-23. *Edit Query in Stream Analytics*

Live Analytics on Stream Data

The last step is to run the code. First, we must run the Stream Analytics job by clicking the Start key (Figure 13-24).

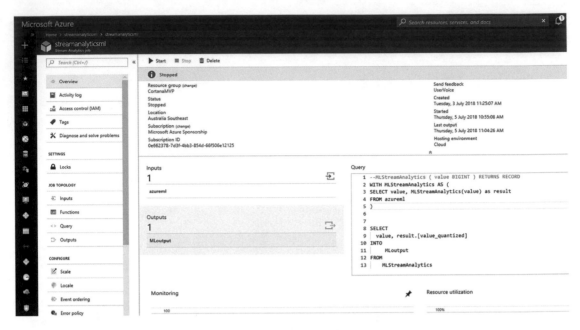

Figure 13-24. *Running the Stream Analytics job*

After running the Streaming Analytics job, open your Power BI service from powerbi.microsoft.com. As you can see in Figure 13-25, a streamed data set has been created in Power BI. To work with it, click the report icon and create an empty report.

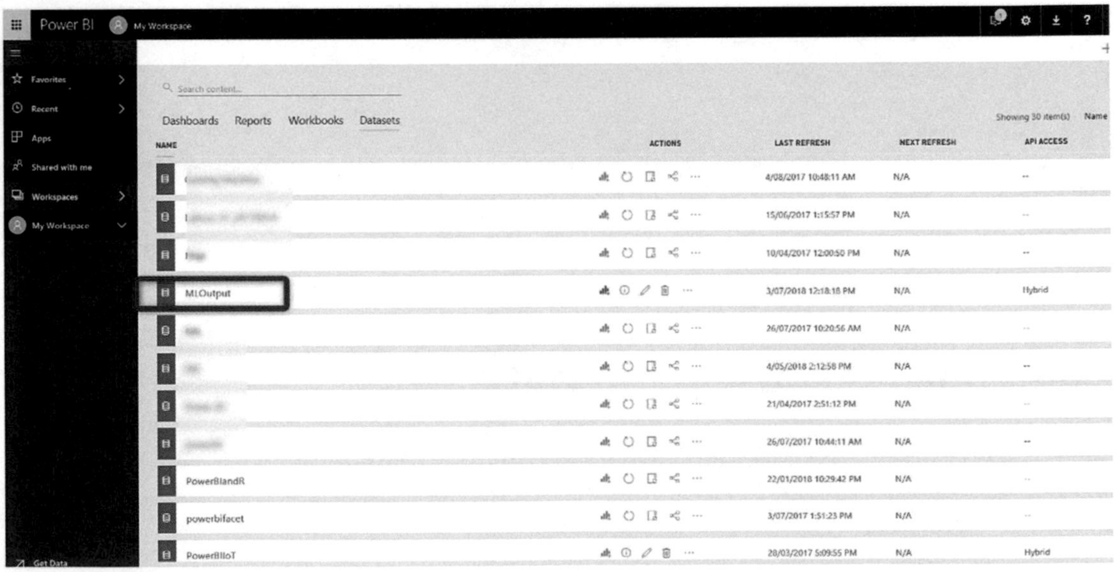

Figure 13-25. *Creating a streamed data set in Power BI*

On the report page, a new Power BI report is shown, with a data set that has two fields: Value and Value_quantized (Figure 13-26).

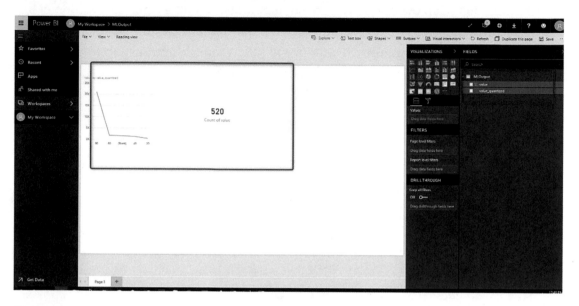

Figure 13-26. *Power BI report with Stream Analytics*

We must now run the code in the .NET application and add the report to the new workspace. After running the code and checking the workspace, you can see the live data coming from the application and the streamed data in Power BI, in addition to the group name and number that each value has been allocated using the Azure ML model (Figure 13-27).

Figure 13-27. *Streamed live data in Power BI*

Summary

This chapter offered an overview of Azure Stream Analytics and a brief explanation of its different components. A use case demonstrated how Stream Analytics can be leveraged for live analytics, using the Azure ML model and API. A sample application to generate a random number was created, then how to use Event Hub, Stream Analytics, Azure ML, and Power BI together to show a streamed live data analysis was reviewed.

References

[1]   Reza Rad, "Stream Analytics and Power BI Join Forces to Real-time Dashboard," RADACAD, `http://radacad.com/stream-analytics-and-power-bi-join-forces-to-real-time-dashboard`, September 12, 2016.

[2]   David Peter Hansen et al., "Install SQL Server 2016 R Services," Microsoft, SQL Docs, `https://docs.microsoft.com/en-us/sql/advanced-analytics/install/sql-r-services-windows-install`, September 30, 2018.

CHAPTER 14

Azure Machine Learning (ML) Workbench

Azure ML Workbench is another tool introduced by Microsoft in 2017. Azure Machine Learning services (preview) integrate end-to-end data science with advanced analytics tools. They help professional data scientists prepare data, develop experiments, and deploy models at cloud scale [1]. First in this chapter, a brief introduction into Azure ML Workbench is provided, then a comparison between Azure ML Studio and Azure ML Workbench is made. The process of installing Azure ML Workbench will be presented next. After, loading, preparing, and visualizing the data will be discussed.

Azure ML Workbench

Azure ML Workbench is an integrated, end-to-end data science and advanced analytics solution. It is a tool for preparing data, developing models and experiments, and, finally, deployment at the cloud scale. Azure ML Workbench is a new version of Azure ML that has some differences from Azure ML Studio. In Table 14-1, I have summarized the principal differences between Azure ML Workbench and Azure ML Studio

© Leila Etaati 2019
L. Etaati, *Machine Learning with Microsoft Technologies*, https://doi.org/10.1007/978-1-4842-3658-1_14

Table 14-1. *Azure ML Workbench vs Azure ML Studio*

	Azure ML Workbench	Azure ML Studio
Users perspective	It is suitable for professional data scientists.	It is a great tool for users who are not experts in machine learning.
Deployment	It is possible to deploy the model in cloud, manage the models, and track their deployment.	The deployment of models in Azure ML Studio is via API creation.
Development language	The only development language is Python.	Model can be developed using R or Python code, in addition to using some existing models and transformation components.
Accessibility	On-premises platform	Cloud-based platform

The five main components of Azure Machine Learning are

- Azure Machine Learning Workbench

- Azure Machine Learning Experimentation Service

- Azure Machine Learning Model Management Service

- Microsoft Machine Learning Libraries for Apache Spark (MMLSpark library)

- Visual Studio Code Tools for AI

Azure ML Workbench is a desktop application that is a command-line tool. It supports Windows and MacOS. With it, it is possible to manage machine learning solutions.

Azure ML Workbench Installation

The first step in installing Azure ML Workbench is to create service accounts for Azure Machine Learning services [2]. Log in to the Azure Portal (`portal.azure.com`) and select Machine Learning Experimentation (Figure 14-1).

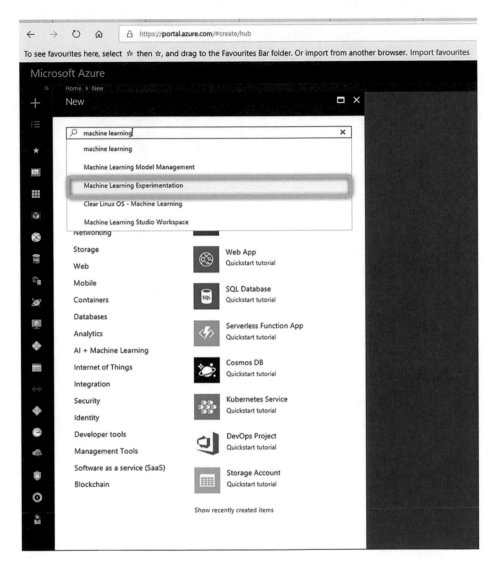

Figure 14-1. *Creating the Azure ML model experimentation*

Next, we must set up the parameters, as shown in Figure 14-2.

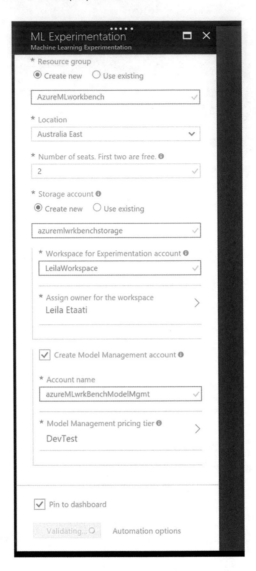

Figure 14-2. Setting up parameters for Azure ML model experimentation

It is possible to download Azure ML Workbench from the overview page. As shown in Figure 14-3, I created Machine Learning Model Management.

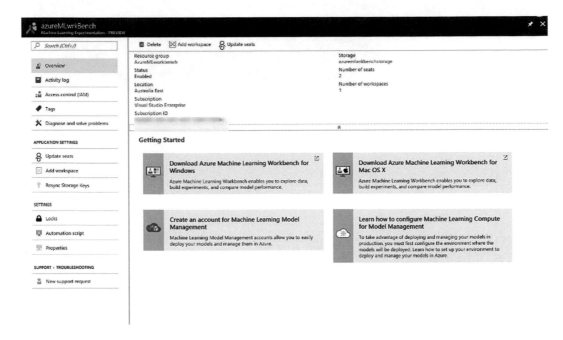

Figure 14-3. *Azure ML model and experiment management*

Download Azure ML Workbench from the Azure portal. The initial installation process may take a few minutes.

Azure ML Workbench Environment

After installing Azure ML Workbench, open it. As you can see in Figure 14-4, at the start, no projects are listed in Azure ML Workbench.

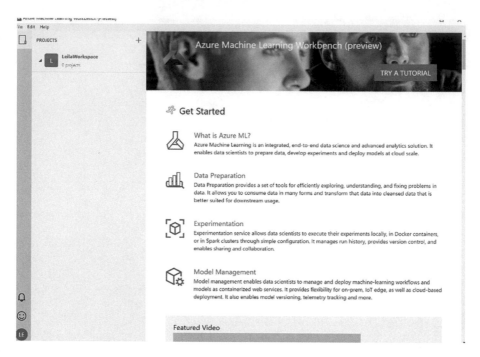

Figure 14-4. *Azure ML model main page*

To start to work with the Azure ML Workbench, there are some sample projects to help users learn more about it. To begin, you must create an empty workspace. To create a new workspace, click the plus sign (+), then click New Workspace (Figure 14-5).

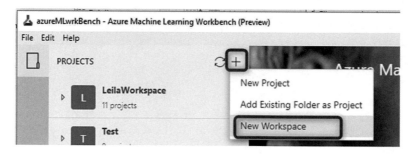

Figure 14-5. *Creating a new Azure workspace*

As you can see in Figure 14-6, to create a new workspace, we must provide some details about the workspace, such as a name and description.

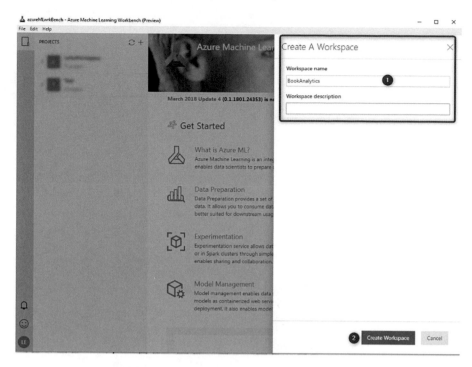

Figure 14-6. *Providing details about the new Azure workspace*

Create a new project under the new workspace. Under the last text box, Search Project Templates, search for Iris Classification (Figure 14-7).

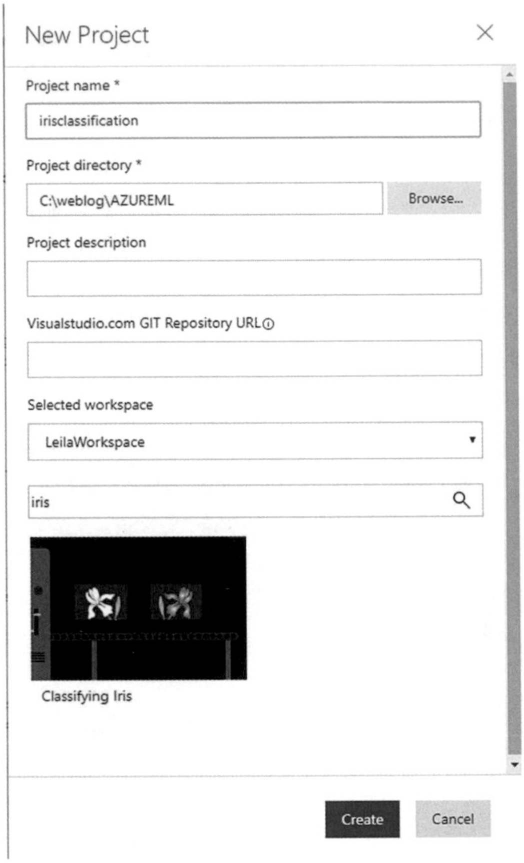

Figure 14-7. *Iris Classification project*

Create the iris classification project. After creating the project, the project environment will be shown. There are five main tabs (Figure 14-8). In the next section, each of these components will be explained.

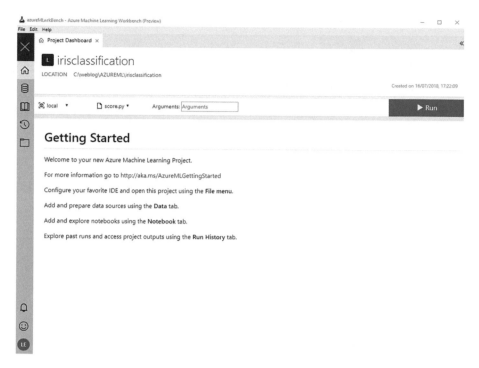

Figure 14-8. *Iris project in Azure ML Workbench*

Azure ML Workbench Import Data

The first step is to import the data into Azure ML Workbench. Click the Data option. There are two main sections there. Data Sources stores the original data source. The Data Preparations option stores the prepared and cleaned data. To import Data into Azure ML Studio, you must click the plus sign (+) at the top of the page (Figure 14-9).

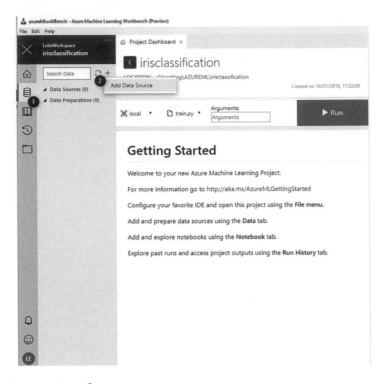

Figure 14-9. *Importing data*

Click Add Data Source, which has four main options to import the data (Figure 14-10):

- Text Files

- Parquet

- Excel Files

- Database

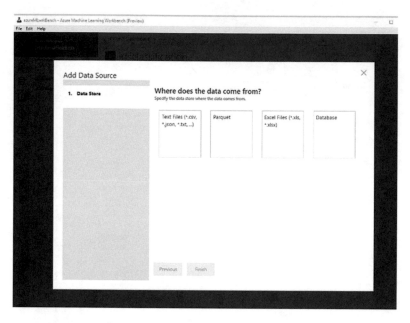

Figure 14-10. *Add Data Source option*

In this example, the iris data (text file) will be imported from the local PC into the Azure ML Workbench environment. Choose the Text file and import the data into Azure ML Workbench (you can download the iris data set file from www.kaggle.com/uciml/iris).

As you can see in Figure 14-11, the iris data set has been imported. The data set in Data Source section stores the raw data. It also shows how many rows have been missed, how many are valid, and so forth.

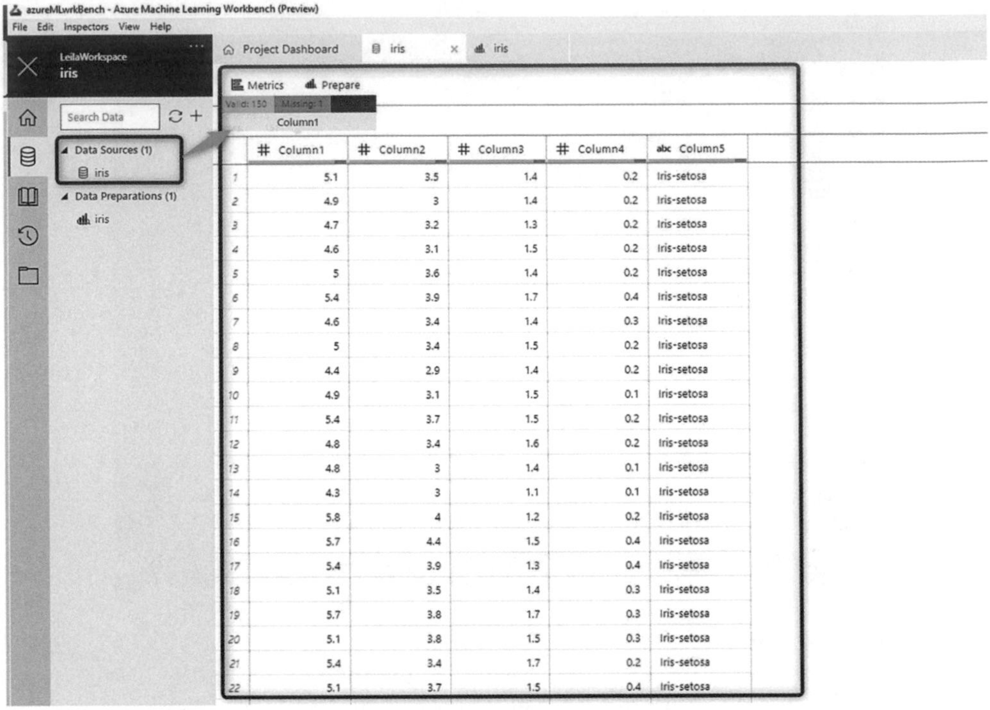

Figure 14-11. *Importing data into Azure ML Workbench*

To prepare the data, click the Prepare option at the top of the window and assign a proper name to the new data set. Then, in the Data Preparations section, a new data will be shown (Figure 14-12).

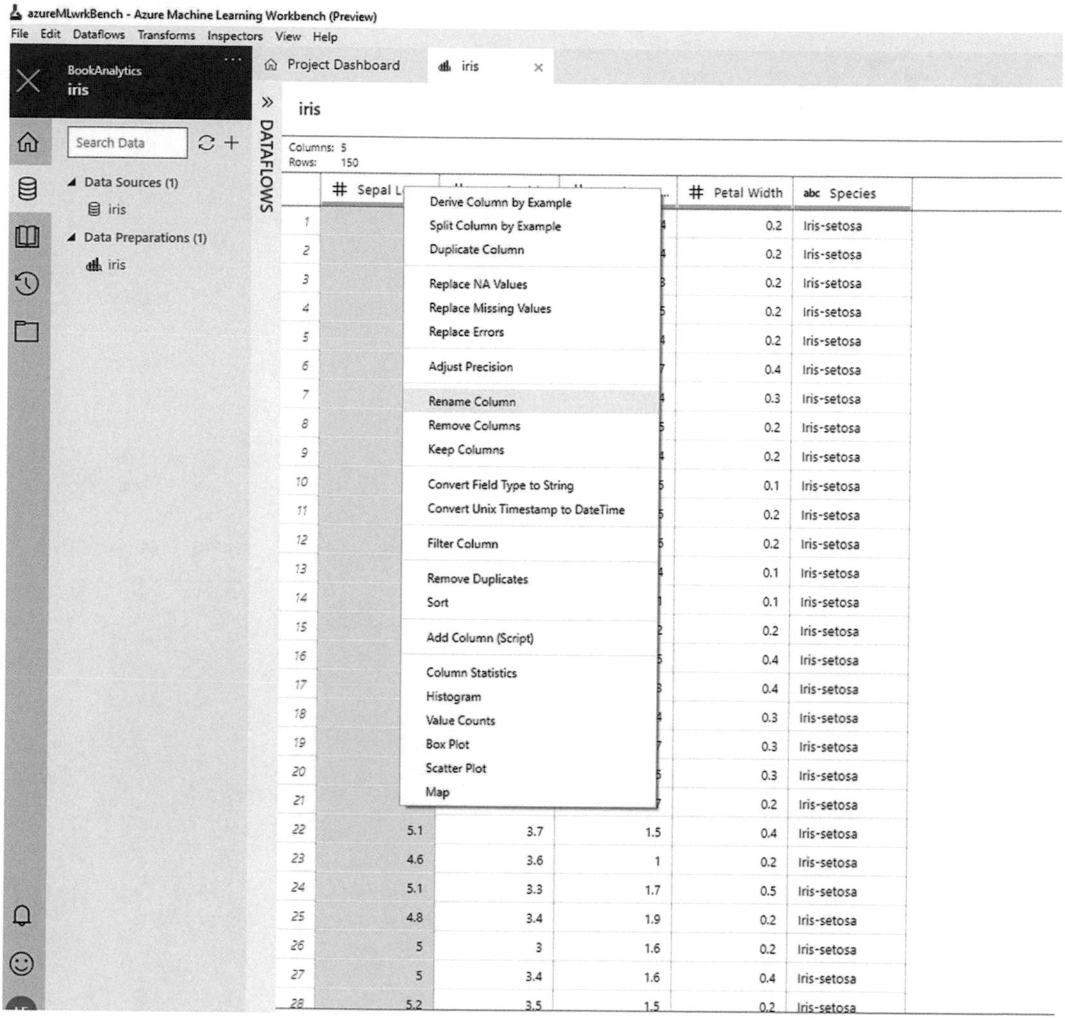

Figure 14-12. *Preparing the data*

Right-click the first column. There are some options for data cleaning, such as Replace NA Values, Replace Missing Values, and so forth. Rename the columns to Sepal Length, Sepal Width, Petal Length, and Petal Width. It is possible to create a chart, to get a better understanding of the data. As you can see in Figure 14-13, at the bottom of the right-click menu, there are some chart options, such as Column Statistics, Histogram, Value Counts, and so forth.

For our example, we can see the distribution of data by choosing a histogram chart.

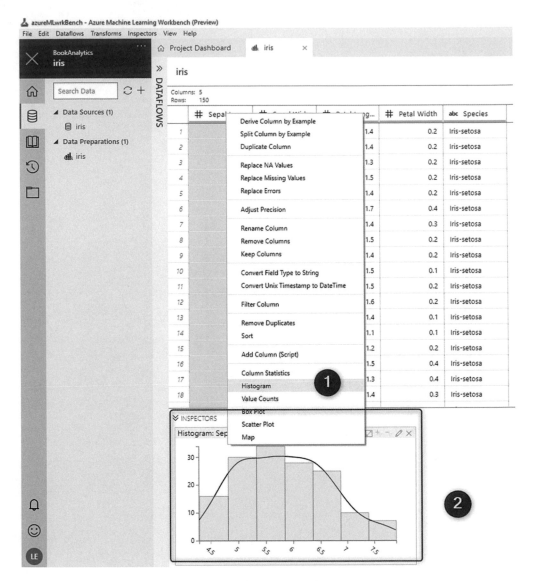

Figure 14-13.   *Histogram chart of iris sepal length*

This editor provides a means for data scientists to better analyze the data and gain a better understanding of the data specifications, such as distribution, outliers, and so forth. Azure Machine Learning Workbench supports interactive data science experimentation through its integration with Jupyter Notebook. After importing and cleaning the data, you must run and train the models. As you can see in Figure 14-14, there is a notebook editor for running the code and testing the models. Click the Notebook option at the left side of the window. A notebook will appear there. (In Chapter 19, a brief introduction to Jupyter Notebooks is presented.)

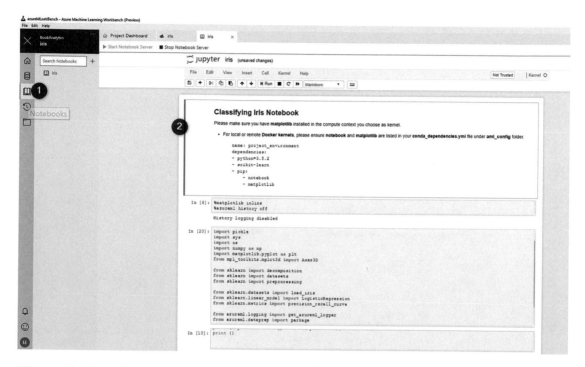

Figure 14-14. *Jupyter Notebook in Azure ML Workbench*

There is an option named Run at the left side of the window. It shows the history of the running model. At the start, there is no run history.

The related files for the iris project have been loaded in the last option on the left side of the window. As you can see in Figure 14-15, all the files related to Iris classification are located there.

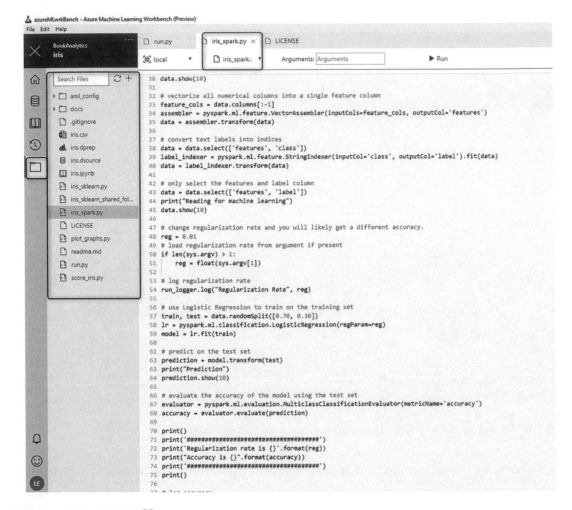

Figure 14-15. *Iris files*

As you can see in Figure 14-15, all files related to the iris project are listed. One of the files is `iris_sklearn.py`. This file contains models and data for Iris classification. It is possible to run the code locally on Docker (Figure 14-16).

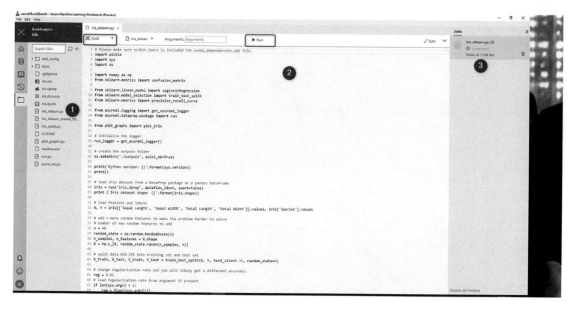

Figure 14-16. *Running the Python code*

Click the Run option and run the model. After running the model, click Run, at the right side of the window. You will be able to see details of the run, including status, run start time, duration, accuracy, and so forth (Figure 14-17).

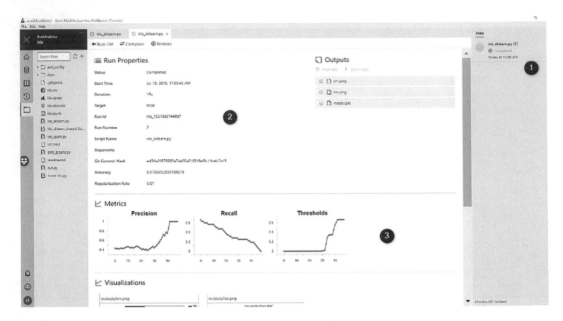

Figure 14-17. *Iris run details*

The details of running the Python code have been shown in Figure 14-16. The evaluation result for Iris classification is shown in Figure 14-18.

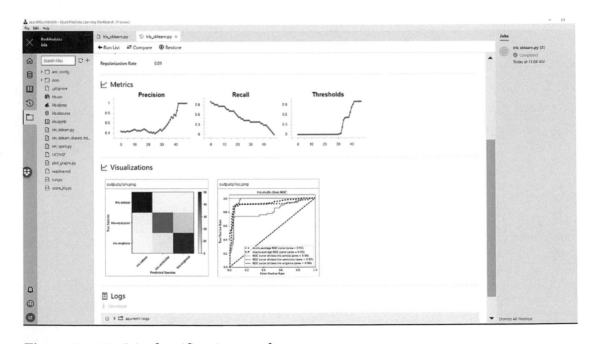

Figure 14-18. *Iris classification result*

Summary

This chapter presented a brief introduction to the Azure ML Workbench environment, including an explanation of how to install it and access the environment. In the next chapter, you will see how to import data from an SQL Server database and then load it to Azure ML Workbench and how to run it in Spark on Docker.

References

[1] Josée Martens et al., "What happened to Azure Machine Learning Workbench?" Microsoft Azure, `https://docs.microsoft.com/en-nz/azure/machine-learning/service/quickstart-installation`, January 8, 2019.

[2] Gary Ericson et al., "What is Azure Machine Learning service?" Microsoft Azure, `https://docs.microsoft.com/en-us/azure/machine-learning/service/overview-what-is-azure-ml`, December 3, 2018.

[3] UCI Machine Learning, "Iris Species," Kaggle, `www.kaggle.com/uciml/iris`, updated 2016.

CHAPTER 15

Machine Learning on HDInsight

In this chapter, an overview of how to use HDInsight for the purpose of machine learning will be presented. HDInsight is based on Apache Spark and used for in-memory cluster processing. Processing data in-memory is much faster than disk-based computing. Spark also supports the Scala language, which supports distributed data sets. Creating a cluster in Spark is very fast, and it is able to use Jupyter Notebook, which makes data processing and visualization easier. Spark clusters can also be integrated with Azure Event Hub and Kafka. Moreover, it is possible to set up Azure Machine Learning (ML) services to run distributed R computations. In the next section, the process of setting up Spark in HDInsight will be discussed.

HDInsight Overview

HDInsight is an open source analytics and cloud-based service. Integration with Azure HDInsight is easy, fast, and cost-effective for processing massive amounts of data. There are many different use-case scenarios for HDInsight, such as ETL (extract, transform, and load), data warehousing, machine learning, Internet of things (IoT), and so forth.

The main benefit of using HDInsight for machine learning is access to a memory-based processing framework. HDInsight helps developers to process and analyze big data and develop solutions, using some great and open source frameworks, such as Hadoop, Spark, Hive, LLAP, Kafka, Storm, and Microsoft Machine Learning Server [1].

© Leila Etaati 2019
L. Etaati, *Machine Learning with Microsoft Technologies*, https://doi.org/10.1007/978-1-4842-3658-1_15

Setting Up Clusters in HDInsight

The first step is to set up HDInsight in Azure. Log in to your Azure account and create an HDInsight component in Azure (Figure 15-1). As you can see in Figure 15-1, there are different modules for HDInsight, such as HDInsight Spark Monitoring and HDInsight InteractiveQuery Monitoring. Among those modules, select the HDInsight Analytics option.

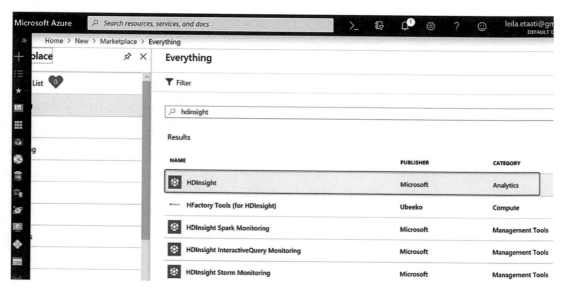

Figure 15-1. *Setting up HDInsight in Azure*

When you create HDInsight, you must follow some steps for setting up the cluster and identifying the size. The first step is to set a name for the cluster, set the subscription, and choose the cluster type (Figure 15-2). Different cluster types are available, including Spark, Hadoop, Kafka, ML Services, and more.

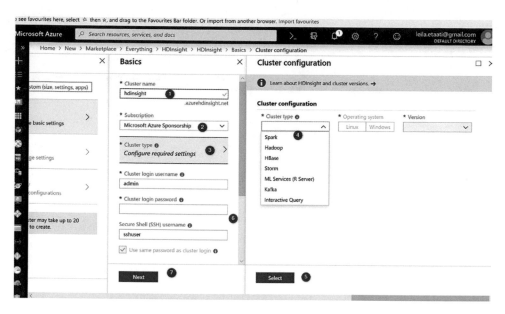

Figure 15-2. *Creating HDInsight in Azure*

The next step is to identify the size and check the summary (Figure 15-3) of the cluster.

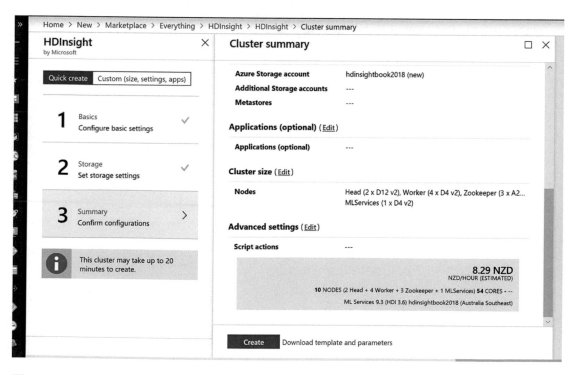

Figure 15-3. *Setting up HDInsight*

Creation of HDInsight may take some time. After creating an HDInsight component, on the main page, in the Overview section, select Cluster dashboards (Figure 15-4).

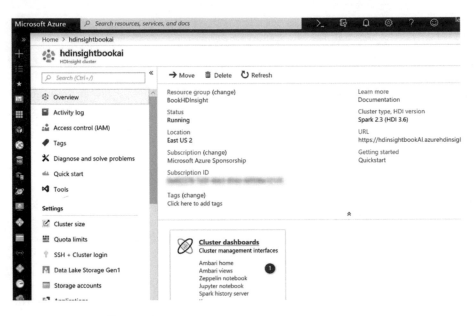

Figure 15-4. *HDInsight environment*

Next, select Jupyter Notebook. On the new page, choose the New option (Figure 15-5).

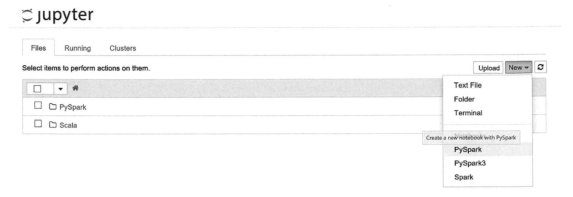

Figure 15-5. *Jupyter Notebook environment*

As you can see in Figure 15-5, there are environment options, such as PySpark, PySpark3, and Spark. You can write the Python code in all of them.

After creating the new page for Spark, you must log in with the username and password that you provided for creating the HDInsight component. The Jupyter environment is like a notebook and, so, like the Azure Databricks environment. As you can see in Figure 15-6, it is possible to write the code there and run the whole cell to see the result.

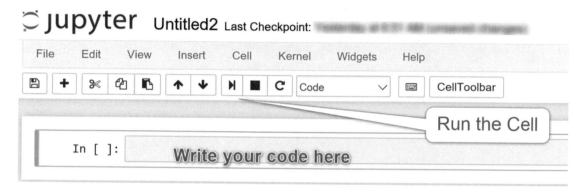

Figure 15-6. *Jupyter Notebook environment*

It is also possible to fetch the data from other Azure components, such as Azure Data Lake Store Gen1 (Figure 15-7). To do this, you must run the following code (in Databricks, you run the same code).

```
spark.conf.set("dfs.adls.oauth2.access.token.provider.type",
"ClientCredential")
spark.conf.set("dfs.adls.oauth2.client.id", "a1824181-e20c-4952-894f-
6f53670672dd")
spark.conf.set("dfs.adls.oauth2.credential", "iRzOkcyahiomc5AKobyVxFdDVF/
mEbS3mqN1moehGOw=")
spark.conf.set("dfs.adls.oauth2.refresh.url", "https://login.
microsoftonline.com/0b414bdb-2159-4b16-ad13-b2d54a1781da/oauth2/token")
val df=spark.read.option("header", "true").csv("adl://adlsbook.
azuredatalakestore.net/titanic.csv")
val specificColumnsDf = df.select("Survived", "Pclass", "Sex", "Age")
val renamedColumnsDF = specificColumnsDf.withColumnRenamed("Sex", "Gender")
renamedColumnsDF.createOrReplaceTempView("some_name")
renamedColumnsDF.show()
```

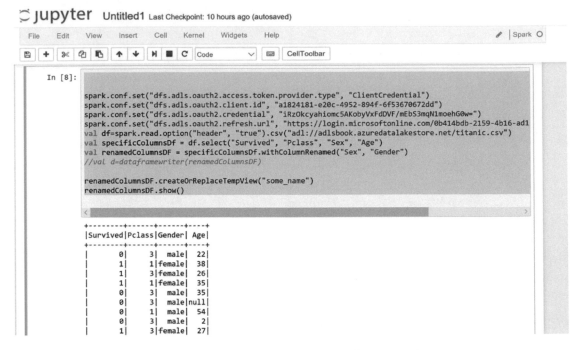

Figure 15-7.   Getting the data from Azure Data Lake Store Gen1

It is also possible to perform machine learning in Jupyter Notebook with Spark. For an example, follow the tutorial available at https://docs.microsoft.com/en-us/azure/hdinsight/spark/apache-spark-ipython-notebook-machine-learning.

Summary

This chapter presented an overview of HDInsight and how to set it up. How to use HDInsight for different purposes was explained briefly, as well as how to set up HDInsight inside the Azure environment and how to access Jupyter Notebook for the purpose of writing codes in a PySpark, Spark, or PySpark3 environment. An example of how to connect to Azure Data Lake Store Gen1 to fetch the data was shown.

Reference

[1]   Microsoft Azure, "Azure HDInsight Documentation," https://docs.microsoft.com/en-us/azure/hdinsight/, 2019.

CHAPTER 16

Data Science Virtual Machine and AI Frameworks

Data Science Virtual Machine (DSVM) is a virtual machine on the Azure cloud that is customized for doing data science. DSVM has some pre-configured and preinstallation tools that help users build artificial intelligence (AI) applications. DSVM assists data science teams to access a consistent setup. In this chapter, a brief introduction to DSVM and how to install it is provided, in addition to an overview of the tools installed.

Data Science Virtual Machine Overview

Data Science Virtual Machine is a preinstalled and pre-configured tool capable of promoting collaboration among data science teams. Installing a set of required tools in the cloud reduces the need for maintaining the software and the cost and time required.

DSVM can help trainers and educators to teach data science with a consistent setup. Having a pre-built setup environment is good for short-term training. DSVM can be useful for learning and comparing different machine learning tools, such as Microsoft ML Server, SQL Server, Visual Studio, Jupyter, deep learning tools, and so forth. DSVM has many different data science and deep learning tools, including the following:

- Microsoft R Open with popular packages preinstalled

- Microsoft ML Server (R, Python) Developer

- Microsoft Office Pro-Plus

© Leila Etaati 2019
L. Etaati, *Machine Learning with Microsoft Technologies*, https://doi.org/10.1007/978-1-4842-3658-1_16

- Anaconda Python 2.7, 3.5

- Relational Database

- Database Tools

- Jupyter Notebook Server with R, Python, Julia, PySpark, Sparkmagic, and SparkR

- Development tools, such as Visual Studio 2017, RStudio Desktop and Server, PyCharm Community, and so forth.

- Power BI Desktop

- Data Movement and Management tools, such as Azure Storage Explorer and Microsoft Data Management Gateway

- Machine Learning tools, such as Azure Machine Learning, Weka, Rattle, and H2O

- Deep learning tools, such as Microsoft Cognitive Toolkit, TensorFlow, and Keras

- Big data platforms, such as Spark and Hadoop [1]

Setting Up the Data Science Virtual Machine

To set up the DSVM, first you must log in to the Azure portal. Choose the AI—Machine Learning, then click Data Science Virtual Machine—Windows 2016 (Figure 16-1).

Figure 16-1. *Data Science Virtual Machine setup*

The next step is to set the size and choose the proper setup. For the purpose of data science, the virtual machine CPU should have more than four cores and 14GB or more of RAM [2] (Figure 16-2). There is a star beside the required service (as shown in Figure 16-2).

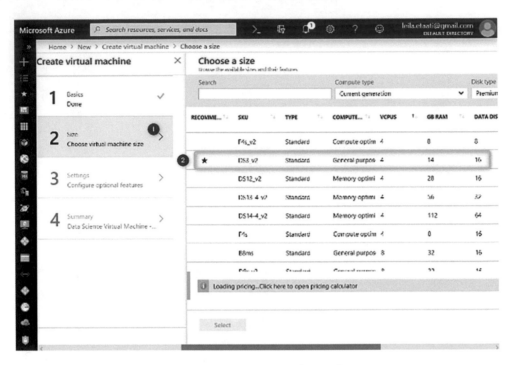

Figure 16-2. *Choosing the Data Science Virtual Machine size*

The next step is to configure the setting, to identify locations and names. Finally, in the last step, the summary of the DSVM will be shown. Deploying the DSVM will take about five minutes to create the service (Figure 16-3). After creating the resource, click Go to Resource.

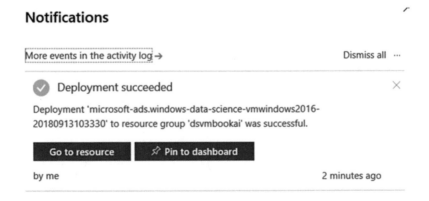

Figure 16-3. *DSVM creation*

An overview of the DSVM will be shown to the end user (Figure 16-4). As you can see in the figure, there is an overview of the location of the DSVM, the size of the virtual machine, and so forth.

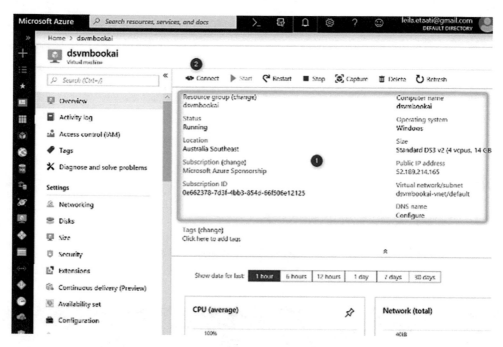

Figure 16-4. *DSVM overview*

To connect to the DSVM, click the Connect option at the top of the window. The related Remote Desktop Protocol (RDP) will be downloaded from Azure (Figure 16-5).

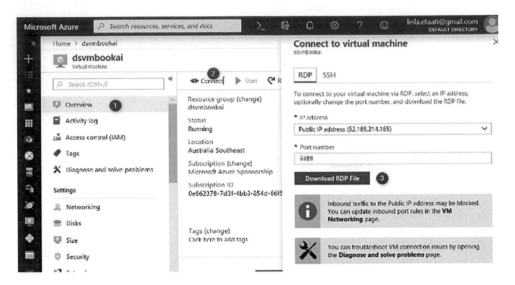

Figure 16-5. *Downloading the RDP*

After downloading the RDP file, open the virtual machine and check the environment (Figure 16-6).

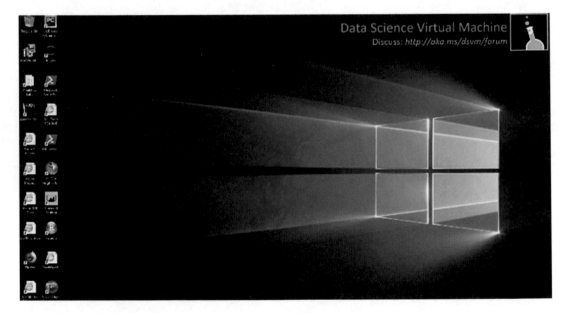

Figure 16-6. *DSVM environment*

In the DSVM, Visual Studio with R and Python tools has been preinstalled (RTVS and PTVS). As you can see in Figure 16-7, you can check for recent updates via Visual Studio [2].

Figure 16-7. *R and Python tools in Visual Studio 2017*

RStudio has been installed in DSVM. You must install all required packages in RStudio, and all users are able to access these packages (Figure 16-8).

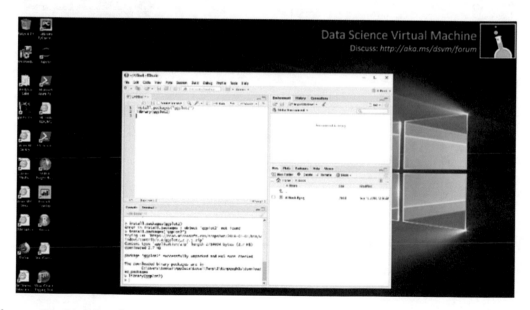

Figure 16-8. *RStudio in DSVM*

Case Study

You can run different machine learning scenarios. In this session, a machine learning scenario on Jupyter Notebook in DSVM will be explained. To access Jupyter Notebook, click the shortcut in the DSVM desktop. Then, in the Jupyter, write the code and run it (Figure 16-9). In the example, I've run the code as follows:

```
library(data.table)
ad <- fread("http://www-bcf.usc.edu/~gareth/ISL/Advertising.csv")
```

The data set is about the cost of advertising on television and radio and in newspapers and how much sales are generated.

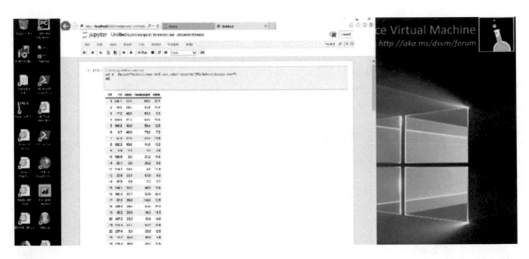

Figure 16-9. *Running R code in Jupyter Notebook*

In the next step, we are going to predict sales based on variables such as number of people impacted by television, radio, and newspapers. Create a model for predicting the number of sales based on the number of advertisements on television, radio, and in newspapers, using linear regression. Use the following code to create a model (Figure 16-10):

```
linearReg<-lm(sales~TV+radio+newspaper,data=ad)
linearReg
summary(linearReg)
```

Figure 16-10. *Creating a model in Jupyter Notebook*

Next, we must create a function that gets the new data from the user and applies the linear regression to it. First, we must create a function for that.

```
newdata<-adv[1:5,]
library(AzureML)
predictfunction <-function(newdata)
{predict(linearReg,newdata)} [2]
```

This function predicts the amount of sales, based on the amount of advertisements on television and radio and in newspapers. The preceding function predicts the new set of data, based on the created model in the preceding codes. Now, for the next step, we must get some identification from WorkSpace and AuthenticationID from the Azure ML Studio environment. To fetch the data, log in to Azure ML Studio, then click Setting, to get information, such as Workspace ID (Figure 16-11).

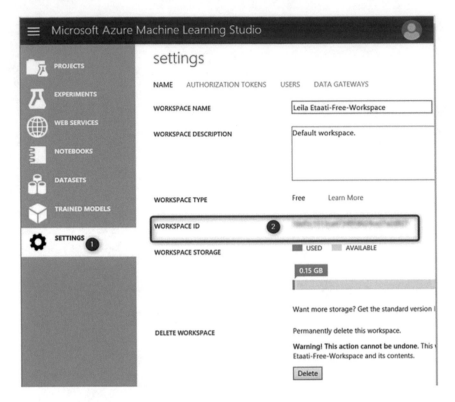

Figure 16-11. *Fetching Workspace ID from Azure ML Studio*

The other information that we need is the Authentication Token, from Primary Authorization Token (Figure 16-12).

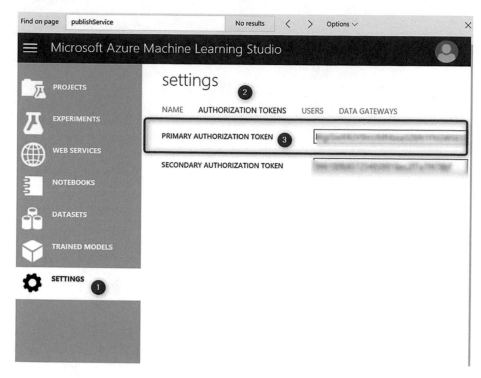

Figure 16-12. *Fetch Authentication Key from Azure ML Studio*

Copy these keys and put the identification in the following codes. The Workspace function is an Azure ML function that creates a connection between the R language and Azure ML Studio.

```
workspace_id<-"Workspace ID"
Authenticationid<-"Authentication Token"
ws<-workspace(workspace_id,Authenticationid)
newdata<-adv[2:5,]
```

The next step is to call another function, publishWebservice, to generate a web service in Azure ML from the created function.

```
data.frame(actual=newdata$sales,prediction=predictfunction(newdata))
ep<-publishWebService(ws=ws,fun=predictfunction,name="SalesPredictionAdvert
isement",inputSchema=newdata)
```

Run the whole code in the Jupyter environment (Figure 16-13).

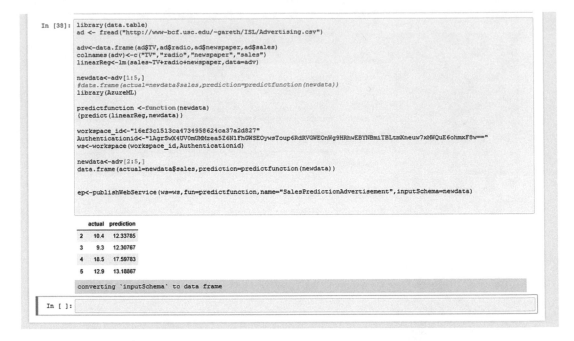

```
In [38]:  library(data.table)
          ad <- fread("http://www-bcf.usc.edu/~gareth/ISL/Advertising.csv")

          adv<-data.frame(ad$TV,ad$radio,ad$newspaper,ad$sales)
          colnames(adv)<-c("TV","radio","newspaper","sales")
          linearReg<-lm(sales~TV+radio+newspaper,data=adv)

          newdata<-adv[1:5,]
          #data.frame(actual=newdata$sales,prediction=predictfunction(newdata))
          library(AzureML)

          predictfunction <-function(newdata)
          {predict(linearReg,newdata)}

          workspace_id<-"16ef3c1513ca4734958624ca37a2d827"
          Authenticationid<-"1AgrSwX4UV0mUMMzea5Z6N1FhGWSEOywsToup6RdRVGWEOnWg9HRhwEBYNBmiTBLtmXneuw7xMWQuE6ohmxF8w=="
          ws<-workspace(workspace_id,Authenticationid)

          newdata<-adv[2:5,]
          data.frame(actual=newdata$sales,prediction=predictfunction(newdata))

          ep<-publishWebService(ws=ws,fun=predictfunction,name="SalesPredictionAdvertisement",inputSchema=newdata)
```

	actual	prediction
2	10.4	12.33785
3	9.3	12.30767
4	18.5	17.59783
5	12.9	13.18867

```
converting `inputSchema` to data frame
```

```
In [ ]:
```

Figure 16-13. *Publish the R ML Code into Azure ML Webservice*

After running the code, check the web service in Azure ML Studio, to see the API created in Azure ML Studio (Figure 16-14).

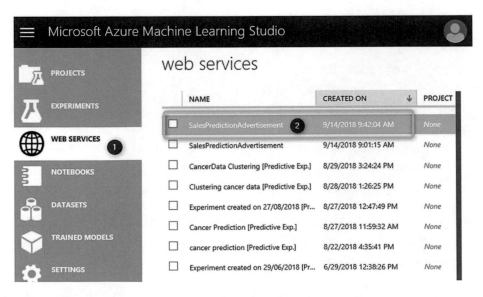

Figure 16-14. *Web service created in Azure ML*

Test the API by clicking the Test button (Figure 16-15).

Figure 16-15. *Testing the web service in Azure ML Studio*

Summary

In this chapter, a brief introduction to DSVM was presented. The process of how to set up DSVM and how to set the related parameters was explained. In addition, a brief introduction to what applications have been preinstalled was provided. Finally, a scenario for machine learning in Jupyter Notebook and then deployed to Azure ML Studio was presented.

References

[1] Gopi Kumar et al., "Introduction to Azure Data Science Virtual Machine for Linux and Windows," Microsoft Azure, `https://docs.microsoft.com/en-us/azure/machine-learning/data-science-virtual-machine/overview`, October 26, 2017.

[2] Gopi Kumar et al., "Samples on Data Science Virtual Machines," Microsoft Azure, `https://docs.microsoft.com/en-us/azure/machine-learning/data-science-virtual-machine/dsvm-samples-and-walkthroughs`, September 23, 2018.

CHAPTER 17

Deep Learning Tools with Cognitive Toolkit (CNTK)

Microsoft Cognitive Toolkit (CNTK) is an open source deep learning tool [1]. In this chapter, an introduction to neural network and deep learning will be provided first. Next, an introduction to what CNTK is and how it is accessed and installed will be provided. Finally, a basic case study using CNTK to solve a simple problem will be elaborated.

Neural Network Concepts

What we expect from a computer is to receive outputs that match our needs, based on our inputs. Scientists attempt to mimic the human brain through intelligent machines. A machine, of course, does reason the same as a human. The principal element of the human brain is neurons. Human brains consist of 75 million neurons. Each neuron is connected to others via a synapse (Figure 17-1). The neural network consists of nodes that are connected to one another. In the human body, if a neuron is triggered by some external trigger, such as high temperature, it will pass the message from the receiver node to other nodes, via synapsis [2].

© Leila Etaati 2019
L. Etaati, *Machine Learning with Microsoft Technologies*, https://doi.org/10.1007/978-1-4842-3658-1_17

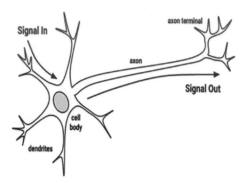

Figure 17-1. *Neural network synapsis[2]*

Neural networks mimic the same concepts as those in the human brain. One node receives input from the user, then the neural network model creates output that produces a result similar to that of a computer system. A neural network has

- A set of input nodes

- A set of output nodes

- Some processing between, to achieve a good result

- A flow of information

- A connection between nodes

To better understand the process, imagine that we are at the summit of a mountain and want to descend from it. The weather is foggy. Under this condition, we able to see only one meter ahead. As a result, we decide to descend only the one meter that is visible. We take a first step based on our current location, then we decide which direction to pursue. We repeat the process until we reach the point where we cannot go on. If that point is the destination, the process is complete, if not, we must go back and try other directions. As a result, for each step, we evaluate the way and choose the best course, until we have descended the mountain.

In a neural network, we undergo the same process. We have input nodes, some hidden nodes (the means to reach the output), and output nodes. Each hidden node has an activation function that processes the input or the resulting output from other hidden nodes (Figure 17-2).

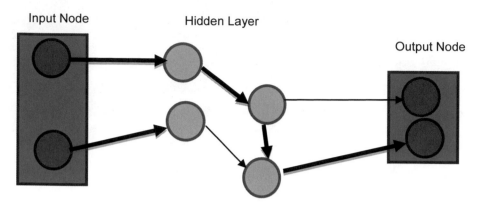

Figure 17-2. *A simple neural network*

To better understand the concept and how it works, let's imagine we want to classify a customer based on whether he or she will shift his or her support to another company. The problem is illustrated in Figure 17-3. As you can see in the figure, there are two groups of people (customers). One is represented by blue dots and the other by green ones. The principal aim is to group people based on one of the colors.

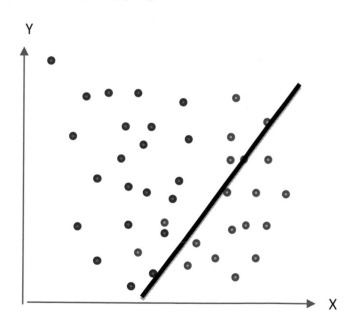

Figure 17-3. *Classification using 2x + y = 2*

As you can see in the figure, we can partially isolate (classify) blue and green dots with a line.

The relevant equation that has been used is $\frac{1}{3}x + y = 2$. This equation is not able to classify the dots completely, so we must try another. The following equation is $x = 4$. As you can see in Figure 17-4, the new equation still does not result in a complete or accurate classification.

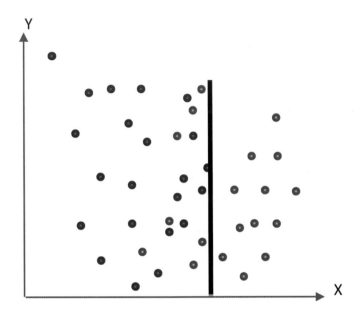

Figure 17-4. *Classification attempted with x = 4*

Both formulae are not good at classifying the data. However, if we apply the first function, then the second, we can classify the dots relatively well.

As you can see in Figure 17-5, we achieved a better result than before.

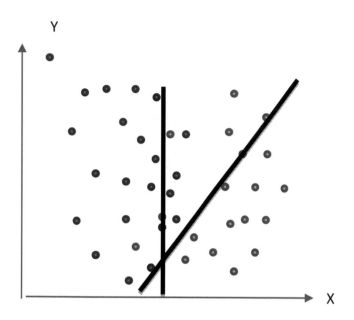

Figure 17-5. *Classifying the data*

So, if we want to illustrate this process as a neural network structure, we will have something similar to what is shown in Figure 17-6.

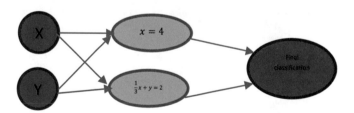

Figure 17-6. *Data Science Virtual Machine (DSVM) environment*

The hidden layer (green nodes) can have different functions that help to classify the data (Figure 17-7). These are called activation functions.

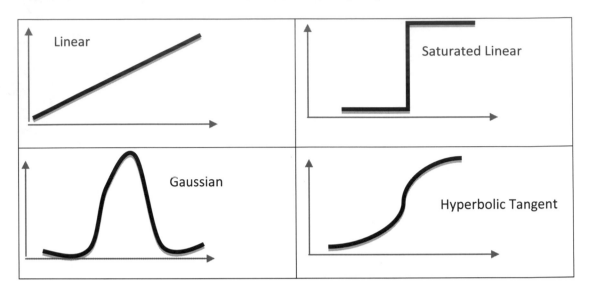

Figure 17-7. *Activation functions*

There are different topologies for neural networks, such as one output (Figure 17-8) or many outputs.

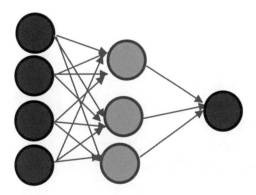

Figure 17-8. *Neural network with one output*

A neural network can also have multiple layers and multiple outputs (Figure 17-9). A neural network with multiple layers reflects what is known as *deep learning* [2].

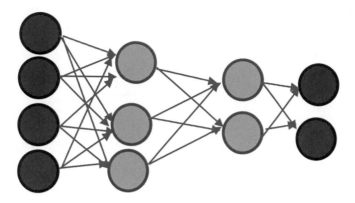

Figure 17-9. *Neural network with multiple outputs and multiple hidden layers*

There are different types of neural networks, such as feed forward deep neural networks (DNN) and convolutional neural networks (CNN), among others.

Microsoft Cognitive Service Toolkit

CNTK is an easy-to-use toolkit to solve problems without much anxiety. This toolkit can handle a large amount of data and is easily extensible. CNTK is a fully open source product. It allows processing over multiple GPUs (graphics processing units). This toolkit has been used in many Microsoft products, such as Cognitive Service, Cortana, Bing search, Skype, Skype Translator, and others. According to many users' experiences, CTNK is fast, and using associated Python language APIs is very intuitive.

CNTK Setup

There are different ways to install CNTK [3]. CNTK supports 64-bit Windows and Linux operating systems. To install CNTK for Python on Windows, you first must open the command prompt and run as an administrator. In the command prompt, insert the following code:

```
pip install cntk
```

After installing the CNTK, the required packages will be installed, and the CNTK version will be appear (Figure 17-10).

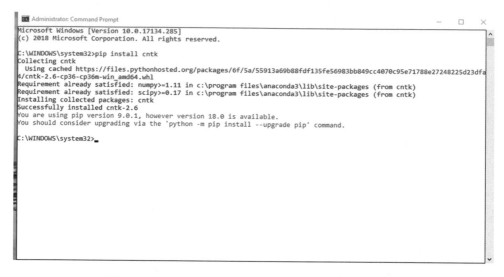

Figure 17-10. *Installing the CNTK*

After installation, you can check the CNTK version via the following code:

```
python -c "import cntk; print(cntk.__version__)"
```

You can access a few examples and tutorials by installing some samples. First, you must go to the C folder and run the following code:

```
python -m cntk.sample_installer
```

Then check the following folder for some samples and tutorials (Figure 17-11):

```
C:\Windows\System32\CNTK-Samples-2-6
```

	Name	Date modified	Type	Size
	Examples	25/09/2018 11:46	File folder	
	Manual	25/09/2018 11:46	File folder	
	PretrainedModels	25/09/2018 11:46	File folder	
	Tutorials	25/09/2018 11:46	File folder	
	LICENSE.md	25/09/2018 11:46	MD File	
	requirements.txt	25/09/2018 11:46	Text Document	

Figure 17-11. *CNTK samples*

Under the Sample folder, you will find Examples, Manual, and so forth.

After installing the CNTK, in the Python environment, you will be able to access the CNTK library, by using the following code in the Python environment:

```
import cntk
```

Another way of using CNTK is through the Azure environment. Likewise, CNTK is preinstalled in DSVM, so you can use it directly. In the next section, I will provide an example from `www.cntk.ai/pythondocs/CNTK_101_LogisticRegression.html` [4] on how to work with CNTK for classification.

Case Study

To proceed with our case study, first you must set up the DSVM, as explained in Chapter 16, then start the virtual machine (Figure 17-12).

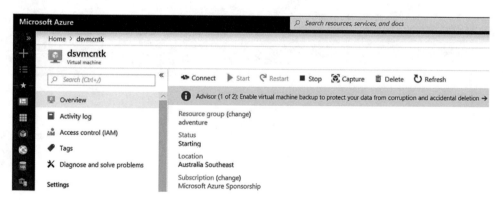

Figure 17-12. *Starting the DSVM*

Next, open the DSVM, by downloading the RDF file (Figure 17-13), and open the virtual machine.

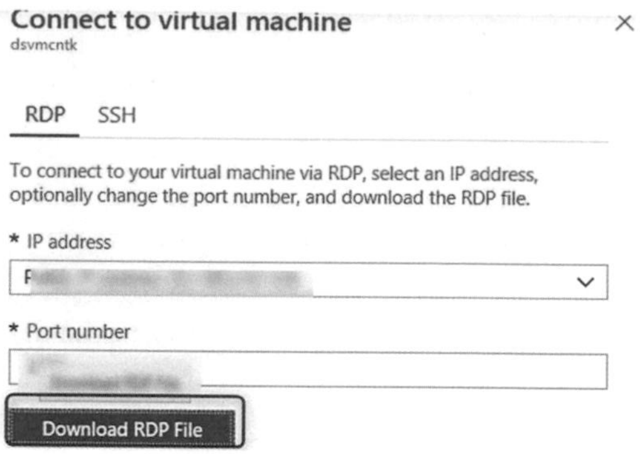

Figure 17-13. *DSVM file and activation*

After opening the DSVM, open Jupyter Notebook in the taskbar, which will navigate to a web-based Jupyter Notebook web site (Figure 17-14).

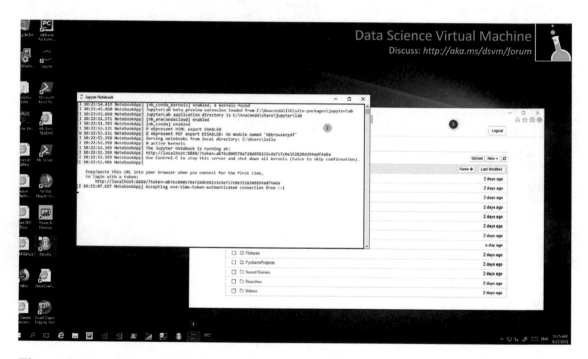

Figure 17-14. *Jupyter Notebook in DSVM*

In the Jupyter Notebook environment, choose Python [conda env:Anaconda] (Figure 17-15).

Figure 17-15. *Jupyter Notebook*

In the next step, we are going to run an example from www.cntk.ai/pythondocs/
CNTK_101_LogisticRegression.html [4]. In this example, the aim is to predict whether
a cancer patient is likely to have a benign (blue) or malignant (red) tumor, based on
the age of the patient and the cancer cell size. As a result, we have two inputs and two
outputs for our neural network (Figure 17-16).

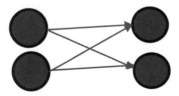

Figure 17-16. *Neural Network Structure*

The first step is to import an appropriate library for showing the result (print_
function), array computation (numpy), and CNTK (cntk), and for the file name and file
paths and directories (sys and os).

```
from __future__ import print_function
import numpy as np
import sys
import os
```

```
import cntk as C
import cntk.tests.test_utils
cntk.tests.test_utils.set_device_from_pytest_env() # (only needed for our
build system)
C.cntk_py.set_fixed_random_seed(1) # fix the random seed so that LR
examples are repeatable [4]
```

Now we must get the data. First, we have to identify the number of inputs and outputs, using the following code:

```
input_dim = 2
num_output_classes = 2
```

Then we create a function to generate some random data. The function gets the sample size and the number of inputs and outputs (see the following codes related to www.cntk.ai/pythondocs/CNTK_101_LogisticRegression.html [4]).

```
np.random.seed(0)

# Helper function to generate a random data sample
def generate_random_data_sample(sample_size, feature_dim, num_classes):
    # Create synthetic data using NumPy.
    Y = np.random.randint(size=(sample_size, 1), low=0, high=num_classes)

    # Make sure that the data is separable
    X = (np.random.randn(sample_size, feature_dim)+3) * (Y+1)

    # Specify the data type to match the input variable used later in the
    tutorial
    # (default type is double)
    X = X.astype(np.float32)

    # convert class 0 into the vector "1 0 0",
    # class 1 into the vector "0 1 0", ...
    class_ind = [Y==class_number for class_number in range(num_classes)]
    Y = np.asarray(np.hstack(class_ind), dtype=np.float32)
    return X, Y
```

Then we call the function, using the following code:

```
mysamplesize = 32
features, labels = generate_random_data_sample(mysamplesize, input_dim,
num_output_classes)
```

You can plot the input data, using the `matplotlib` library in Python.

```
import matplotlib.pyplot as plt
%matplotlib inline
```

```
# let 0 represent malignant/red and 1 represent benign/blue
colors = ['r' if label == 0 else 'b' for label in labels[:,0]]
```

```
plt.scatter(features[:,0], features[:,1], c=colors)
plt.xlabel("Age (scaled)")
plt.ylabel("Tumor size (in cm)")
plt.show()
```

After running the code, you will get a two-dimensional representation of the data (Figure 17-17).

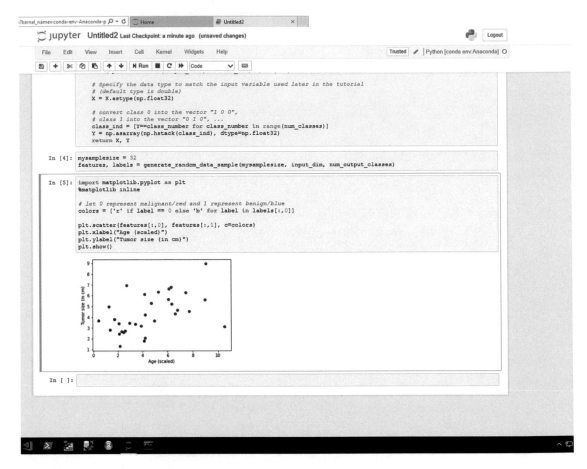

Figure 17-17. *The actual data represented*

The next step is to create a neural network model. To create the model, first we must identify the input variable and assign it to the feature variable, specifying the data type.

```
feature = C.input_variable(input_dim, np.float32)
```

The next step is to set up the network. We are going to use logistic regression as an activation (formula) to classify the data (Figures 17-5 and 17-4). To do that, we must define a function that identifies the layers of the neural network structure. As was shown in Figure 17-4 and the discussion related to it, we require an equation for classifying the data.

The formal parameters can be as follows:

$$z = \sum_{i=1}^{n} w\mathrm{i} * \mathrm{Xi} + \mathrm{b} = \mathrm{w.x} + \mathrm{b}$$

or

Z=W∗X+b

The equation used is the same as was illustrated in Figure 17-3: 2x+y=2.

```
mydict = {}
def linear_layer(input_var, output_dim):
    input_dim = input_var.shape[0]
    weight_param = C.parameter(shape=(input_dim, output_dim))
    bias_param = C.parameter(shape=(output_dim))
    mydict['w'], mydict['b'] = weight_param, bias_param
    return C.times(input_var, weight_param) + bias_param
```

So, the output would be as follows:

```
output_dim = num_output_classes
z = linear_layer(feature, output_dim)
```

The next step after creating the network structure is to train the data, based on the data behavior and the probabilities, so as to be as close as possible to the observed data. There is a concept named *Entropy* [5] to train the data, an example of which follows:

```
label = C.input_variable(num_output_classes, np.float32)
loss = C.cross_entropy_with_softmax(z, label)
```

After creating the model, we must evaluate it via the following code:

```
eval_error = C.classification_error(z, label)
```

For additional examples, check the relevant samples and resources from the Microsoft web site.

Summary

The aim of this chapter was to introduce neural networks and associated deep learning concepts. How to set up CNTK and how to run it in a DSVM was then discussed. Some elaboration of concepts related to neural networks, their structure, and so forth, was provided. Next, how to set up CNTK in Windows for the Python language was covered. Finally, a very brief explanation on how to use the CNTK library for prediction was given.

References

[1]   Microsoft Teams, "The Microsoft Cognitive Toolkit",
      https://docs.microsoft.com/en-us/cognitive-toolkit/

[2]   https://www.amazon.com/Machine-Learning-R-Brett-Lantz/
      dp/1782162143

[3]   Chris Basoglu et al., "Setup [sic] CNTK on your machine,"
      https://docs.microsoft.com/en-us/cognitive-toolkit/
      setup-cntk-on-your-machine, March 6, 2018.

[4]   Python API for CNTK, "CNTK 101: Logistic Regression
      and ML Primer," www.cntk.ai/pythondocs/CNTK_101_
      LogisticRegression.html, 2017.

[5]   Python API for CNTK, "cntk.ops package," https://cntk.ai/
      pythondocs/cntk.ops.html#cntk.ops.cross_entropy_with_
      softmax, 2017.

PART V

Data Science Virtual Machine

CHAPTER 18

Cognitive Services Toolkit

Microsoft Cognitive Services are collections of APIs and services that help developers create smarter applications and reports. By using Cognitive Services, developers can add such intelligent features as face recognition, emotion recognition, text analytics, and so forth, to their applications. This chapter first presents an overview of Cognitive Services and then explains how to use them for text analytics in Power BI Report. Finally, how to use Cognitive Services in a Windows application is explored briefly.

Overview of Cognitive Services

There are different Cognitive Services that you can use by receiving a web service URL and a key. To check out the available services, you must navigate to the Cognitive Services web site [1]. As you can see in Figure 18-1, there are five main categories for solving business problems: Vision, Knowledge, Language, Speech, and Search.

© Leila Etaati 2019
L. Etaati, *Machine Learning with Microsoft Technologies*, https://doi.org/10.1007/978-1-4842-3658-1_18

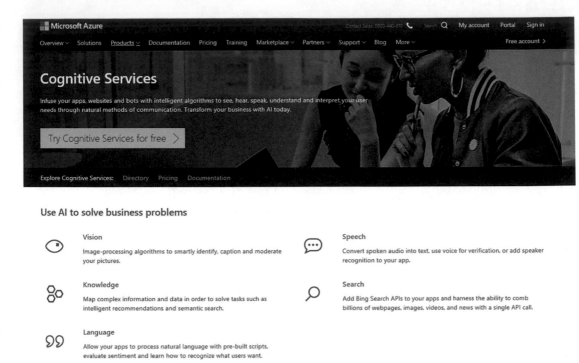

Figure 18-1. *Main Cognitive Services categories*

As you can see in Figure 18-2, there are five different APIs for business language problems. Text Analytics is one of the most popular features for language detection, identifying main keywords in text, topic extraction, and checking how much text is positive or negative in context (sentiment analysis).

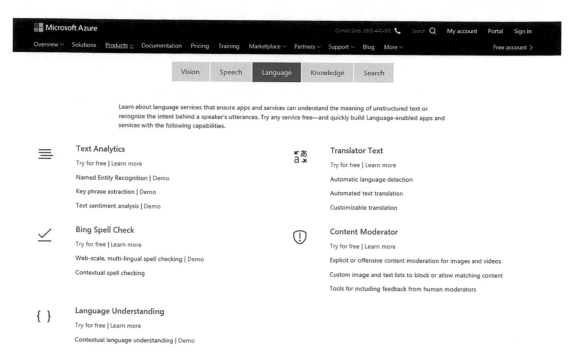

Figure 18-2. *Language category in Cognitive Services*

The other services in the Language category are about translating a text, identifying the primary intent, and objectives in conversations and texts.

These features can be combined. For example, it is possible to integrate the Language Understanding service with the Speech service, for instant speech-to-intent processing, and, with a Bot application (Chapter 19), to develop a more sophisticated application.

In this chapter, you will see how you can perform text analytics for the purpose of detecting main keywords in customer feedback, how much of the feedback is positive, detecting the language in Power BI, by using Text Analytics services.

First, we must set up the environment in which to use Cognitive Services. To use Cognitive Services, you can sign up for a free trial. The trial services are free for seven days and do not require a credit card. The other way to access Cognitive Services is to use a free Azure account for a month, which provides a $280 credit on Azure, and all data and customization will be saved. The final approach is to use an existing Azure account (Figure 18-3).

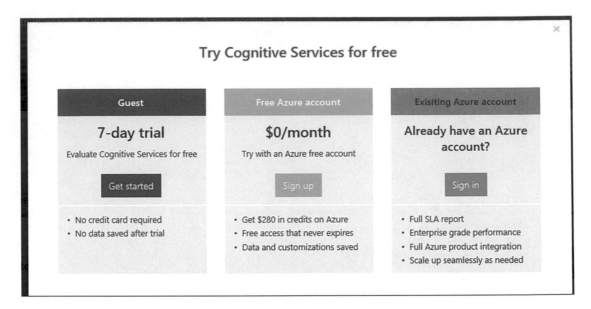

Figure 18-3. *Different Cognitive Services accounts*

To set up Cognitive Services in Azure, you must log in to your Azure account and search for the services you want. After logging in to the Azure portal, you must create a Text Analytics service. To create a Text Analytics service, you must create a new service in Azure, by clicking the top left of the page. In the New page, the main service categories will be shown (Figure 18-4). AI + Machine Learning is one of the main services in Azure. Click it to see the available options. As you can see in Figure 18-4, Computer Vision, Face (recognition), Text Analytics, Language Understanding, Translator Speech, Bing Search, and Azure Search are among the main topics under AI + Machine Learning.

Figure 18-4. Different Cognitive Services features

Text Analytics Services

Not all collected data is about numbers and structured data. To gain a more holistic perspective about a customer, products, and so forth, collecting and analyzing the text can be used, to enhance company performance. Text Analytics is the process of converting unstructured text data into meaningful data, to understand customer needs and feedback [2].

In this section, a case study will be presented that explains the process of using the Text Analytics API in Power BI and is applied to customer feedback.

The first step is to set up a Text Analytics service in the Azure portal (Figure 18-5).

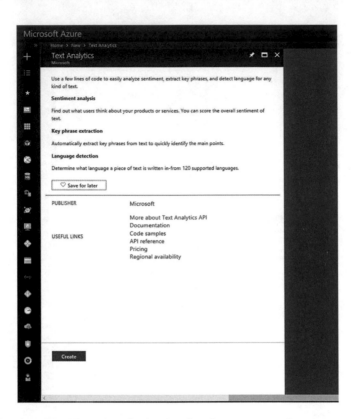

Figure 18-5. *Setting Up Text Analytics in the Azure portal*

There are different pricing tiers for this service. The first is a free tier that allows users to apply the Text Analytics service on 5K rows of data a month (Figure 18-6).

Figure 18-6. *Pricing tiers for Text Analytics*

After creating the Text Analytics service, we get the API URL and key access from the created service. Figure 18-7 shows how to access the URL and the access key in the Text Analytics service.

Figure 18-7. *Accessing the URL and key*

After creating the service from the Azure portal, we must call it inside the Power BI Desktop and apply it on the available data there.

Data Set

Fabrikam is a mock production company. It has received e-mails from customers regarding shipping, tech support, and other concerns. The business intelligence (BI) manager wants to perform some analytics on the e-mail the company is receiving from customers, to better understand the main points of customers' e-mails and to determine whether they are satisfied with the company's services. You can download the data set from `https://github.com/Kaiqb/KaiqbRepo0731190208/blob/master/CognitiveServices/TextAnalytics/FabrikamComments.csv` [3].

The first step is to open Power BI Desktop and load the data set, as a Text/CSV file, into Power BI (Figure 18-8).

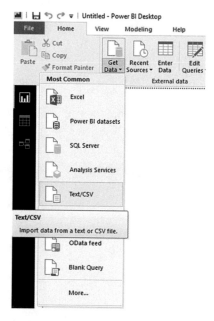

Figure 18-8. *Getting a CSV file from Power BI*

Then, instead of loading the data, click the Edit option to navigate to the Power Query environment for data transformation (Figure 18-9). As you can see in Figure 18-9, an overview of the data set is shown. There are about 20 rows of data about customer e-mails, names and IDs, e-mail subjects, and comments.

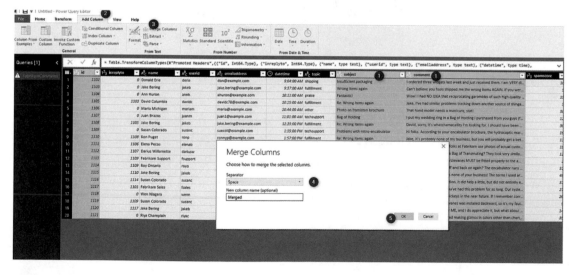

Figure 18-9. *Editing data in Power Query*

First, we are going to combine the Subject and Comment columns in Power Query, using Merge Columns under the Add Column tab. The general procedure is shown in Figure 18-10.

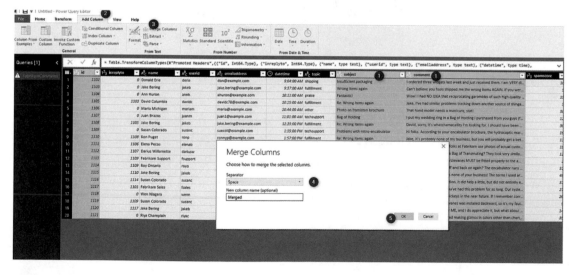

Figure 18-10. *Merging Subject and Comment columns*

After creating a new column, we must rename it to Customer Feedback.

Create a Text Analytics Function

It is possible to create a function in Power Query that applies Text Analytics to a specific column in Power Query. To create a function, we must click the whitespace in a query, at the left side of the main page, and choose the Blank Query option (Figure 18-11).

Figure 18-11. *Creating a blank query*

Rename the created query Sentiment Analytics. The next step is to convert the blank query to a function. To do that, we must access the M Query behind the created query, by clicking on the Home tab, then Advanced Editor (Figure 18-12). Here there is an editor that we are going to use to write some M scripts and change the query to a function.

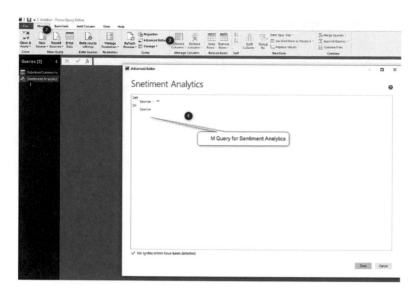

Figure 18-12. Power BI Query Editor

The next step is to add the following code:

```
(text) => let
    apikey      = "<API Key>",
    endpoint    = "https://<Location of Your Azure>.api.cognitive.
                   microsoft.com/text/analytics/v2.0/sentiment",
    jsontext    = Text.FromBinary(Json.FromValue(Text.Start(Text.
                   Trim(text), 5000))),
    jsonbody    = "{ documents: [ { language: ""en"", id: ""0"", text: " &
                   jsontext & " } ] }",
    bytesbody   = Text.ToBinary(jsonbody),
    headers     = [#"Ocp-Apim-Subscription-Key" = apikey],
    bytesresp   = Web.Contents(endpoint, [Headers=headers, Content=bytesbody]),
    jsonresp    = Json.Document(bytesresp),
    sentiment   = jsonresp[documents]{0}[score]
in  sentiment
```

As you can see in the preceding code, the first line is about the function input which is text. In line 2, the API key collected from Azure Service must be pasted here. In line 3, the required URL for connecting to the API must be provided. As you can see at the end of the URL, the service that we are going to use from Cognitive Services is shown. In this example, we are using sentiment analysis. Lines 4 to 11 indicate the required code for connecting to Cognitive Services and getting the result in JSON format. The last line is the result column that shows the sentiment score for each comment.

Now, replace the preceding code with the previous one and click OK. The blank query will change to a function type, and a page with a text box will appear. You can test it by writing a sentence, such as "the weather is so nice today," and click the Invoke button, to see the result.

As you can see in Figure 18-13, the result of sentiment analysis is 0.92.

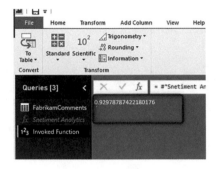

Figure 18-13. *Text Analytics function test in Power Query*

The output of the sentiment analysis is a number from 0 to 1. A number closer to 1 means that the comment is positive, one closer to 0 means the feedback is negative.

For a final step, we can apply the function to the customer feedback (Comments) column. Click the Fabrikam data set, the Add Column tab, and then Invoke Custom Function. On a new page, choose an appropriate name for the new column, then choose the function in the drop-down. From the last drop-down item, choose the column you want to apply the function to (Figure 18-14).

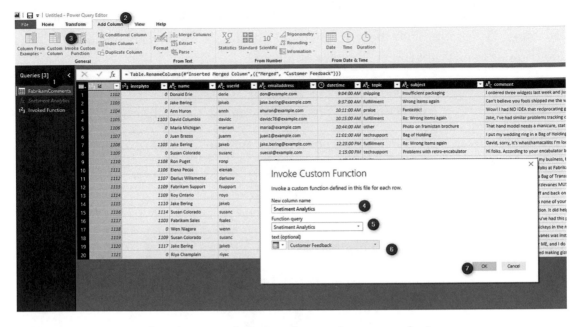

Figure 18-14. *Invoke a custom function for sentiment analysis*

A new column will be shown at the end of the data set overview that shows the numeric result for sentiment analysis. As you can see in Figure 18-15, the number varies from 0 to 1. You can click the Home tab and Close and Apply to see the result in Power BI Desktop.

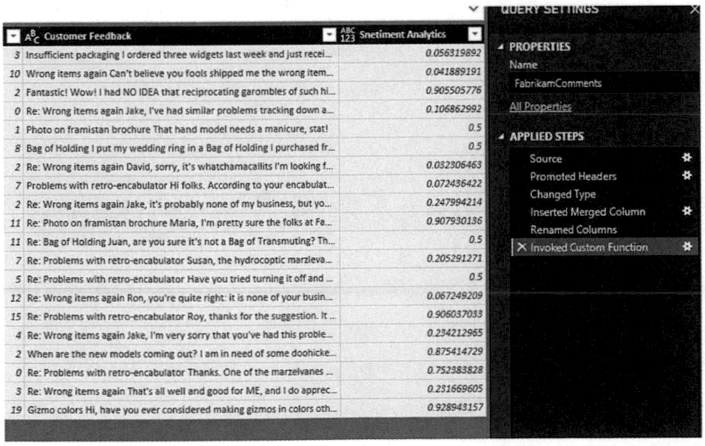

Figure 18-15. *Sentiment analysis result in Power BI Desktop*

The process of using the other features, such as language detection and key phrase extraction, is the same. Only the URL end point will change slightly. For language detection, the end point URL will change as follows:

```
endpoint    = "https://<Location of Your Azure>.api.cognitive.
              microsoft.com/text/analytics/v2.0/languages",
```

For key phrase extraction, the end point URL would be

```
endpoint    = "https://<Location of You Azure>.api.cognitive.microsoft.com/
              text/analytics/v2.0/keyPhrases"
```

In addition, the last line of code will change to show a different variable. For language detection, this would be as follows:

```
language    = jsonresp[documents]{0}[detectedLanguages]{0}[name]
in  language
```

For the key phrase, it would be as follows:

```
keyphrases  = Text.Lower(Text.Combine(jsonresp[documents]{0}
              [keyPhrases], ", "))
in  keyphrases
```

The preceding example was about using Cognitive Services in Power BI. In the next section, I will show you how to use the Face (that is, face recognition) service in a Windows application.

Intelligence Application, Face Recognition Services

Another feature in Cognitive Services is the Face (facial recognition) API. This API performs face detection from an image, in addition to emotion detection and finding similar facial features of faces from two images.

It is possible to try the Face API before using it in an application. To see a demo, navigate to the Cognitive Services web site, then to the Vision category (Figure 18-16). Under the Vision category, click the Emotion recognition in images demo. To test the API, browse to a picture and then submit it. After uploading the image, click the Submit button.

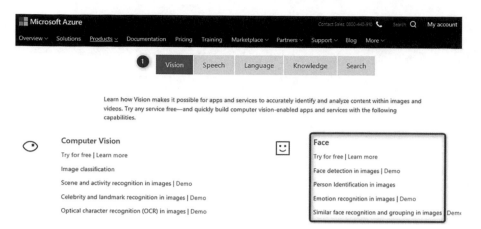

Figure 18-16. *Cognitive Service Face Recognition*

As you can see in Figure 18-17, after uploading the image, the API shows the emotion, such as anger, contempt, disgust, fear, happiness, neutral, sadness, and surprise, indicated by a number between 0 to 1. As you can see in Figure 18-17, the only measure that has a higher number is for happiness, and the person in the picture is smiling.

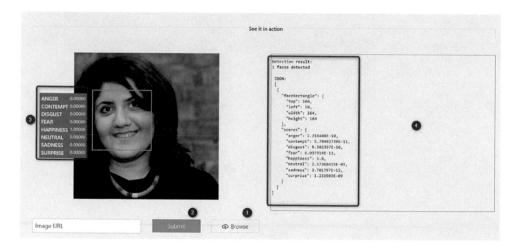

Figure 18-17. *Image emotion detection demo*

We are going to create a Windows application that is able to detect the image using the Face API in Cognitive Services.

The process of creating the Face API is like that for Text Analytics. First, we must log in to the Azure portal, then search for the Face API under *AI + Machine Learning* (Figure 18-18).

Figure 18-18. *Face recognition feature in Azure*

After creating the service, click the Key tab at the left side of the page and grab the key (Figure 18-19).

Figure 18-19. *Collecting the Face API key*

We are going to create a Windows application that employs face recognition [4]. To write the code, you must first download one of the free versions of Visual Studio 2015 or 2017 [5]. Then you must create a Windows application (Figure 18-20). For this case study, I am using Visual Studio 2015.

Figure 18-20. *Create a Windows Application*

The next step is to install the Microsoft Azure Cognitive Service Face API in a Windows application. To install it, we must navigate to the Tools tab, then navigate to NuGet Package Manager, and choose the Package Manager Console. Next, we must type in the following code in the console editor (Figure 18-21).

```
Install-Package Microsoft.Azure.CognitiveServices.Vision.Face -Version
2.0.0-preview
```

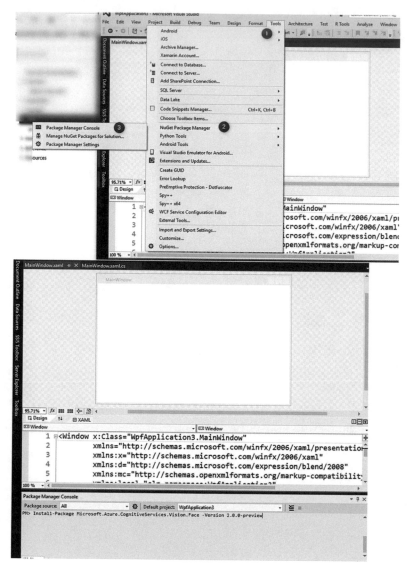

Figure 18-21. *Installing the Face API in Windows*

Then we must create the interface for the application. We have to add a button to the screen. To do that, we change the code. Right-click the MainWindow.xaml page, choose View Designer, and change the code to the following (Figure 18-22):

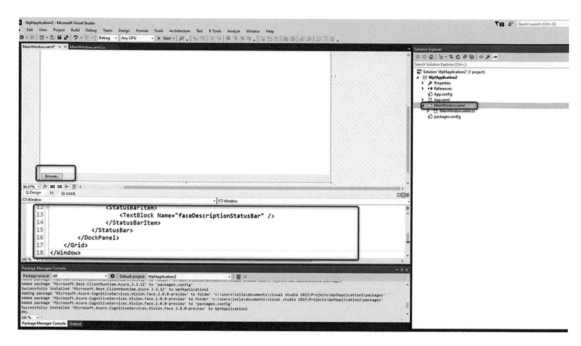

Figure 18-22. *Changing the code*

```
<Window x:Class="FaceTutorial.MainWindow" xmlns="http://schemas.microsoft.
com/winfx/2006/xaml/presentation" xmlns:x="http://schemas.microsoft.
com/winfx/2006/xaml" Title="MainWindow" Height="700" Width="960">
<Grid x:Name="BackPanel"> <Image x:Name="FacePhoto" Stretch="Uniform"
Margin="0,0,0,50" MouseMove="FacePhoto_MouseMove" /> <DockPanel DockPanel.
Dock="Bottom"> <Button x:Name="BrowseButton" Width="72" Height="20"
VerticalAlignment="Bottom" HorizontalAlignment="Left" Content="Browse..."
Click="BrowseButton_Click" /> <StatusBar VerticalAlignment="Bottom">
<StatusBarItem> <TextBlock Name="faceDescriptionStatusBar" />
</StatusBarItem> </StatusBar> </DockPanel> </Grid> </Window>
```

After changing the code, the visualization will change. We must change the C# code
to access the Face API. First, a reference to Azure Cognitive Services for FACE API has to
be added.

```
using Microsoft.Azure.CognitiveServices.Vision.Face;
using Microsoft.Azure.CognitiveServices.Vision.Face.Models;
```

To change the code, click MainWindows.xaml.cs, then add the preceding code to the reference part (Figure 18-23).

Figure 18-23. *Add Libraray for Face Recognition*

We must now change the code, as follows:

```
namespace FaceTutorial
{
    public partial class MainWindow : Window
    {
        private const string subscriptionKey = "<SubscriptionKey>";
        private const string baseUri =
            "https://<Local>.api.cognitive.microsoft.com/face/v1.0";
        private readonly IFaceClient faceClient = new FaceClient(
            new ApiKeyServiceClientCredentials(subscriptionKey),
            new System.Net.Http.DelegatingHandler[] { });
        IList<DetectedFace> faceList;    // The list of detected faces.
        String[] faceDescriptions;       // The list of descriptions for the
                                         // detected faces.

        double resizeFactor;             // The resize factor for the
                                         // displayed image.
```

```csharp
public MainWindow()
{
    InitializeComponent();
    if (Uri.IsWellFormedUriString(baseUri, UriKind.Absolute))
    {
        faceClient.BaseUri = new Uri(baseUri);
    }
    else
    {
        MessageBox.Show(baseUri,
            "Invalid URI", MessageBoxButton.OK, MessageBoxImage.
            Error);
        Environment.Exit(0);
    }
}
// Displays the image and calls UploadAndDetectFaces.
private async void BrowseButton_Click(object sender, RoutedEventArgs e)
{
    // Get the image file to scan from the user.
    var openDlg = new Microsoft.Win32.OpenFileDialog();
    openDlg.Filter = "JPEG Image(*.jpg)|*.jpg";
    bool? result = openDlg.ShowDialog(this);
    // Return if canceled.
    if (!(bool)result)
    {
        return;
    }
    // Display the image file.
    string filePath = openDlg.FileName;
    Uri fileUri = new Uri(filePath);
    BitmapImage bitmapSource = new BitmapImage();
    bitmapSource.BeginInit();
    bitmapSource.CacheOption = BitmapCacheOption.None;
    bitmapSource.UriSource = fileUri;
```

```
        bitmapSource.EndInit();
        FacePhoto.Source = bitmapSource;
    }
    // Displays the face description when the mouse is over a face
        rectangle.
    private void FacePhoto_MouseMove(object sender, MouseEventArgs e)
    {
    }
}
}
```

We must now change the subscription key and the location of the API. To detect and upload the image, we write a function, as follows:

```
private async Task<IList<DetectedFace>> UploadAndDetectFaces(string
imageFilePath)
{
    // The list of Face attributes to return.
    IList<FaceAttributeType> faceAttributes =
        new FaceAttributeType[]
        {
            FaceAttributeType.Gender, FaceAttributeType.Age,
            FaceAttributeType.Smile, FaceAttributeType.Emotion,
            FaceAttributeType.Glasses, FaceAttributeType.Hair
        };

    // Call the Face API.
    try
    {
        using (Stream imageFileStream = File.OpenRead(imageFilePath))
        {
            // The second argument specifies to return the faceId, while
            // the third argument specifies not to return face landmarks.
            IList<DetectedFace> faceList =
                await faceClient.Face.DetectWithStreamAsync(
                    imageFileStream, true, false, faceAttributes);
```

```
        return faceList;
    }
}
// Catch and display Face API errors.
catch (APIErrorException f)
{
    MessageBox.Show(f.Message);
    return new List<DetectedFace>();
}
// Catch and display all other errors.
catch (Exception e)
{
    MessageBox.Show(e.Message, "Error");
    return new List<DetectedFace>();
}
}
```

We can draw a rectangle around the face of each person in the picture. In the
BrowseButton function, write the following code:

```
Title = "Detecting...";
faceList = await UploadAndDetectFaces(filePath);
Title = String.Format(
    "Detection Finished. {0} face(s) detected", faceList.Count);
if (faceList.Count > 0)
{
    // Prepare to draw rectangles around the faces.
    DrawingVisual visual = new DrawingVisual();
    DrawingContext drawingContext = visual.RenderOpen();
    drawingContext.DrawImage(bitmapSource,
        new Rect(0, 0, bitmapSource.Width, bitmapSource.Height));
    double dpi = bitmapSource.DpiX;
    resizeFactor = (dpi > 0) ? 96 / dpi : 1;
    faceDescriptions = new String[faceList.Count];
```

```csharp
for (int i = 0; i < faceList.Count; ++i)
{
    DetectedFace face = faceList[i];
    // Draw a rectangle on the face.
    drawingContext.DrawRectangle(
        Brushes.Transparent,
        new Pen(Brushes.Red, 2),
        new Rect(
            face.FaceRectangle.Left * resizeFactor,
            face.FaceRectangle.Top * resizeFactor,
            face.FaceRectangle.Width * resizeFactor,
            face.FaceRectangle.Height * resizeFactor
            )
    );
    // Store the face description.
    faceDescriptions[i] = FaceDescription(face);
}
drawingContext.Close();
// Display the image with the rectangle around the face.
RenderTargetBitmap faceWithRectBitmap = new RenderTargetBitmap(
    (int)(bitmapSource.PixelWidth * resizeFactor),
    (int)(bitmapSource.PixelHeight * resizeFactor),
    96,
    96,
    PixelFormats.Pbgra32);
faceWithRectBitmap.Render(visual);
FacePhoto.Source = faceWithRectBitmap;
// Set the status bar text.
faceDescriptionStatusBar.Text =
    "Place the mouse pointer over a face to see the face description.";
}
```

The description of the face must be shown at the bottom of the image. By using the following function, you can show the face description, such as by different emotions, at the bottom of the page.

```csharp
private string FaceDescription(DetectedFace face)
{
    StringBuilder sb = new StringBuilder();
    sb.Append("Face: ");
    // Add the gender, age, and smile.
    sb.Append(face.FaceAttributes.Gender);
    sb.Append(", ");
    sb.Append(face.FaceAttributes.Age);
    sb.Append(", ");
    sb.Append(String.Format("smile {0:F1}%, ", face.FaceAttributes.Smile * 100));
    // Add the emotions. Display all emotions over 10%.
    sb.Append("Emotion: ");
    Emotion emotionScores = face.FaceAttributes.Emotion;
    if (emotionScores.Anger >= 0.1f)
        sb.Append(String.Format("anger {0:F1}%, ", emotionScores.Anger * 100));
    if (emotionScores.Contempt >= 0.1f)
        sb.Append(String.Format("contempt {0:F1}%, ", emotionScores.
        Contempt * 100));
    if (emotionScores.Disgust >= 0.1f)
        sb.Append(String.Format("disgust {0:F1}%, ", emotionScores.Disgust * 100));
    if (emotionScores.Fear >= 0.1f)
        sb.Append(String.Format("fear {0:F1}%, ", emotionScores.Fear * 100));
    if (emotionScores.Happiness >= 0.1f)
        sb.Append(String.Format("happiness {0:F1}%, ", emotionScores.
        Happiness * 100));
    if (emotionScores.Neutral >= 0.1f)
        sb.Append(String.Format("neutral {0:F1}%, ", emotionScores.Neutral * 100));
    if (emotionScores.Sadness >= 0.1f)
        sb.Append(String.Format("sadness {0:F1}%, ", emotionScores.Sadness * 100));
    if (emotionScores.Surprise >= 0.1f)
        sb.Append(String.Format("surprise {0:F1}%, ", emotionScores.
        Surprise * 100));
    // Add glasses.
    sb.Append(face.FaceAttributes.Glasses);
    sb.Append(", ");
```

```
    // Add hair.
    sb.Append("Hair: ");
    // Display baldness confidence if over 1%.
    if (face.FaceAttributes.Hair.Bald >= 0.01f)
        sb.Append(String.Format("bald {0:F1}% ", face.FaceAttributes.Hair.
        Bald * 100));
    // Display all hair color attributes over 10%.
    IList<HairColor> hairColors = face.FaceAttributes.Hair.HairColor;
    foreach (HairColor hairColor in hairColors)
    {
        if (hairColor.Confidence >= 0.1f)
        {
            sb.Append(hairColor.Color.ToString());
            sb.Append(String.Format(" {0:F1}% ", hairColor.Confidence * 100));
        }
    }
    // Return the built string.
    return sb.ToString();
}
```

The last code is about showing the description of the face when hovering a mouse over the picture.

```
private void FacePhoto_MouseMove(object sender, MouseEventArgs e)
{
    // If the REST call has not completed, return.
    if (faceList == null)
        return;
    // Find the mouse position relative to the image.
    Point mouseXY = e.GetPosition(FacePhoto);
    ImageSource imageSource = FacePhoto.Source;
    BitmapSource bitmapSource = (BitmapSource)imageSource;
    // Scale adjustment between the actual size and displayed size.
    var scale = FacePhoto.ActualWidth / (bitmapSource.PixelWidth /
    resizeFactor);
```

```
    // Check if this mouse position is over a face rectangle.
    bool mouseOverFace = false;
    for (int i = 0; i < faceList.Count; ++i)
    {
        FaceRectangle fr = faceList[i].FaceRectangle;
        double left = fr.Left * scale;
        double top = fr.Top * scale;
        double width = fr.Width * scale;
        double height = fr.Height * scale;
        // Display the face description if the mouse is over this face
            rectangle.
        if (mouseXY.X >= left && mouseXY.X <= left + width &&
            mouseXY.Y >= top  && mouseXY.Y <= top + height)
        {
            faceDescriptionStatusBar.Text = faceDescriptions[i];
            mouseOverFace = true;
            break;
        }
    }
    // String to display when the mouse is not over a face rectangle.
    if (!mouseOverFace)
        faceDescriptionStatusBar.Text =
            "Place the mouse pointer over a face to see the face description.";
}
```

If you ensure that all libraries and reference work are in order, you will gain proper access to the Azure Cognitive Service Library inside the .NET application.

Now you must run the code, by clicking the Start button, then click the Browse button and import a picture, to see the description of the image at the bottom of the page (Figure 18-24). As you can see, the software provides a description, such as my age, emotion, hair color, and so forth.

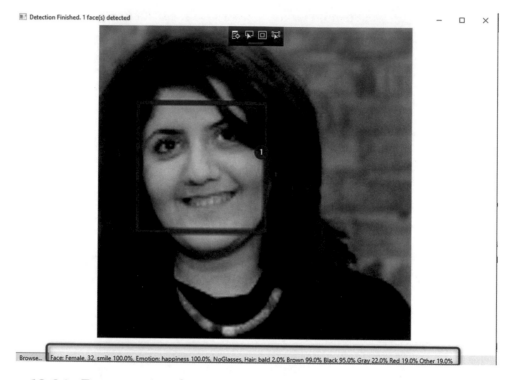

Figure 18-24. *Face emotion detection*

Summary

This chapter presented a brief introduction to the easy-to-use AI tools available in Microsoft Cognitive Services. A brief description of Cognitive Services and how they can be accessed was provided. Then how to use Cognitive Services Text Analytics API in some other Microsoft tools, such as Power BI, was explained. Next, the process of using Cognitive APIs in a Windows application was discussed, and all related codes were shown. In the next chapter, Bot Framework, another tool for creating smart applications, will be explored.

References

[1]   Microsoft Azure, "Cognitive Services," `https://azure.microsoft.com/en-us/services/cognitive-services/`, 2019.

[2]   PAT Research, "What is Text Analytics," `www.predictiveanalyticstoday.com/text-analytics/`.

[3]   Kamran Iqbal, Fabrikam data set, GitHub, `https://github.com/Kaiqb/KaiqbRepo0731190208/blob/master/CognitiveServices/TextAnalytics/FabrikamComments.csv`, September 6, 2017.

[4]   Patrick Farley et al., "Tutorial: Create a WPF app to display face data in an image," Microsoft Azure, `https://docs.microsoft.com/en-us/azure/cognitive-services/face/tutorials/faceapiincsharptutorial`, February 5, 2019.

[5]   Microsoft Visual Studio, "Visual Studio 2019," Downloads `https://visualstudio.microsoft.com/downloads/`, 2019.

CHAPTER 19

Bot Framework

A bot is an application that is able to interact with users conversationally [1]. It can be a very simple application that supports dialog and basic questions, or it can be sophisticated, capable of understanding language. In Microsoft Azure, it is possible to create a bot in C# or Node.js. You can create a bot using .NET SDK [2] and test it via such tools as Emulator [3]. In addition, some bot components help you to add more features [4]. In this chapter, a very simple bot using an Azure component will be presented. First, how to create a bot service in Azure will be shown, then how to create a simple bot for questions and answers will be presented, as well as a more complex one.

Bot Creation in Azure

Log in to your Azure account and create a new service name: Web App Bot (Figure 19-1).

On creating a new Bot service, you must provide some information, such as a bot name, subscription, resource group, location, and so forth. One of the main fields that you have to choose at the start is Bot template. The default option is Basic (C#). In our scenario, we are going to change the default option to Form, which helps us to create a bot application to guide end users.

© Leila Etaati 2019
L. Etaati, *Machine Learning with Microsoft Technologies*, https://doi.org/10.1007/978-1-4842-3658-1_19

Figure 19-1. *Web App Bot service in Azure*

As you can see in Figure 19-2, the Form option should be selected.

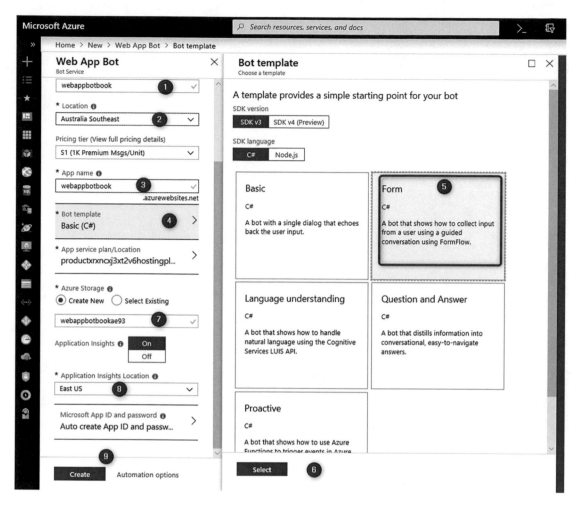

Figure 19-2. *Bot Framework for questions and answers*

After completing the bot application, the resulting services have three main categories: Bot Management, App Service Setting, and Support and Troubleshooting. First, check the output of the created bot. Go to Bot Management ➤ Test in Web Chat.

To see the default result of Bot Framework, click Test in Web Chat and write Hi. The result will be shown as "Welcome to the simple sandwich order bot!" Then list the sandwich option (Figure 19-3).

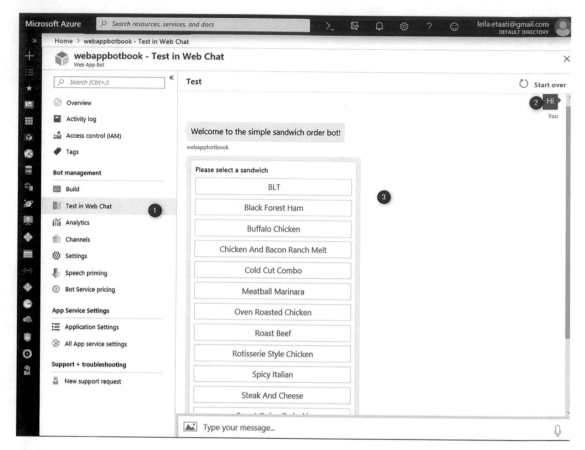

Figure 19-3. *Bot Framework test*

Under the Bot management section, the first option is Build, which provides all the source code for creating a bot framework. The first option is Open Online Code Editor. Using this option, developers are able to see code in the online code editor.

As you can see in Figure 19-4, under Online code editor, the code behind the bot is shown.

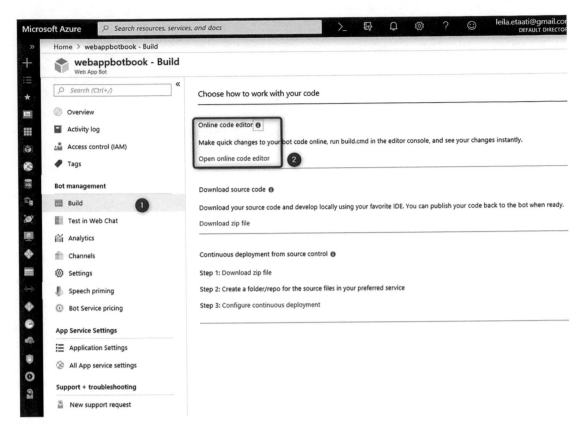

Figure 19-4. *Build section of Bot Framework*

To see the code, click Open online code editor. The code for the Web App bot framework will be shown (Figure 19-5). As you can see in Figure 19-5, under the Model folder, in the Sandwiches file, the list of the dialog that users may ask is shown.

In addition in Figure 19-5, each of the questions and possibilities has been represented following an *enumeration* data structure. Each enumeration defines different questions that may occur in a dialog with end users. You can change online the questions and types of offerings in code. For example, you can change the Sandwiches option to Chicken, Ham, Lamb, Pork, or Veggie.

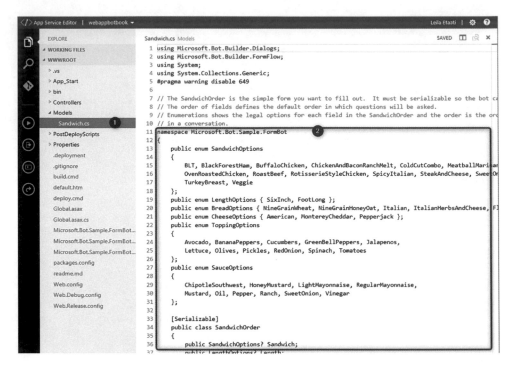

Figure 19-5. *Online editor for dialog bot framework*

Changes to the file will be saved. You must build and compile them in a .NET application. To build the file, click Open Console and type "build.cmd" (Figure 19-6).

Figure 19-6. *Building the Bot online editor*

Now we have to test and check the changes in Test in Web Chat. Type "Hi" for the first time, after building the framework. As you can see in Figure 19-7, the first option regarding the sandwich type has been changed.

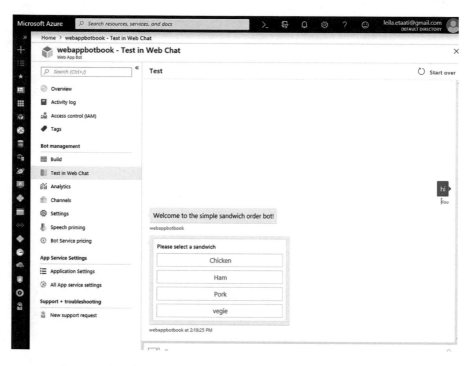

Figure 19-7. *The result of changes in the bot framework*

Now, when you choose the Ham option, the next sandwich option will be shown, which is a question about selecting the sandwich length. It is possible to embed the code in a channel, such as Facebook, Telegram, Skype, and so forth (Figure 19-8).

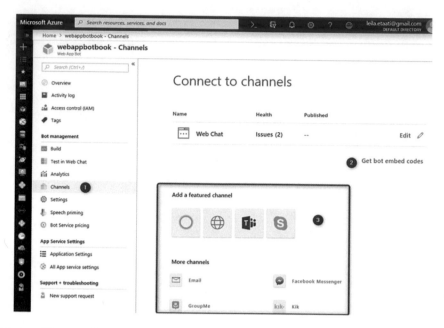

Figure 19-8. *Channels in chatbot*

Click Channels and note the different ways to embed the bot in different channels. One of the ways is embed the bot in a web application is to use Get Bot Embed Codes. If you want to embed the code in an HTML page, you must copy the embed code and replace the secret code with the secret key shown in the windows above (Figure 19-9).

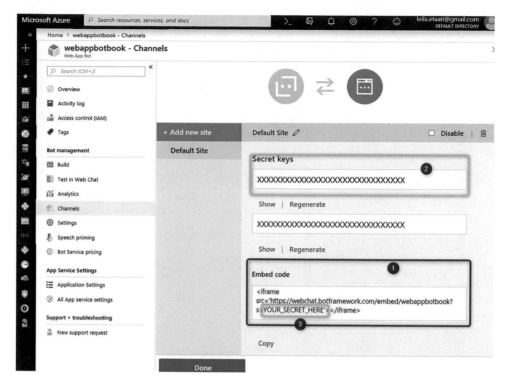

Figure 19-9. *Embed code in Channel*

Now you have a code, as follows, using Secret keys.

```
<iframe src='https://webchat.botframework.com/embed/webappbotbook?s=YOUR_
SECRET_HERE'></iframe>
```

Now you can embed the code in any web site. In the following section I will show how to create a question-and-answer chatbot and embed it in another web site.

Question-and-Answer Chatbot

A question-and-answer (QnA) chatbot can be used for any web site, to guide users. The procedure for creating a chatbot is the same as that followed in the previous section. First, we create a Web App Bot service and choose the Question and Answer bot template (Figure 19-10).

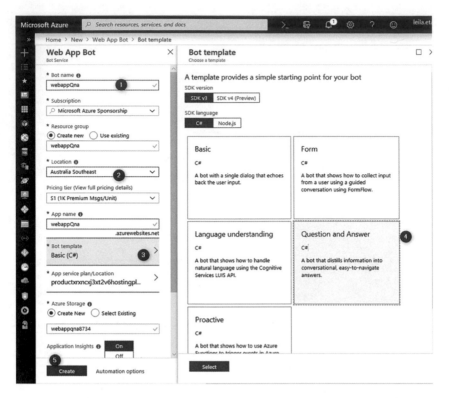

Figure 19-10. *Web App Bot for QnA chatbot*

By creating the QnA chatbot, as shown in Figure 19-10, we must test it in Test in Web Chat. By testing the chatbot, you will receive an error message (Figure 19-11) asking you to set up some parameters, such as `QnAKnowledgebaseId`, `QnAAuthKey`, and `QnAEndpointHostName`.

Figure 19-11. *Testing a web QnA chatbot*

To set up these parameters, we must create a QnA Maker service in Azure. In your Azure account, set up the QnA Maker service (Figure 19-12).

Figure 19-12. *QnA Maker*

After creating QnA Maker in Azure, you must set up a knowledge database [5]. Using your Azure account, log in to the qnmaker.ai web site (Figure 19-13).

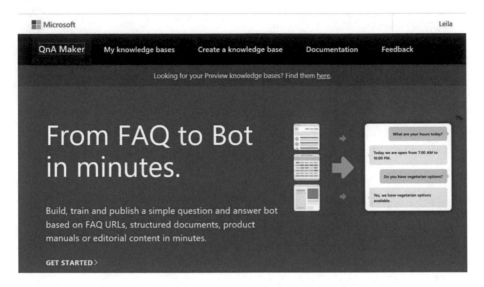

Figure 19-13. *QnA Maker web site*

Click the Create a Knowledge Base at the top of the page (Figure 19-13). The first step is to create a QnA service (as = in the last section). The second step is to connect the knowledge service to the QnA component in Azure. The third step is to choose the related Azure Directory ID, Azure Subscription Name, and Azure QnA Service. Then you must choose a name for the knowledge base (Figure 19-14).

STEP 2

Connect your QnA service to your KB.
After you create an Azure QnA service, refresh this page and then select your Azure service using the options below.

* Microsoft Azure Directory ID

| leilaetaatigmail (Default Directory) | ⌄ |

* Azure subscription name

| Microsoft Azure Sponsorship | ⌄ |

* Azure QnA service

| QnAleilabookAI | ⌄ |

STEP 3

Name your KB.
The knowledge base name is for your reference and you can change it at anytime.

* Name

| Conference Knowledge Base | × |

Figure 19-14. *Connecting the knowledge base (KB) with Azure*

Next, we have to upload some knowledge base as a URL or in a file format (.et, .pdf, .doc, .docx, .xlsx). The file contains some frequently asked questions (FAQ). I have created a word file that contains some FAQs for a conference (Figure 19-15).

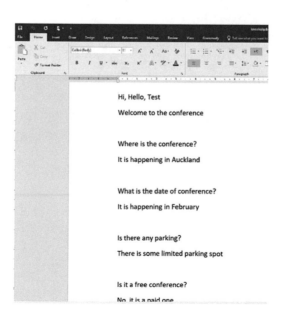

Figure 19-15. *FAQs*

Now you must upload the file to the web site and create the knowledge base
(Figure 19-16).

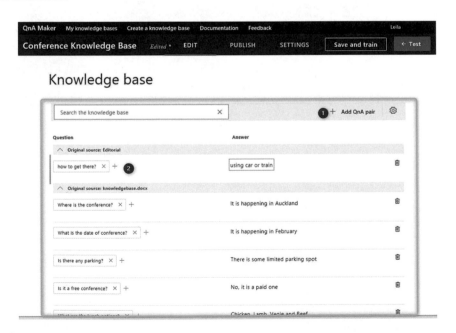

STEP 4

Populate your KB.
Extract question-and-answer pairs from an online FAQ, product manuals, or other files. Supported for
containing questions and answers in sequence. Learn more about knowledge base sources. Skip this s
after creation. The number of sources and file size you can add depends on the QnA service SKU you

URL

> http://

+ Add URL

File name

knowledgebase.docx   ❶

+ Add file

STEP 5

Create your KB
The tool will look through your documents and create a knowledge base for your service. If you are n
create an empty knowledge base table which you can edit.

Create your KB   ❷

Figure 19-16. *Creating a knowledge base*

After creating the knowledge base, you can extend the knowledge base questions,
by clicking Add QnA Pair (Figure 19-17). In addition, it is possible to add more questions
and more answers.

Figure 19-17. *Adding a QnA pair*

After uploading and adding the question, you must "Save and train" the knowledge base. After training the model, click Test. Type "Conference," and the knowledge base returns the result (Figure 19-18).

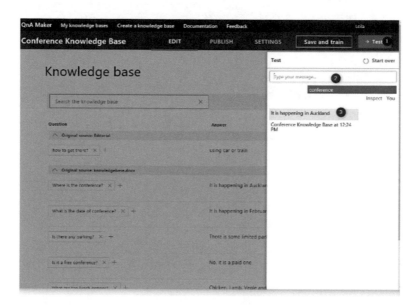

Figure 19-18. *Testing the knowledge base*

After testing the knowledge base, we must publish it. After publishing the knowledge base, an HTTP request will build. The created request contains all the required information, such as the knowledge base ID, end point link, and authentication key (Figure 19-19).

QnA Maker   My knowledge bases   Create a knowledge base   Documentation   Feedback

Looking for your Preview knowledge bases? Find them here.

Success! Your service has been deployed. What's next?

You can always find the deployment details in your service's settings.

Use the below HTTP request to build your bot. Learn how.

Sample HTTP request	POST /knowledgebases/ QnAKnowledgebaseId c/generateAnswer Host: https://qnaleilabookai.azurewebsites.net/qnamaker — QnAEndpointHostName Authorization: EndpointKey QnAAuthKey Content-Type: application/json {"question":"<Your question>"}

Need to fine-tune and refine? Go back and keep editing your service.

[Edit Service]

Figure 19-19. *Creating an HTTP request*

These parameters can be viewed in Figure 19-11. In webappqnabook (Figure 19-20), click Application Settings and fill the parameters with HTTP Request parameters (Figure 19-20).

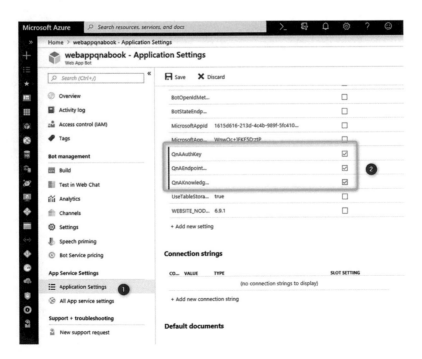

Figure 19-20. *Application Setting Parameters*

Now we have to test the chatbot. Click Test in Web Chat and type "Conference." The output will be displayed in the test window (Figure 19-21).

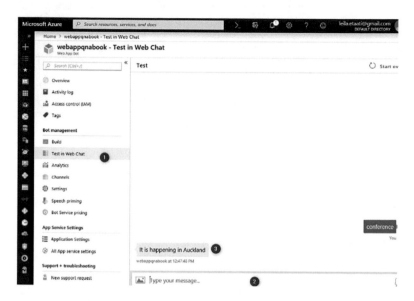

Figure 19-21.   *Testing the chatbot*

You can embed the questions and answers on any page and channel. In this example, this chatbot has been embedded in the conference web site, to guide users. To embed the chatbot in the web site, we must get the embed code. To get the embed code, follow the same procedure related to Figure 19-9.

Next, copy the code and put it in the web page (Figure 19-22).

```
<iframe src='https://webchat.botframework.com/embed/webappqnabook?s=YOUR_
SECRET_HERE'></iframe>
```

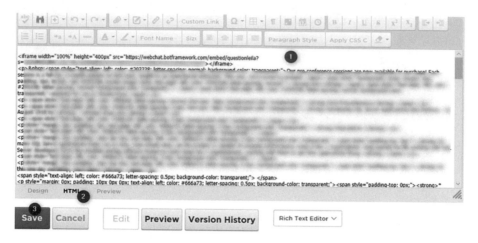

Figure 19-22. *Copying the embed code in a web page*

Test the code, and you will see the chatbot on the web page (Figure 19-23).

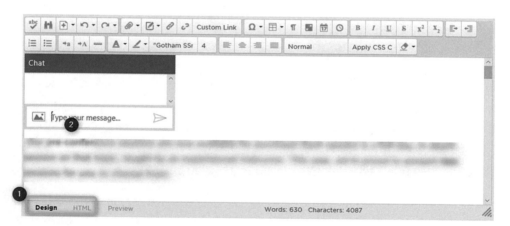

Figure 19-23. *Chatbot embeded in the web page*

Summary

In this chapter, the general procedures for creating a chatbot were explained.

References

[1]   Kamran Iqbal et al., "About Azure Bot Service," Microsoft Azure, `https://docs.microsoft.com/en-us/azure/bot-service/bot-service-overview-introduction?view=azure-bot-service-3.0`, April 17, 2019.

[2]   Bot Builder, `https://marketplace.visualstudio.com/items?itemName=SkillBotBuilder.SkillBotBuilder`.

[3]   Tony Anziano, "Bot Framework-Emulator," GitHub, `https://github.com/Microsoft/BotFramework-Emulator/releases`, 2019.

[4]   Microsoft Visual Studio, Downloads, `https://visualstudio.microsoft.com/downloads/`, 2019.

[5]   Microsoft QnA Maker, `www.qnamaker.ai/`, 2019.

CHAPTER 20

Overview of Microsoft Machine Learning Tools

The last 19 chapters were an overview of how you can undertake machine learning with different Microsoft products. First, an introduction to machine learning approaches, such as descriptive, predictive, and prescriptive analytics, was provided. The R language, as one of the principal languages for machine learning was then discussed. Following was a brief explanation of how to do machine learning using such tools as Power BI, Azure ML Studio, SQL Server, and others.

This chapter offers a summary of machine learning technologies and best practices when using particular approaches.

Overview of Microsoft Machine Learning Technologies

Artificial intelligence (AI), and specifically machine learning, can bring lots of benefits to businesses. Many have been using Microsoft data platform tools for years. Microsoft employed machine learning to create such products such as Xbox, Bing Search, and others. However, from 2014, Microsoft began to provide a facility for power users and end users to embed machine learning in their reports and software.

Previous chapters categorized the relevant Microsoft tools, based on the way machine learning is used. In this chapter, technologies are categorized according to the following:

- The need to write R or Python code

- Cloud or on-premises computing

© Leila Etaati 2019
L. Etaati, *Machine Learning with Microsoft Technologies*, https://doi.org/10.1007/978-1-4842-3658-1_20

The first classification is based on the degree to which these tools are easy to use and accurate.

We can classify the associated products into two main groups:

- *Pre-built AI*: Microsoft machine learning tools that do not require that you write any R or Python code to generate a machine learning scenario.

- *Custom AI*: Microsoft machine learning tools that require you to know how to write R or Python code

The first group is easy to use, and you need only follow the instructions provided. The main benefit of using pre-built AI tools is that there is no need to know the machine learning concepts, or at least by knowing some, most anyone is able to create an AI application. Pre-built AI tools can address general problems and issues, but for some business problems, other categories of tools (e.g., for writing R or Python code) are more efficient. In this book, the Cognitive Services (Chapter 18) and Bot Framework (Chapter 19) are the tools that you can embed in Power BI, Windows, or other web applications without writing any R or Python code. As mentioned in the relevant chapters, there is no direct way to access the code behind pre-built custom AI tools, so there is no way to alter that code and change the algorithms.

In contrast, to use Custom AI tools requires knowing how to code and how to write code for the purpose of machine learning. However, for some tools, such as Azure ML Studio, it is possible to conduct machine learning without writing R or Python code, although at least some understanding of how machine learning works is necessary. Some Custom AI tools address writing R or Python code inside other Microsoft tools, such as R or Python in

- Power BI (Chapters 6, 7, and 8)

- SQL Server 2016 for R Services and SQL Server 2017 for Machine Learning (ML) Services (Chapter 9)

- Azure Data Lake Analytics (Chapter 11)

- Azure Databricks (Chapter 10)

- Azure HDInsight (Chapter 15)

- .NET applications (Chapter 13)

- And others

For Azure machine learning tools, it is possible to write R or Python code as well. In addition, the drag-and-drop environment is quite easy to use.

The second classification is about cloud vs. on-premises AI tools. Many companies still prefer to keep their tools on-site, while some others prefer to move all their business products to the cloud. Between the two, some companies have both cloud and on-premises tools.

If the main strategy of a company is to keep everything on-premises, using Power BI or SQL Server for writing R or Python can be more suitable. However, if the preference is to do machine learning in the cloud, the Azure ML Studio (Chapter 12), for writing R or Python on Databricks, and Azure Data Analytics can be most helpful.

The third categories of tools address solutions to business problems. The nature of a problem and the scenario that we want to enrich with AI also matter when selecting specific tools, for example

- Applying machine learning on Internet of things (IoT) use case scenarios

- Using Text Analytics, speech, images, and so forth, for analysis

- Applying machine learning to an ETL (extract, transform, load) project

- Fast tracking a prototype for a client with Azure Machine Studio

IoT Scenario

Analyzing real-time data is a need that has been addressed by such Microsoft tools as Event Hub, Stream Analytics (Chapter 13), Databricks (Chapter 10), and others. With Power BI, it is possible to create a live stream report based on the real data that flows from sensors, applications, and so forth.

For most of this scenario, there is a need to identify anomalies in the data or classify prospective data into different groups. By using Azure Machine Learning with Stream Analytics or Databricks, we can apply machine learning to IoT scenarios.

Image, Text, and Voice Analytics

There are different tools for image, text, and voice analytics in the Microsoft stack. Cognitive Services (Chapter 18) is one of the popular tools for text, voice, and image analytics that provides APIs to use in other applications.

However, it is also possible to do image processing and voice recognition using the CNTK platform, which is covered in Chapter 17. These Microsoft packages and libraries provide facilities for developers to employ for performing machine learning with a deep learning approach.

Machine Learning on ETL

Another possible requirement is to apply machine learning to data that has been loaded and transformed with the aim of visualization and creating reports. There is always a need to apply some descriptive or predictive analytics on data before showing it to the final users. As a result, those who use Power BI self-service BI can leverage the machine learning, using R and Python scripts to make reports more insightful. Another approach is to use R or Python in SQL Server 2016 or 2017. In addition, if the data is on the cloud, it is possible to use Databricks for ETL and machine learning at the same time.

Machine Learning Prototype

For companies that want to use machine learning on their data for the first time, Azure Machine Learning Studio is a great tool that demonstrates the real process of machine learning, from collecting data to training and testing models. Moreover, managers and stakeholders are able to fast track the machine learning process and see how it can be used as an API in other applications or a simple Excel file.

To sum up, tool selection for machine learning depends on the architecture being used, how much effort is willing to be expended on programming, and what scenario is to be put in place. Tools related to the first requirement are based on pre-built AI and custom AI. Those for the second depend on the current architecture in place, whether on-premises or cloud-based. Finally, the last requirement to consider relates to appropriate tools for a specific scenario that is to be implemented, such as for IoT, ETL, or prototype creation.

Index

A

Activation functions, 95, 291, 292
Apache Spark, 159, 267
Application programming
      interface (API), 11, 211
Artificial intelligence (AI), 3, 273, 355
Automated machine learning
    advanced editor, 111
    association rules, 130
    attributes, 130
    cancer data set
      call classification function, 118
      prediction result, 118
    Changed Type, 113
    Chiclet slicer, 134
    creating function, Power
      Query, 110
    customer purchasing behavior, 129
    data set, transformation, 112
    duplicate data set, 109
    final code, 114
    importing data set, 131
    parameters setting, 133
    permission request, 116
    Power Query Editor, 106
    Power Query filter value, 133
    prediction analysis, 108
    report, 134
    result analysis, 132
    rpart library, 107
    R scripts editor, 131
    RStudio, 107
    run R Script, 112
    selecting columns, 115
    titanic data set, 107
Azure Databricks
    chart option, 165, 166
    cluster page, 161, 162
    environment module, 159, 160
    import data, 166, 167
    launch workspace, 161
    new cell creation, 169, 170
    R notebook creation, 163, 164
    run code, 165
    Scala language, 167, 168
    scheduling a process, 171
Azure Data Lake
    Analytics sample scripts, 180, 181
    create resource, 176, 177
    creating Analytics resource, 179, 180
    Data Explorer option, 178
    definition, 175
    Microsoft Cloud components, 176
    R scripts in U-SQL language, 184–188
    into RStudio
      Active Directory, create
        connection, 194, 195
      Azure Active Directory, application
        registration, 190
      Azure Active Directory, create, 188

© Leila Etaati 2019
L. Etaati, *Machine Learning with Microsoft Technologies*, https://doi.org/10.1007/978-1-4842-3658-1

M

Machine learning (ML)

   AI, 3, 4

   approaches

      supervised learning, 6

      unsupervised learning, 6

   descriptive analysis, 69, 70

   languages and platforms, 9–12

   life cycle, 7–9

   predictive analysis, 70–72

   prescriptive analysis, 5, 72, 73

Matplotlib, 35, 299

merge function, 84

Microsoft Cognitive Toolkit (CNTK), 274, 358

   case study

      actual data, 300

      DSVM, 295

      Jupyter Notebook, 297

      random data, 298

   definition, 293

   neural networks

      activation functions, 292

      classifying data, 290

      deep learning, 292

      DSVM environment, 291

      model, 288

      synapsis, 287

      topologies, 292

   setup, 293, 295, 296

Microsoft machine learning

   custom AI tools, 356

   data platform tools, 355

   ETL, 358

   IOT, 357

   pre-built AI tools, 356

   prototype, 358

   voice analytics, 358

N, O

Neural networks, 288

   computer system architecture, 94

   concrete data set, 96

   package library command, 98

   machine learning with R, 95

   mountain climbing,

      comparison, 95

   normalization, 97

   output data set, 98

   Power BI report, 100

   prediction result, 99

   Python codes, pivot, 97

   structure, 99

   training data set, 97

Normalization

   MinMax approach, 87

   normalized data, 90

   R scripts, 88

NuGet packages, 232, 321

P

Packages, R

   installation, 18

   machine learning, 23, 24

Power BI, 227, 229

   data visualization, 38, 39

   R code

      CSV file, import, 41

      ggplot function, 46

      mpg data set, 42

      Python environment, 43

      scatter chart result, 46–48

      script editor, 44, 45

      whitespace area, 42

   setting up R, 39–41

Printed in the United States
By Bookmasters